Tools for Ideas

Christian Gänshirt

Tools for Ideas

AN INTRODUCTION TO ARCHITECTURAL DESIGN

Birkhäuser

Basel • Boston • Berlin

Design and production: Atelier Fischer, Berlin

Translation: Michael Robinson, London
Copyediting: Julian Reisenberger, Weimar
Lithography: LVD GmbH, Berlin
Printing: Druckhaus Köthen
Binding: Kunst- und Verlagsbuchbinderei, Leipzig

This book is also available in a German edition:
ISBN 978-3-7643-7576-8

Bibliographic information published by The Deutsche Nationalbibliothek
The Deutsche Nationalbibliothek lists this publication in the Deutsche
Nationalbibliografie; detailed bibliographic data are available in the
Internet at http://dnb.ddb.de.

Library of Congress Control Number: 2007925789

© 2007 Birkhäuser Verlag AG
Basel · Boston · Berlin
P.O.Box 133, CH-4010 Basel, Switzerland
Part of Springer Science+Business Media
Printed on acid-free paper produced from chlorine-free pulp. TCF ∞

Printed in Germany
ISBN-13 978-3-7643-7577-5

www.birkhauser.ch
9 8 7 6 5 4 3 2 1

Contents

7 **Preface**

9 **DESIGN AND RESEARCH**
12   TEACHING ARCHITECTURAL DESIGN
16   RESEARCH IN ARCHITECTURAL DESIGN

20 **ARCHITECTURAL DESIGN**
24   EXAMPLES, PRINCIPLES, THEORIES
24   WHAT ONE CAN DESIGN
27   HOW ONE CAN DESIGN
34   HOW DESIGN CAN BE ACCOUNTED FOR
40 **Terms and definitions**
41   PLATO, ARISTOTLE, PLOTINUS: *IDEA*
43   VITRUVIUS AND ALBERTI: *COGITATIONE* AND *INVENTIONE*
45   VASARI AND ZUCCARI: *DISEGNO*
48   OSTENDORF, RITTEL, UHL: *DESIGNING, PLANNING*
52   AICHER AND FLUSSER: *NEGATION* AND *TRANSCENDENCE*
57 **Ways of designing**
59   PERCEPTION AND THOUGHT
65   DESIGNING AS A PROCESS
72   DESIGNING AS AN INDIVIDUAL ACT
78   THE DESIGN CYCLE

81 **DESIGN TOOLS**
82   SYMBOLS OF CREATIVITY
88   FLUSSER: THE GESTURE OF MAKING
90   THE AMBIVALENCE OF TOOLS
94   "DESIGN TOOLS" AS A METAPHOR
100   VISUAL AND VERBAL TOOLS
105 **Gesture**
108   STARTING FROM GESTURES
113 **Sketch**
114   PARCHMENT AND PAPER
117   CREATIVE IMPRECISION
121   VISUAL-SPATIAL THINKING
125 **Language**
126   TRAINING AND PRACTICE
129   CREATING METAPHORS, INTERPRETING, ABSTRACTING

134 **Design drawing**

134   GEOMETRY AND ABSTRACTION

140   MEDIA SWITCH

142   DESIGNING OR DRAWING

145   DIGITALIZATION OF DRAWING

149 **Model**

151   RELATIONSHIP WITH REALITY

154   THE IMPORTANCE OF MATERIALS

160 **Perspective view**

161   THE DISCOVERY OF THE WORLD

165   AMBIVALENT REALISM

168   PERSPECTIVE AS AN ATTITUDE

173 **Photograph, film, video**

175   FROM RECORD TO RE-PRESENTATION

177   SIMULATING IMAGES DIGITALLY

181 **Calculation**

183   CALCULATION IS INTERPRETATION

186 **Computer, program, simulation**

187   FROM CALCULATING MACHINE TO MASS MEDIUM

191   DESIGNING DIGITALLY

194   NETWORKING THE DESIGN TOOLS

196 **Criticism**

199   A TEACHING TOOL

201 **Criteria and value systems**

201   *FIRMITAS, UTILITAS, VENUSTAS*

207   INNOVATION AND THE ENIGMATIC

209 **Theory**

212   AICHER: THEORY FROM BELOW

219   OPEN QUESTIONS

223   DESIGNING THEORY

225 **Trying to address the whole**

         Appendix

231   BIBLIOGRAPHY, PART A (GENERAL)

240   BIBLIOGRAPHY, PART B (TOOLS)

245   ILLUSTRATION CREDITS

247   INDEX OF NAMES

251   INDEX OF SUBJECTS

Preface

This book is based on a metaphor: "design tools". Perhaps the most immediate way of describing design would be in terms of the individual activities carried out in the process of designing. However, by looking at this process through the lens of "design tools", it is possible to distance oneself from personal working methods. This book is not written from the point of view of an architect trying to justify his design approach or to present a specific design method. It is much more a view of the interplay between designers, the "tools" at their disposal and the "materials" those tools will work upon.

Tools, in German, are *Werkzeuge*, objects that "create works", and as such they are fundamental to all human tasks. This book will first undertake a survey of current knowledge about design, outline the essential terms and definitions as a basis for understanding and then describe the basic features of the design process. The second part of the book identifies the basic ideas behind "design tools" and describes the way they emerged and their specific qualities, in order to analyse their current significance as working "design tools" and to critically examine their use and future significance, especially with regard to the present digitalization of all tools. I hope that this procedure will make it possible to recognize and systematically explore the many planes of meaning involved in designing.

In the long years I have been working on this book I have been supported and encouraged from many quarters. My thanks go first of all to Prof. Jörg J. Kühn, who took me on for six years at the Design Institute of the Brandenburg Technical University in Cottbus, thus giving me the opportunity to conduct this work. The enthusiasm generated by the fresh start of what was then a young department gave me the courage to address fundamental design questions in a new way. Another first thank you goes to the editorial board of the internet architecture magazine *Cloud-Cuckoo-Land* [cloud-cuckoo.net], and especially its editor Prof. Dr. Eduard Führ, who triggered key stimuli for this work and accompanied its gestation with great interest in the early years in particular. My very special thanks go to the Berlin *Tagesspiegel* journalist Holger Wild, who has tried to teach me to write comprehensibly for over twelve years now, and Prof. Ralph Johannes, who spurred me on with research literature reference for many years and asked after my progress with unwavering patience.

I would like to thank all my friends, colleagues and students for inspiring conversations, tips on research literature, criticism and encouragement, especially Ulrich Ackva, Florian Aicher, Karyn Ball, Raimund Binder, Nicolau Brandão, Peter Böke, Axel Buether, Jorge Carvalho, Ariane Epars, Christian Federmair, Anton Graf, Matthias Gorenflos, Tobias Hammel, Dagmar Jäger, Cornelia Jöchner, Christian Keller, Nico Knebel, Gereon Legge, Claudia Moddelmoog, Norbert Palz, Constanze A. Petrow, Jörg Petruschat, Ute Poerschke, Riklef Rambow, Hinrich Sachs, Eran Schaerf, Astrid Schmeing, Andreas Schwarz, Jürgen Schwinning, Melanie Semmer, Álvaro Siza, Sandra Staub, Peter Testa, Yvonne Wuebben and Ulrike Wulf-Rheidt.

Special thanks to everyone whose illustrations I have been allowed to use, they are mentioned in the relevant picture captions. As publisher's editor, Andreas Müller has supported the book farsightedly and with great commitment in the last eighteen months, and made a vital contribution to its success. It would not have achieved its present compelling form without his concentrated and productive criticism. Bernd Fischer has shown extraordinary commitment to the production and graphic design of the book, and captured its basic ideas outstandingly well. Our thanks to Michael Robinson for his fine, precise translation into English. Finally and above all I thank my parents, Martin and Elfriede Gänshirt, who supported me even when no one else did, and who ultimately made this book possible with their contribution to the printing and translation costs.

DESIGN AND RESEARCH

Ultimately, all theory means what points beyond it. Hans-Georg Gadamer (1986, p. 50)

9   Architecture has featured as a fully accredited faculty at universities for
some time now. Given the centuries-old history of these institutions, this is
a new phenomenon whose significance has not been thoroughly explored to
date, either by architects or the universities. Until a few decades ago, architectural design and construction were mainly taught at art academies, engineering schools, specialist colleges and technical colleges. In European countries where architecture has increasingly found its way on to university syl-
labuses since the mid eighties, many art colleges and technical colleges that
used to run such courses have developed into fully-fledged universities. This
acknowledges the assertion by artists and architects since the beginning of
the modern age that they should be treated not just as specialist craftsmen,
as artists and engineers, but also as scientists.

Unifying teaching by introducing bachelor's and master's courses is currently facing some European countries with great challenges, especially in the field
of architecture. The question arises in the universities about the extent to which
the introduction of new, strongly pre-structured courses threatens to restrict
teachers' freedom to teach and students' freedom to learn. On the other hand,
a longer period of practical experience between the bachelor's and master's
courses, as is customary in the USA, would make it possible to accumulate the
skills needed for design work. Certainly making courses internationally com-
patible promotes the mobility of both students and teachers. But it also
demands new forms of design teaching devised to impart generally applicable
subject matter, rather than ideas born of personal preference or local specifics.

This process of unification necessitates the streamlining of study curricula,
often at the expense of the "soft" subjects in architectural studies. Cultural
and creative subject areas are gradually being displaced by technical and
commercial subject areas. This tendency is a direct result of an economic climate that honours creative achievement only when money can be earned
from it. The promise of creative self-realization inherent in all creative professions is a fundamental myth within this economic order adhered to by

designers, authors, fine artists, musicians and film makers alike. It remains to be seen to what degree the notion of a creative profession will be reflected in future study programmes.

Astonishingly enough, even today architects, and particularly those who see themselves as designers, make little of the original university idea of combining teaching and research. They are sceptical about a systematic analysis of fundamental questions relating to design, especially as research approaches appropriate to this particular activity are not yet anywhere near to being in place. It is not considered usual to do a doctorate as a so-called design architect, indeed it may even be seen as counter-productive. What really counts for designers and design teachers nowadays seems to be winning competitions and realizing projects.

There is a good reason for this: as many of the mental processes involved in design (or any other creative activity) happen subconsciously and can only be practised indirectly and in complex contexts, any research activity can only indirectly extend the skills needed for design. It creates knowledge that is of a fundamentally different kind to that of the design abilities of a particular person. For this reason, all architects working in academic fields should consider the objection raised by the German architect Egon Eiermann that in our profession academic achievement is of only little importance compared with the

Jaspers 1946 (The Idea of the University), Adorno 1971 (Education for Maturity and Responsibility), Bourdieu 1984 (Homo Academicus): an idealistic, a theoretical and a socio-ethnographic view of the university

basic human attitude that should inform this profession from start to finish. (Eiermann 1994, p. 39) Theoretical knowledge and knowledge that informs actions are not the same thing, and one can often be applied to the other only with great difficulty. (Dörner 1989, p. 65) However, this *"grey"* knowledge (loc. cit., p. 304) can serve as a basis for talking about designing and building – it can produce *"communicable, verifiable, discussable"* (Karl Jaspers, after Saner 1970, p. 69) insights that in their turn can provide a basis for teaching. Design is so centrally significant in today's society that research into it can no longer be neglected. The architect and journalist Wolfgang Bachmann wrote recently that *"merely glancing out of the window shows us that we have reached a state of near-emergency regarding architectural design. Every expansion of the urban periphery, every business park reveals the absence of architectural design."* (Bachmann 2006)

The position of architects at universities and other architecture schools is primarily that of teaching staff. This is problematic from the outset. In his lecture *Taboos about the teaching profession*, Theodor Adorno described typical deficits associated with being a teacher: it is quite obvious that the teaching profession, compared with other academic professions such as lawyers or doctors, carries a certain aroma of something that is not wholly socially accepted. According to Adorno, teachers have perhaps subconsciously been perceived as cripples of a kind, as fundamentally immature people who have no function within actual life and the real reproductive processes of society. (cf. Adorno 1971, p. 71 ff.) Gregory Bateson is even more radical, expressing the suspicion that many teachers don't really have anything to say:

"Is it that teachers know that they carry the kiss of death which will turn to tasteless-ness whatever they touch or teach, and therefore they are wisely unwilling to touch or teach anything of real-life importance? Or is it that they carry the kiss of death because they dare not teach anything of real-life importance?" (Bateson 1979, p. 15)

But Adorno sees university teachers as exempt from this odium. He says it is significant that the teachers who enjoy the greatest respect are in fact those academics who still pursue productive research, or at least the idea and public perception of what that is, in other words those who are not trapped in the educational sphere, which is suspected of being secondary and illusory. Adorno cites the example of a university teacher who reflects that he was only able to educate his students because he never acted like a teacher. What makes a successful academic teacher is obviously based on the absence of any desire to influence, on not attempting to persuade. Not only from this point of view is academic research a factor that makes university teaching particularly credible and relevant. In architecture faculties it is the teacher's own designs and realized buildings that are generally regarded as being equivalent to academic research – rather than an analyti-cal approach to the teacher's own activities or a theory of design derived from this. The general view is that the status and esteem of a university design teacher is measured by built designs, which have thus proved that they can be realised, are functionally useful and culturally valuable. But the quality of design teaching does not derive solely from the quality of what

Leonardo da Vinci: Old man seated, with vertebra studies, c. 1513, pen and ink, 15.2 x 21.3 cm, Windsor Castle, The Royal Collection 12579r

teachers have designed and built, but also from their ability to reflect on their own practice and transform its implicit practical knowledge into *"communicable, verifiable, discussable"* knowledge–as in Karl Jaspers' previously quoted description of academic insight. Only this makes it teachable.
In this respect, two deficits would signify a design teacher's "immaturity": not having proved the quality of their designs by building them, and not having ensured the quality of their teaching through systematic studies. Both have to be overcome, as *"the demand for mental maturity seems evident in a democracy"*. (Adorno 1971, p. 133)

Leonardo da Vinci had to overcome a comparable kind of–alleged or real–"immaturity" in his day. If in today's climate it is a lack of academic reflection that often marks the limitations of design teaching, in the social hierarchy of Leonardo's day, artists and architects were not rated much more highly than craftsmen, a status certainly not comparable with that of scholars. Leonardo's wish to be acknowledged as a scholar and not just as little more than a craftsman, as a *"huomo sanza lettere"*, (Arasse 1997, p. 69) manifested itself in extended scientific research that he saw as the basis for his artistic work, and at the same time reinforced his claim for a higher social status. As the personification of the combination of artistic work, technical and architectural design and scientific research, Leonardo da Vinci became a *"figure symbolizing modern man".* (Mittelstrass 1994, p. 159) Leonardo the *"projector"* (Schumacher 1981, p. 41) can serve as a model for architects who see themselves as generalists, as *"specialists in not specializing"* (Álvaro Siza) in a climate of an ever-increasing pressure to specialize. Leonardo, who as a left-hander was inclined towards spatial, pictorial, associative and simultaneous thinking, is worth renewed study to examine how art and technology, design and research, architecture and science can once more be brought together in an up-to-date way. Any teaching has an inherent tendency to simplify and abbreviate for the sake of presenting material more concisely, with the danger of consequently becoming dogmatic. If one follows the historic development of architecture teaching, it becomes clear that attempts were regularly made to break with this tendency and mount a counter-movement in order to return to reality. The attempts to incorporate current knowledge and working methods in teaching provided the most fruitful impetus for the further development of design teaching in the long term. One historic example is the English Arts and Crafts movement, which specifically linked art and craft, and still continues to be relevant today in the legacy of the Bauhaus and Hans Poelzig. The desire to create a direct and concrete link with reality became the basis for many innovations in Poelzig's role-plays or the material studies that László Moholy-Nagy conducted at the Bauhaus. In the course of the

enlightenment and industrialization, two parallel traditions with different focuses have developed in Europe since the French Revolution, one placing more emphasis on the artistic side of design and building, and the other on the engineering aspects. The artistic side was represented by the studios of the École des Beaux-Arts, which was founded in Paris in 1793 as successor to the Académie Royale d'Architecture. Design was taught at this school as an art, with each studio as a sworn company subordinated to an architectural personality and a hierarchy characterized by a traditional master-pupil relationship. This line of tradition can be

Students' workrooms in the faculty of architecture at Oporto University (FAUP), Álvaro Siza, 1986–1995 traced via the art colleges of our day down to the *units* of the British Architectural Association.

The other approach taught design from the perspective of the technical basis of architecture. This teaching was committed to the principles of enlightenment, modern science and ultimately the modern university. The corresponding institution, the École Polytechnique, was founded in 1794, a year after the École des Beaux-Arts, and thus also in the aftermath of the French Revolution and with the unbroken enthusiasm of the Enlightenment. The teachers at this school were obliged to write down the subject matter they taught and to justify it scientifically. (Pfammatter 1997) This led to publications including Jean-Nicolas-Louis Durand's famous and influential *Précis des leçons d'architecture données à l'École Polytechnique* (Paris 1802). Teaching no longer took place only in the studio, but also in lectures and seminars, and an effort was made to underpin design teaching with theoretical work. Here the principle of academic research was set against the master-pupil relationship of artistic training.

The students of the day were aware of the split into two educational systems, and thus also that they needed to concern themselves intensively with both aspects of building. Many trained under both systems, and occasionally, as in the case of Durand, also taught in both systems. This dichotomy between the artistic and technical-scientific aspects of architecture is still either poorly or wrongly understood and continues to be a cause of uncertainty in the self-perception of architects today. While some see themselves as functional-rational technicians at the service of their clients, with no responsibility for the project as a whole, others are happy to overlook the fact that scientific, technical and economic rationalities are part of the human culture with which we make this world habitable – or uninhabitable.

Architecture is more committed to concrete reality than to any theory. According to this notion, it is best placed at the opposite end of the scale to philosophy on the spectrum of faculties (what Jaspers terms the cosmos of the sciences and humanities). While philosophy sums up and evaluates the results of research work from a theoretical point of view, architecture is able to direct this summing up and evaluation towards concrete realization. Just as philosophy moves in a world of ideas *beyond* the exact sciences, architecture can make a contribution to relating the exact sciences to the concrete world we live in. The idea of a *Synthèse des Arts* as formulated by Le Corbusier would be extended in this way into a *Synthèse des Arts et des Sciences*.

Architecture's role in the university would then be not to complete the totality of the sciences, but actually to bring such a totality into being from the perspective of concrete realization. In order to achieve this, systematic research – the precise meaning of which is still to be defined–needs not only to be rated much more highly in architecture faculties, but also needs to be anchored within the self-comprehension of designing architects.

RESEARCH IN ARCHITECTURAL DESIGN

One of the most concise definitions of scientific research was proposed by the biologist Edward O. Wilson who says that natural science "is the organised, systematic enterprise that gathers knowledge about the world and condenses it into testable laws and principles". (Wilson 1998, p. 53) The natural sciences represent ideal academic activity employing criteria such as methodological rigour, repeatability, predictability and conclusive general validity. Gregory Bateson identifies the limitations of this ideal:

"Whenever we pride ourselves upon finding a newer, stricter way of thought or exposition [...] we lose something of the ability to think new thoughts. And equally, of course, whenever we rebel against the sterile rigidity of formal thought and exposition and let our ideas run wild, we likewise lose. As I see it, the advances in scientific thought come from a combination of loose and strict thinking, and this combination is the most precious tool of science" (Bateson 1972, p. 116 f.)

According to Bateson, the indispensable basis of scientific research is to be clear about the precise requirements when a problem is approached, as academic enquiry never proves anything. It simply sets up hypotheses that it either improves or refutes as the research proceeds (Bateson 1979, p. 37). It is only when the researcher is aware of what is required that it becomes possible to question it. In the *Book of Disquiet*, which Fernando Pessoa, the modernist Portuguese writer, attributes to his heteronym Bernardo Soares, a fragment of a sentence suddenly crops up between two longer sections, and without any further comment. It says: "... *o sagrado instinto de não ter teorias.*" (... the sacred instinct to have no theories ...). (Pessoa 1991, p. 77) These words give a sense of the ideal view of an artist or scientist exposing him or herself to the totality of human existence, in an attempt to absorb the world without the filter of theoretical categories.

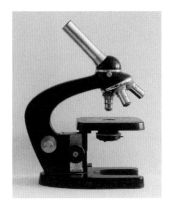

Symbol of scientific research: the microscope

Human freedom, which Karl Jaspers once characterized as an *"existence of freedom inaccessible to all research"*, (Jaspers 1946, p. 50) manifests itself above all in the creative act of design. One aim of this book is to describe the freedom of design, in the hope of making it more accessible, able to be experienced and communicable. What must be avoided at all costs is to constrain design in a predefined methodology. On the contrary, the world of design should be understood as open, and at the same time as complete in itself, as a realm containing a wide variety of languages, and of forms of thought and work. This should contribute to a development that Wolfgang Welsch identifies in academic theory as a whole, where the artistic element is not just a programme for art, but also for its opposite pole, science itself. (Welsch 1988, p. 18 f.)

How do research and design relate to each other? What can research do for designers? Both activities produce knowledge, but of different kinds. Design, seen by many artists as a means of providing insight, can definitely not be replaced by research. Research, and scientific and technical research in particular, does contribute to the knowledge that may inform a design. But the process of design can claim to be scientific only to the extent that it is based on scientific insights. The relationship between design and science can be seen as analogous with the relationship between medical treatment and natural science: medical practice is based on scientific practices and insights, but itself is not a pure, but an applied science. Design is an art that is essentially compelled to rely on personal knowledge about actions and experience, one that goes beyond secured facts and beyond craft and technical knowledge. So, on the one hand, design is not a science in its own right, but draws on technical and scientific insights as well as artistic skill and ability. On the other hand design, although not a science, can be the object of systematic research.

Any research that addresses design is not so much concerned with isolating and analysing existing objects or repeatable phenomena for detailed study. Rather, it addresses the relationship between the thoughts and actions of design, and the future, and inherently uncertain, realization of what has been designed. Such a "design science" goes beyond the academic disciplines of art, culture and engineering, and encompasses a sphere in which both scientific and artistic approaches are relevant. The problems of design, and thus also of an academic discipline for design, are of a fundamentally different structure to those of traditional academic disciplines. Horst Rittel also defined the categorical difference between an academic approach to design and traditional academic approaches by distinguishing between "tame" and "tricky" or "wicked" problems which because of their complex and contradictory nature can be neither unambiguously defined nor completely solved.

A scientific argument is normally abandoned when an irresolvable contradiction, a paradox is identified in its logical structure. In contrast to this, the activity of design is characterized by the problem that the designer is expected to devise acceptable solutions despite obvious contradictions. Any academic approach addressing design must therefore look for ways of identifying paradoxes, decoding their structure and significance and working with them productively. For example, it could do this, as Rittel suggests, by redefining the problems to be solved or as Vilém Flusser demonstrates, by looking for solutions on another level of meaning.

Research of this kind can support design and design teaching by constructing theory. One of its essential aims would be to make implicit knowledge from actions and experience *"communicable, verifiable, discussable"*. The architect's ability to bring together different disciplines, scales and levels of consideration when designing and building is increasingly in demand in the sciences. Jürgen Mittelstrass writes that science is no longer interested in recognizing what holds the world together in its innermost workings, but in

the by no means less important and increasingly urgent task of holding the world together. (Mittelstrass 1994, p. 32) In this context, nothing less than a new translation of the Greek word *architekton* is proposed. The verb *arkhein* is usually translated as *"to take the lead"*, but its original meaning is simply *"to begin, to rule"*. The term *tekton* does iden-

36 research works on the subject of design

tify the carpenter, and *tectonics* is also *"pertaining to building or construction"*. (Onions 1996, p. 906) But when these two concepts are related to architecture and science as a whole, their meaning is extended significantly. Being an architect would then mean not just being a master builder "lording it over the carpenters," but means acting as an artist, engineer and scientist at the same time– *as someone who starts to fit individual parts together to form a harmonious whole.*

ARCHITECTURAL DESIGN

Of course there's a contradiction. It's within the contradictions and ambiguities that we must find our work. John Cage (after Mau 2000, p. 427)

This book came into being as the result of a search for new ways of describing design. Design theories usually prescribe certain methods or systematic procedures, or they present the architectural elements from which a design could be devised. An attempt is made below to identify the aids and possible ways of acting available to design, to analyse them and to discover their potential for further critical development on a higher and at the same time more concrete level. The fact that it does not seem possible to formulate generally valid design methods – a dream of old, comparable with the medieval search for the philosophers' stone, or Modernism's search for a world formula that explains everything, or the search for software that would solve all communication problems – should not put us off trying to widen the boundaries within which design thinking can operate.

In the "horizontal section" through various areas of knowledge we are undertaking here, the level at which we are directing our attention is defined by two questions: "What is design?" followed by "What are the tools of design?" This process is related to the way architects work. When designing and planning a building they link countless pieces of information from different disciplines without losing sight of the project as a whole. These thoughts started with approaches made to design theory by the designer Otl Aicher and the philosopher Vilém Flusser. Aicher's writings in particular have set new standards for the systematic discussion of design. Flusser's texts, above all his study of the *Geste des Machens* (Gesture of Making) (Flusser 1991) and of the relationships between tool, machine and apparatus, can be read as complementary, theoretically well-versed and deeper explorations of Aicher's less systematic approaches.

Architect drawing. Photograph: Marianne Kristen, 2002

To a certain extent, this book follows the structure of many works on engineering, in which the first part is devoted to the theoretical basis for the tools, usually developed by the particular author, and these are then described in detail in the second half – with the difference that in this book none of the tools are new, instead existing ones are considered anew. Here our fundamental concern is to see the whole picture. This corresponds with the approach taken by designers, who repeatedly make sure they have an overview of the context they are moving in, in order to set individual details and the whole, the design and its context, in a convincing relationship.

Two sentences in particular caught my attention, because they suggest a new view of design, and one determined neither stylistically nor ideologically. The first comes from Álvaro Siza, who declared in an interview:

"One should not make oneself the slave of one tool only. That is why I always work with proper drawings from the drawing board, with sketches and with models at the same time." (Bauwelt 1990, p. 1470)

Doubts about the fitness of the tools available can be noted here, and as a response to this, the idea of relativizing these as part of the everyday design work, and thus compensating for their deficiencies. And a second sentence struck me in Otl Aicher's book *analog und digital (analogous and digital):*
"we must move from thinking to making and learn to think in a new way by making." (Aicher 1991/1, p. 76) Aicher talks about the cultural and ideological limitations of thought, and thus also of design, and at the same time shows how these can be questioned by actual work.

Design processes are infinitely complicated and rich in detail, and hard to predict in terms of their crucial elements. Every individual designs differently. Everyone knows different things, sees things in different ways, thinks in different structures and follows different criteria, and expresses thoughts differently. Simple rules or compact theories of design, even if there were any, and even if they were right, would remain either too detailed or too general to be much help in day-to-day practice. But a theory is able to help formulate a range of questions, to think them through and differentiate them sufficiently in order to find appropriate answers to the questions raised in practice. A theory of this kind can place a large number of observed details in sensible contexts, make their mutual relationships and dependencies recognizable and help to draw a picture of architectural design that can always be

Exhibition gallery in the faculty of architecture at Oporto University (FAUP), Álvaro Siza, 1986–1995

corrected and differentiated further. Each question is at the same time a challenge to readers to reflect on their own way of working and formulate their personal responses.

Designers are working towards the future, looking at the relationship between what they are designing at a particular moment in the present and its future realization. Essentially the design process involves translating theory into practice. But the relationship between the original design idea and its future realization cannot be grasped with the same analytical rigour as problems in the natural or even the social sciences. On the contrary, the ability to deal with a lack of rigour reflectively is an essential skill for competent design.

Architects use the factual knowledge – classified by Aristotle as *episteme* – they have gained from the natural sciences for their work, but the work itself is based on abilities that would be called *poiesis* (Greek: making, manufacturing, producing) and *praxis* (Greek: acting, behaviour) in Aristotle's terminology. While *poiesis* relates to the *"skilful craft knowledge"* (Gadamer 1998, p. 6) of *techne*, the basis of *praxis* is knowledge of another category that Aristotle calls *phronesis* and defines as *"directive, true behaviour based on reasons in the sphere of what is good and bad for man"*. (after Ebert 1995, p. 167)

Aristotle clarifies the distinction between these two categories by taking the example of the craftsman whose expertise, restricted to his trade and manufacturing skills (*poeiesis*), he distinguishes from the architect's good and reasonable behaviour (*praxis*); he still knows what to do for the best when *techne* and its rules fail (cf. Nichomachean Ethics VI, 1141b 20). In this context, Aristotle mentions *architektonike* as a *"supreme art of direction"*. (Gadamer 1998, p. 12) The actual problem of design, it can be said now these definitions have been established, is not just a question of *poiesis* and *techne* (expert manufacture), but above all of *praxis* and *phronesis* – that good and reasonable behaviour that grows out of *empeiria* (Greek: experience). Unlike the natural sciences, which see themselves as value-neutral, when dealing with design the question of value, whether the value of a piece of knowledge, of a skill, an action or a tool, is of central importance.

Designers addressing concrete problems thus find terse definitions by the book relatively unhelpful, what they need is differentiated knowledge of the possibilities for design action. In general, both classical architectural theory and current design theory discuss the role of criteria, examples and the results of design work. However, here we will discuss tools and cultural design techniques.

EXAMPLES, PRINCIPLES, THEORIES

A broad spectrum of specific knowledge is required for design, differing according to subject. All disciplines share general knowledge about the activity of designing that is regrettably seldom exchanged outside the individual subject areas. This survey concentrates on the sphere of architecture, and is complemented by references to related areas. The structure of the fields of knowledge laid down here also applies to other design disciplines.

What literature is currently available about design, and what part of it is of particular relevance to designers? There are enough design-related publications to fill entire libraries. It is not just architects, designers and engineers who are concerned with questions of design, so too are town planners and landscape architects, historians of architecture, technology and art, mathematicians, psychologists and neurologists, fine artists, musicians, managers and philosophers. This may be why the discourse on the subject is so little ordered or generally just loosely linked.

The wide range of research approaches available to design are presented for the English-speaking world by Groat and Wang in the book *Architectural Research Methods* (2002) and Laurel in *Design Research* (2003). Groat and Wang examine seven different research methods in detail, while Laurel collects several dozen independent pieces of research on the subject. She uses a matrix in which categories of methods, contexts, objects and spheres available for research intersect with the subject areas of person, form, process and action to show (Laurel 2003, p. 8 f.) that most of these studies touch on several themes and several categories. In this book we have simplified this and distinguish between three categories: views based on examples, on principles and on theories. These are arranged in several sub-groups in each category, on a scale from the general to the personal. Those publications most important for the current discourse are dealt with below, and some further 300 publications are listed in the bibliography.

WHAT ONE CAN DESIGN

Design approaches that are informed by *what* can be designed use concrete, realized examples and are generally not seen as design doctrine or design theory. As a rule such publications stress the artistic and visual aspects of architectural design. Their predecessors are the 19th century's portfolios and submissions. For many designers these are a favourite source of information.

Based on examples (what one can design)

Based on individual buildings (the making of ...)
Based on **typologies**
Based on styles, formal languages, genealogies, trends
Based on regions, countries or periods
Based on the œuvres of **individual designers**

Based on principles (how one can design)

Based on design teaching
Based on the **design process (methodology)**
Based on rules, **standards,** regulations
Based on building materials or construction methods
Based on **graphic representation**
Based on formal design principles
Based on an analysis of the **architectural elements**
Based on individual designers' working methods

Based on theories (how design can be accounted for)

Based on approaches from the **natural sciences**
Based on approaches from the life sciences
Based on approaches from the humanities or **cultural science**
Based on **social and political subjects**
Based on art, architectural and design theory

Approaches to design research (relating to architecture)

They are usually easy to consume, conveying straightforward and applicable examples that can be imitated without critical study and absorbed into the designer's own work without difficulty. In the worst cases, such literature can lure practitioners into superficial imitation. At best, when coupled with other questions, they provide insight into the deeper motivations behind design solutions.

Working on the basis of **individual buildings** makes it possible to show a design emerging in full detail. Fiederling's book (1975) does not do justice to its ambitious title *Theorie des Entwerfens* (Design Theory), as all it does is show how a design for a detached house is developed step by step. But Nägeli and Vallebuona (1992) demonstrate how a factory complex comes into being in exemplary fashion. In *The Making of Beaubourg*, Silver (1994) examines the "biography" of the Centre Pompidou by Piano and Rogers over a decade after its construction. Books by Foster (2000) and Behnisch and Durth (2005) do not just introduce the story of the buildings they have converted and the institutions they house, but also the political background to their design work. In many cases, publications addressing individual buildings are little more then self-presentations by building firms, architects and their clients.

Product design, for example, conducts intensive market and user-oriented design, both in advance of the design phase and afterwards as a subsequent evaluation by independent institutions. This is uncommon in the field of architecture. There are, however, studies based on **typological questions**, which select projects on the basis of certain functional criteria, impose some order on them and thus lay them open to comparison. For example, the *Floor Plan Manual: Housing* (Schneider 1994, 2004) offers numerous floor plans for homes at a scale of 1:200, complemented by sections, photographs and technical information to provide a good overview. Similar volumes are available for industrial buildings (Ackermann 1988, 1993, 1994) as well as for offices, high-rise buildings and museums. The Bechers' numerous books on the architecture of the mining industry, or Höfer's (2001, 2005) on interior design for public buildings make valuable contributions using the resources of documentary photography.

There are so many studies based on architectural trends, individual regions or particular periods that it would be go beyond the scope of this book to mention them individually. As with works on individual personalities, they shed light on the cultural, geographical and political contexts of design.

Upper floor and stairs in the Lello & Irmão bookshop, Oporto

HOW ONE CAN DESIGN

The approaches discussed so far see design in terms of its results, while the second group's approaches and publications are based on principles that are readily identified and can serve as examples. They ask how and by what means designs can be made and look at the methods followed, and the points of view, rules, regulations, standards and laws that have to be taken into consideration. They attempt to record the parameters and laws of design rationally. Almost all these contributions can be classified under one of the individual aspects mentioned below, and even if many publications discuss elements from several approaches, none of them successfully provides a comprehensive account of the wide range of specialist knowledge and the broad spectrum of different cultural techniques required for designing.

Another difficulty lies in the fact that knowing and acknowledging these rules and principles is not always essential and in no cases a guarantee for producing good designs. Their sphere of validity is always limited, but these limitations are almost never indicated. An enlightened treatment should particularly stress the relativity of such rules. Rules for applying rules are seldom given, and according to a polemic by Francisco de Goya, *"in art no rules apply anyway"*. (after Hofmann 2003, p. 119) In fact many of them are more like recipes or rules of thumb that are now presented as universally valid.

Architecture faculty library at Oporto University (FAUP), Álvaro Siza, 1986–1995

One simple example: the formulae Neufert gives for staircase pitch (1992, p. 176) are certainly adequate for the dimensions of standard stairs in flats or offices, but of no use for stairs in prestigious public buildings, gardens or parks – or for that matter for double-decker buses. They take no account of the width of the stairs, which makes a crucial difference in terms of safety, nor of the speed at which they are usually climbed or descended. But above all they do not consider the architectural significance that a particular pitch can convey.

Many of these books reduce architectural design to something technical. Artistic and cultural aspects are neglected, as are historical ones, and no attempt is made to prioritise methods. One positive aspect is the attempt to make generally valid statements about those aspects of design that are independent of a person, or of formal language. This approach originated in the Enlightenment and freed design teaching from the master-pupil relationship by developing rational design theory based upon scientific principles. It can be traced back to Durand and the early days of the École Polytechnique in Paris. (Pfammatter 1997)

In the context of this approach, a first group of publications concentrates on the design process and its systematisation in design methodology. This approach was already the subject of study by the Design Method Movement in the 1960s whose story is recorded by Prominski in his dissertation on *Komplexes Landschaftsentwerfen* (Complex Landscape Design, 2003).

Reading room in the Cottbus University library, Herzog & de Meuron, 1994–2005

The approach taken by Joedicke (1970, 1976) describes a functionalistic design methodology based on process, using complex *"evaluation and decision-making techniques"*, (1976, pp. 33–34) but without adequately presenting the procedures of design itself. In his book *Creativity as an Exact Science, The Theory of the Solution of Inventive Problems* (1984), the Russian academic

Altschuller develops algorithms for solving invention problems that help to systematically determine the parameters of such tasks and suggest ways of solving them. His approach is now pursued in the engineering disciplines, but also offers many ideas for the sphere of design.

Design methodology is also still pursued today. For example, Engel (2003) uses numerous diagrams in his attempt to present *"the methodology of architectural planning as a rational procedure, transparent and predictable"*. (loc. cit, p. 230) By contrast, Gerkan suggests that *"the assertion that design could be explicitly effected in terms of methodology is charlatanism"*. (Gerkan 1995, p. 39) Kücker also criticizes the *"so-called scientific approach to design"*: he says that cutting the dimensions of design down to something comprehensible on the basis of a rational planning process is bound to fail, as designing is an artistic act. (Kücker 1998, p. 19, p. 92 f.) Schön examines design processes, but without going back to the

Reading room in the Aveiro University library,
Álvaro Siza, 1988–1995

nebulous concept of the artistic. He decodes the involved and often unpredictable sequences by observing architects, engineers and town planners in detail, but also includes scientists, psychotherapists and managers. He ends up with a description of design as a *"Reflective Practice"*, (Schön 1983, 1987) which he says is characterized by a constant reflective oscillation between rules and their evaluation. But above all, Schön shows the categorical difference between applying rules, to which he also attributes scientific principles and theories, and a *"reflective"* design that cannot be enshrined in rules because of its complexity. Dorst (1997) also compares rational problem-solving strategies with the "reflective" practice described by Schön, as two fundamentally different ways of describing design processes. Starting out from the everyday practice and theory of design, his book *Understanding Design* (2003) collects 150 short essays, each one page long, to form a mosaic that provides a good overview and conveys a variety of inspiring insights.

The **rules, standards, regulations and laws** of architectural design form the basis on which Neufert (1936, 2005) developed his design-oriented *Architects' Data* handbook, which is still very popular today. However, he devotes only few lines to the actual design process. In the German edition he describes design using the metaphor of a birth:

"And now the labour pains of the first house design begin, first in the mind, as a deep immersion in the organizational, organic intricacies of the task and the intellectual motivations behind them. Out of this, a shadowy idea of the intellectual approach to the building and its atmosphere as a set of spaces starts to emerge for the designer, and out of this the physical quality of its appearance in ground plan and elevation. A rapid charcoal sketch is the first result of this labour for one designer, a filigree scribble for another, according to temperament. The result may seem like just a scrawl for most people but for those who know how to read it, it is a living thing from which the design for the building is refined, becoming ever more transparent and intelligible." (Neufert 1992, p.42)

Here the design process is rendered somewhat mystically as something in the mind, experienced almost passively. In this respect, the value of the book lies not so much in the way it presents design but in the abundance of technical data it offers in compact form – a similar function to the one fulfilled today by the volume *Time-Saver Standards for Architectural Design Data* by Watson,

Crosby and Callender or the *Metric Handbook* by Adler (1986, 1999). The numerous publications, beloved of students, by the US classic Ching (1979, 1989, 1998, 2002) introduce design principles based on formal creative approaches, on **presentation** (especially drawing and perspective) and on building analysis. His books contain many examples inviting imitation, but little explanation, classification or analysis. A related but more analytical approach is contributed by Ermel (2004) in German. His *Grundlagen des Entwerfens* (Fundamentals of Architectural Design) presents design methodology using formal principles and the functional basis of architecture, but without going into any detail about design itself or its tools. Schricker (1986) and in particular Knauer in *Entwerfen und Darstellen* (Designing and Presenting, 1991, 2002), operate rather like Ching, focusing entirely on drawing as a medium. Despite its subtitle that refers to drawing as a means of architectural design, drawing is treated as a means of presentation rather than a design tool. As with Porter and Goodman's *Manual of graphic techniques for architects, graphic designers and artists* (1980), the account thrives on the numerous examples intended for imitation.

But in practice certain spheres of presentation or "visual representation" have long been separated from the process of design. In addition to architectural draughtsmen, there are now also specialists for drawing perspectives, model-making and digital presentation. Rodrigues (2000) analyses drawing as a specific design tool for imposing order on architectural thinking. De Lapuerta examines sketches by Spanish architects (1997) in a similarly analytical way; Smith (2004) and Moon (2005) do the same for architectural models.

Fonatti (1982) also takes **formal design principles** as his starting point, as do the above-mentioned publications by Ching (1979) and Ermel (2004, vol. 1). Fonatti analyses the basic design principles using basic geometrical forms and possible ways of dividing them up and exploring them creatively as ground plans for buildings. Von Meiss (1984) looks at general formal design principles such as order, contrast, proportion and symmetry, combining these with the architectural dimensions of path and place, material and space in his building type studies.

As with Ching (1989) and Ermel (2002, vol. 2), **building typology**, seen as an analysis of architectural elements, is the starting point for Alexander, who makes analysing individual architectural situations the basis of his design theory in A *Pattern Language* (1977). Fuhrmann links functionalistic building analysis with a description of planning processes in *Bauplanung und Bauentwurf – Grundlagen und Methoden der Gebäudelehre* (Architectural Planning and Building Design – the Basics and Methods of Building Theory, 1988). His book is more an examination of the general conditions that need to be adhered to, the physiological, sociological and ecological bases of building, rather than the process of design itself, which receives only marginal attention and is dismissed in five pages using some diagrams. Accounts of design that describe outstanding practice from the **working methods** of individual architects may seem particularly promising. This requires the author to be very close to the designer's everyday work. Unfortunately, such studies are often undertaken only posthumously. For example, Klaus-Peter Gast (1998, 2001) analyses the principles and methods underlying the works of Louis I. Kahn and Le Corbusier. In *Der Sinn der Unordnung* (The Meaning of Disorder, 1989), Michels researches the work forms in Le Corbusier's studio. One exception is Rodrigues, who with *Obra e Método* (Work and Method, 1992) devoted a revealing study to the personal design methods of Álvaro Siza. Eames Demetrios, the grandson of Charles and Ray Eames, provides a detailed picture of work in the Eames Office in his book *An Eames Primer* (2001), based on conversations with family members and many former employees.

Many authors explain their **personal working methods** in remarkable texts that admittedly tend to be more self-glorifications of the "brilliant designer" than precise studies. A large number of texts are worth reading in relation to design, including those by Alvar Aalto, (Schildt 1997) Buckminster Fuller, (Krause 2001) Jean Prouvé (2001), Renzo Piano (1997), Norman Foster, (Jenkins 2000) Peter Eisenman (1995, 2005), Álvaro Siza (1997) and Otl Aicher (1991, 1993). The engineers Peter Rice and Cecil Balmond pass on many inspiring insights into their thought and work in their books *An Engineer Imagines* (Rice 1994) and *Informal.* (Balmond 2002)

Designers also provide information about the rules and principles of design in **interviews**. Lawson (1984) asked architects including Santiago Calatrava, Herman Hertzberger or Ken Yeang about their design processes. Robbins pursues a similar approach: in *Why Architects Draw* (1994) he presents interviews with eminent architects on their treatment of drawing as a central design process. A less convincing book is Lorenz's *Entwerfen: 25 Archi-tekten, 25 Standpunkte* (Architectural Design: 25 Architects, 25 Viewpoints, 2004), which despite the sweep of its title scarcely achieves more than an image-enhancing presentation of the featured architecture practices. Although not directly related to architecture, the conversations and photographs that Koelbl uses to present the working methods of well-known German language authors in her volume *Im Schreiben zu Haus. Wie Schriftsteller zu Werke gehen* (At Home in Writing. How Writers Approach Their Work, 1998) reveal much about creative work.

Last but not least, the rules and principles of design can also be presented from the point of view of **teaching**. The two most important 19th century institutions, the Paris École des Beaux-Arts and its opposite number the École Polytechnique are described by Cafee (1977) and Pfammatter (1997). Wick (1982) examines teaching at the Bauhaus and Blaser (1977) introduces Mies van der Rohe's teaching. Since Lindinger's publication in 1987 there have been numerous publications about the hochschule für gestaltung in Ulm. (including Spitz 2002, Form+Zweck no. 20/2003, Ulmer Museum/hfg-Archiv 2003) The volume edited by Jansen (1989) gives a detailed account of Bernhard Hoesli's modernistic courses in the architecture department of the Swiss Federal Institute of Technology in Zurich. Kleine and Passe (1997) provide a record of *Positionen zur Entwurfsgrundlehre* (Positions on the Fundamentals of Architectural Design) as practised in Germany in the 1990s.

Design textbooks like Schricker's *Raumzauber* (Spatial Magic, 1999) are aimed directly at students. Schricker discusses the design of rooms and products for the teaching of interior design taking a conceptual approach based on presentation methods and design methodology. In *Opening Spaces* (2003) Loidl presents a series of design principles derived from analysing the elements of landscape architecture. Dominick's *Tools and Tactics of Design* (2000), a textbook for engineering students, offers a detailed description of tools and procedures, but restricts itself to engineering design.

The approaches discussed above deal with concrete *donnés*. The authors in the third group draw on artistic or scientific theories as a basis for design. They ask how design can be given a conceptual basis, and look for the premises and theories, criteria and paradigms that should be used for design. Most practitioners find these texts too abstract and too little suited to practical application. As such they are primarily the subject of discussion and development in the context of research, teaching and criticism.

Scientific approaches like mathematics, cybernetics, model theory, complexity and chaos theory and information technology form the basis for the works of authors like Broadbent (1973), Rittel (1992) and Kalay (2005). Broadbent introduced a wide variety of new approaches to discussing design methodology in the 1960s in the rich material included in his study *Design in Architecture – Architecture and the Human Sciences* (1973). This discussion is driven by the tendency to transfer new methods developed in the sciences and space travel to architectural design. Broadbent combines a broad thematic spectrum including statistics, cybernetics, model theory, Computer-Aided Design and "New Maths" with general design practice questions and methodology, user needs and the environment. However, with all of these approaches the problem still remains that some key parameters of architectural design cannot be either quantified or predetermined.

Horst Rittel taught at the hochschule für gestaltung in Ulm and later at the universities of Berkeley and Stuttgart. He was a trained mathematician and theoretical physicist, and published numerous essays on planning and design theory, touching on various specialist areas. The most important of these were collected in a single volume posthumously. It contains a number of remarkable theoretical approaches, even if no over-arching theory of design is formulated. As a mathematician, Rittel successfully identifies the categorical differences between the "tricky" and "wicked" nature of design problems and the comparatively simply structured problems faced by the exact sciences. Relating to Rittel to an extent, Kalay (2004) offers a very detailed and comprehensive design theory, focused on CAAD, presenting the *"Principles, theories and methods of computer aided design"* using mathematical or methodological approaches. Despite this Kalay, like the two authors mentioned previously, touches on design tools only cursorily.

There are numerous studies that are relevant to design, although of course seldom written by or for designing architects, that are based on **life science approaches** as pursued by psychology and neurology, on the subjects of mental strategy, emotionality, creative techniques or game theory. Neurological insights by Sperry (1968), Eccles (1966, 1973) and others show that different thought patterns predominate in the two halves of the human brain. In *Lateral Thinking*, De Bono (1970) describes a series of mental strategies complementing traditional thought structured according to linear and analytical logic, which he classifies as *vertical*, with *lateral* thinking, i.e. thinking using generative, speculative patterns that employ mental leaps, a method particularly suitable for solving design problems. He uses this method very successfully to develop teaching methods, which he presents in numerous subsequent publications. The neurologist António Damasio examines the meaning of emotions for rational thought in his acclaimed works (1994, 1999). His case studies make it clear how emotions are fundamental to rational behaviour: the patients' intelligence is entirely uncompromised, but they are unable to feel emotions – and as a consequence are no longer capable of rational thought and action.

One central theme of design is dealing with **complexity**. The psychologist Dietrich Doerner has published a great deal of material on thinking and problem-solving (1974, 1976, 1983, 1989), and Schönwandt related this to architects' activities and developed it further in *Denkfallen beim Planen* (Thought Traps for Architects, 1986). Vester also published on these subjects (1975, 1980, 1988): in *Die Kunst vernetzt zu denken* (The Art of Networked Thinking, 1999) he describes tools for a systematic treatment of complexity, combining cybernetic, ecological and computer-oriented approaches. Lawson's much-read volume *How Designers Think* (1980, 1990, 1997, 2006) relates to the activities of architects in particular. It examines the thought processes involved in design from the point of view of psychology and design methodology. In this way he creates a comprehensive account of design that also addresses the most important design tools. His key topic is *"Design Thinking"*, and complements the approach followed here of presenting design from the point of view of tools. Lawson develops the themes of his first book further in *Design in Mind* (1994), analysing concrete design processes by contemporary architects, and in *What Designers Know* (2004), an account of selected designers' specific knowledge.

The **perception** and communication processes through which all information incorporated in a design is ultimately acquired are also fundamental to design. Two works by Arnheim, *Art and Visual Perception: A Psychology of the Creative Eye* (1974), and *Visual Thinking: About the Unity of Image and Concept* (1969) are indispensable here. Wiesing's *Philosophie der Wahrnehmung* (Philosophy of Perception, 2002) examines the difficulty of defining the concept of perception satisfactorily – comparable with the difficulty of defining design. Spengemann's *Architektur wahrnehmen* (Perceiving Architecture, 1993) presents "experiments and studies of the many areas of interplay between man, architecture and the environment" (subtitle), but this is directed more at the reception of towns and architecture rather than their design. The same applies to Seyler's *Wahrnehmen und Falschnehmen* (Perceiving and Mis-perceiving, 2003), which develops "formal criteria for architects, designers and art educators" (subtitle) on the basis of Gestalt psychology. However, focusing as exclusively on this aspect as this author does would mean ignoring the complexity of design problems. The theme of contradictory demands emerges particularly clearly in the communication between laymen and experts, which the psychologist Riklef Rambow examines taking practising architects as examples (2000).

Studies based on the **humanities' and cultural science' approaches** consider design from the point of view of philosophy, sociology, media and culture theory, and the history of architecture, technology and art. The works of the designer and theoretician Otl Aicher and the philosopher Vilém Flusser, which are seen as complementary to each other, contribute to the fundamentals of the approach developed here. Related to these are some of the texts addressing tools and cultural techniques in the volume *Bild – Schrift – Zahl* (Image – Text – Number, 2003) edited by Krämer and Bredekamp, as is the fine seminar report compiled by Adamczyk *Rezeptfreies Entwerfen: Auf der Suche nach persönlichen Gesichtspunkten im Entwurfsprozess* (Design without a Recipe: Looking for Personal Viewpoints in the Design Process, 1998). In contrast, the collection of essays edited by Mattenklott and Weltzien *Entwerfen und Entwurf: Praxis und Theorie des künstlerischen Schaffensprozesses* (Designing and Design: Practice and Theory in the Artistic Creative Process, 2003) remains bogged down in academic meticulousness driven by a series of highly specialized, usually historical studies, without linking them to any broader discussion. Ferguson (1992) offers an account of the history of design from the point of view of the engineering sciences that is well worth reading. The conference volume *Bauplanung und Bautheorie der Antike* (Building Planning and Building Theory in Antiquity, DiskAB 4, 1984) from the German Archaeological Institute brings together a series of remarkable contributions.

The great interest in design shown by **philosophers and sociologists** indicates that the subject is by no means a special ability shared only by artists, architects, engineers and designers, but a fundamental human activity. The French sociologist Pierre Bourdieu provides some valuable insights in *Homo Academicus* (1984) and *Les Règles de l'Art* (1992) which, although they do not relate specifically to design, do contribute a great deal to understanding individual aspects. Making reference to John Dewey and the philosophy of pragmatism, the sociologist Hans Joas lays down the principles of a *"pragmatic action theory"* with creativity at its core in *Die Kreativität des Handelns* (The Creativity of Action, 1996). Lenk also devotes himself to this subject matter in *Kreative Aufstiege* (Creative Ascents, 2000), in which he writes about the *"philosophy and psychology of creativity"*. He combines the concepts of creativity and metaphor to make "creataphor", which he uses to define the human urge *"to keep on creating, to keep transcending boundaries and strata symbolically"* (p. 338). These themes are extended into a differentiated spectrum in the two wide-ranging volumes on "Creativity" that form the report, edited by Günter Abel, on the 20th German Philosophy Congress. (Abel 2005)

Astonishingly, design as an activity is seldom a central them in the **theory of art and architecture**, presumably because it was long felt to be unsusceptible to theory. But a number of texts provide valuable information about the motivation and reasoning designers employ. Publications in which authors expound and defend their own artistic and theoretical positions regularly influence architectural debate to a considerable extent. The significance of architects like Adolf Loos, Le Corbusier, Robert Venturi, Aldo Rossi, Oswald Mathias Ungers, Rem Koolhaas or Peter Eisenman derives not least from the way their theoretical work is linked to what they have built. A good view of this is provided by the numerous collections of texts that have appeared in recent years, including Kruft (1986), Nesbit (1996), Jencks / Kropf (1997), Neumeyer / Cepl (2002), Evers / Thoenes (2003),

 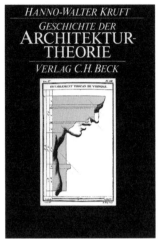 

Text collections on the theory of architecture

Moravansky / Gyöngy (2003), De Bruyn / Trüby (2003), Lampugnani / Hanisch / Schumann / Sonne (2004).

Although none of the above-mentioned anthologies address design in particular, the topic is of greater importance to **theory in the field of graphic and industrial design**. This is presumably due to the influence of the hochschule für gestaltung Ulm. The theoretical studies undertaken there are continued in work including that by Aicher (1991), Rittel (1992) and Bense (1998). Schneider (2005) combines a design history of the 20th century with theoretical ideas about design, while Thackara in his book *In the Bubble – Designing in a Complex World* (2005) addresses predominantly the criteria for future design. Fischer and Hamilton (1999) have published a collection of basic texts.

A forum for the subject of design research in the German-speaking countries is largely non-existent, there being a lack of specialist institutions and of academic periodicals devoted to the subject. As well as this, the individual research areas are not linked to any extent, even though an interdisciplinary approach to the subject would seem to be urgently needed. **Trade journals** do devote individual articles to the subject of design, and sometimes even entire issues (see Thesis no. 2/1999: *Architektonisches Entwerfen*, *Cloud-Cuckoo-Land* no. 1/1999: *Design* and no. 2/2000: *Design Teaching*, *Graz Architecture Magazine GAM* 02/2005: *Design Science*, *Form & Zweck* 21/2005:

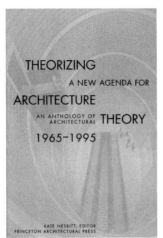

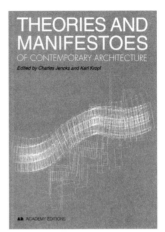

Entwerfen). The *Design History Society* of Great Britain, founded in 1977, publishes the *Journal of Design History* (London: Oxford University Press). The magazine *Design Issues* (Cambridge, Mass.: MIT Press) has appeared on a quarterly basis since 1984, dealing with *"design history, theory, and criticism"*. The *Architectural Research Quarterly* (Cambridge, UK: Cambridge University Press) has been published since 1995, and contains numerous articles discussing fundamental architectural research questions. The *Journal of Architectural and Planning Research* (Chicago: Locke), *Design Studies* (Oxford: Elsevier) and the Harvard *Design Magazine* should also be mentioned here. *Architectural Design* (London: Wiley) devotes occasional issues to design (no. 176, 4/2005: *Design Through Making*). The European Association for Architectural Education (EAAE) addresses questions of design education, and publishes a quarterly Newssheet. Networks have come into being in countries including Switzerland (Swiss Design Network, SDN) and in Holland where the Doors of Perception design network arranges conferences in Amsterdam and Delhi alternately.

Terms and definitions

Terms are programmes. Horst Rittel (1992, p. 249)

40

Terms in design are often bandied about with a considerable lack of precision. Only the context makes it clear what an author actually means by designing, developing, inventing, creating, making, shaping, modelling, drawing, planning, conceiving, projecting, presenting, calculating, describing and so on. Each of these terms emphasizes particular aspects of design that seem to be essential from a particular point of view; it is only when seen as a whole that this conceptual field indicates the broad range of possible design actions. One reason for this may be that the term design in the sense of architectural design is not widely used in everyday language, and thus scarcely defined by habitual usage, while at the same time it is used in very different ways in various professions – architecture, interior design and engineering, landscape architecture, town planning, IT, graphics and industrial design, but also fine art, theatre direction and design, writing, science and politics. Another reason for the lack of precision in the term is the fundamental ambiguity of design itself. It is not possible to determine from the outside whether someone is only scribbling or tinkering at a particular moment, or "really designing", and often the person doing it will not know either. As Flusser shows, designing is a gesture, an arbitrary act that can be "true", but also "untrue". It is only by its future consequences – solving a single design problem, winning a competition, a completed and approved design, difficulties that occur or do not occur during the building phases, the qualities of the completed building, the cultural quality accruing to it – that the quality of such a gesture can be gradually measured.

Title page of Walter Ryff's German translation of Vitruvius: *Vitruvius Teutsch*, Nuremberg, 1548

PLATO, ARISTOTLE, PLOTINUS: *IDEA*

The concept of what design is, and how and by whom it should be practised, has been formulated differently in every epoch. The art historian Erwin Panofsky attempts to show by studying the history of the term *"idea"* that every notion about what design is can relate to two opposite positions.

41 (Panofsky 1924) The first of these draws on empirical reality, where ideas emerge as mimesis and a perfecting force of nature; for example, Socrates says that *"the painter should be obliged and enabled to combine the most beautiful parts from a number of human bodies in order to make the figure to be represented appear beautiful".* (loc. cit., p.15) This view, which is influenced by a sensual perception of the world, was criticized in Plato's counter-argument as being merely imitative, based on deceptive appearances. His theory of ideas is based on the hypothesis that the fluctuating, deceptive appearances of the sensual world are confronted by an unchanging world of perfect ideas as the *"true reality"*. These serve as *"immutable models and causes for the imperfect objects of the world of appearances".* (after Metzler, p. 249) Both points of view are problematical in terms of the relationship between *mimesis* (imitation) and *poiesis* (creation). The dualism between the world of ideas and the world of appearances postulated by Plato is toned down by Aristotle to a *"synthetic interaction between form and material".* (loc. cit., p. 17) He argues that everything comes into being *"by the entrance of a definite form into a definite substance",* so works of art differ from works of nature only in that their form is in the soul of man before it enters the material. (loc. cit., p. 17)

In Plotinus, the Platonic idea becomes the *"living vision of the art,"* (loc. cit, p. 26) and as such claims metaphysical validity and objectivity as it is identical with the principles in which nature originates and *"that reveal themselves to the artist in an act of intellectual contemplation".*

(loc. cit., p. 26) In the early Middle Ages a shift of accent was enough to make what for antiquity was a *"philosophy of human reason"* into a *"logic of divine thinking",* and to establish the idea as a theological concept. Augustine defines the concept in almost the same way as Plato, but with a crucial reversal:

Leonardo da Vinci: Structural scheme of the duodecedron, from: Pacioli (1509)

A distorted polyhedron: the Casa da Música in Porto, OMA / Rem Koolhaas, 1999–2005

"For they [the ideas] are the original forms or principles of things, constant and unchangeable, that themselves have not been formed. They are therefore eternal, persisting in one and the same condition and contained in the divine intelligence, and while they themselves do not arise and perish, everything that can and does arise and perish is said to be formed according to them." (Augustine, after Panofsky, p. 38–9)

Thus it was scarcely possible any longer to speak of an artistic idea in the actual sense. And beyond the doctrines of the philosophers and theologians, the master builders of the Middle Ages did not see themselves as designers either, but identified their task as building on the basis of existing predecessors. Once a building type was established, its basic idea often remained unchanged for a long time:

"Thus the building pre-existed in the mind of the architect; and this can be designated as the Idea of the house because the artist tends to assimilate the real building to the same form that he has conceived in his mind." (St. Thomas Aquinas, after Panofsky, p. 41)

Design was not a central theme for classical architectural theory. Thus Vitruvius may not seem substantially important for the philosophical discourse presented by Panofsky. In his *De architectura libri decem (Ten books on architecture)* the Roman author devotes himself exclusively to the questions of how and what is to be built, but the activity of design itself is discussed only in passing. He manages it in just two sentences, albeit very fine ones. He does not yet use the Latin term for design *projectare* at this juncture; in the context of drawing he speaks only of "analysis" and "invention".

43

"The species are produced by analysis and invention. Analysis is devoted concern and vigilant attention to the pleasing execution of a design. Next, invention is the unravelling of obscure problems, arriving through energetic flexibility, at a new set of principles." (Vitruvius I, 2,2)

By "forms" Vitruvius means *"the forms of Dispositio, which the Greeks call* μδεασ *(ideas)"*: by this he understands the ground plan largely reduced in scale, the front view and the perspective view – in other words not *"immutable primal forms"* in Plato's sense, but representations created by individual reflection and individual invention. So Vitruvius is not moving back to "eternally valid" ideas, but basing himself on the possibility of being able to create something new. Another remarkable feature is the reference to a feeling of happiness, suggesting the emotional side of design.

More careful reading of Vitruvius *Ten books on architecture* will detect many more scattered hints and statements about individual aspects of design, for example the story of Callimachus, who was inspired to design the Corinthian capital by the sight of a basket standing on acanthus leaves:

"Callimachus [...] passed by this monument and notices the basket and the fresh delicacy of the leaves enveloping it. Delighted by the nature and form of this novelty, he began to fashion columns for the Corinthians on this model, and he set up symmetries and thus he drew up the principles for completing work of the Corinthian type." (Vitruvius IV 1,10)

Here transferring a formal principle from the sphere of biology into architecture by imitation becomes a kind of primal design narrative. Vitruvius describes architects knowledge and tools in many other places, formulates

Callimachus, from: Roland Fréart 1650 (detail)

fundamental criteria, criticizes working on models and describes, often in anecdotal form, how design problems are solved. His descriptions are often succinct and substantial, and they show how little the problems he deals with are anchored to a specific time.

In the English translation of Leon Battista Alberti's *De re aedificatoria libri decem (Ten books on architecture)* few pages are in fact devoted to the subject of design in the broadest sense. One must, he writes *"weigh up repeatedly and examine, the work as a whole and the individual dimension of all the parts".*
(Alberti 1485, p. 34)

Alberti is concerned to remind us that design decisions should be weighed up carefully to avoid mistakes when realizing the building. Unlike Vitruvius, he considers that building models is very important. Ultimately Alberti says very little about design itself, but simply recommends considering, over and over again, the whole building and the dimensions of each individual part, and

"by the time-honoured custom, practised by the best builders, preparing not only drawings and sketches but also models of wood or any other material". (Alberti 1485, p. 33 ff.)

His book *De pictura (On Painting)*, completed in 1435 and first published in 1540, contains the first description of perspective, which will be discussed in a later chapter.

VASARI AND ZUCCARI: *DISEGNO*

The term *disegno* acquired its central significance in theoretical discourse in Florentine and Roman art theory in the second half of the 16th century. As Wolfgang Kemp explains in his study of conceptual history, (Kemp 1974), an argument flared up about the form that the seal should take for the Accademia del Disegno founded in Florence c. 1562. A definition that Giorgio Vasari had formulated shortly before this emphasizes two aspects: he says that design is *"the father of our three arts, which emerges from the intellect"*, but at the same time, whether its quality is recognized *"depends on hands that have been practised for years in drawing"*. (Vasari 1568, after Kemp 1974, p. 226) Benvenuto Cellini, a member of the academy, put forward several designs based on this definition, including one that embodied design in the figure of Apollo. According to Cellini, just as Apollo represented illumination, disegno is the light of all human actions. He adds that *disegno* is the father of all fine arts, painting, sculpture and architecture, and of the goldsmith's art. (Cellini, after Kemp 1974, p. 222)

Kemp shows how at that time a second meaning was added to the original meaning of the term, and this was soon accorded considerably more importance than the first. *Disegno* originally means drawing or plan, and relates to *forma* and *pratica*, to the visible form of the drawing, and the practical ability to draw. It was understood as the *scienza delle linee*, (Vasari, after Kemp 1974, p. 225) as the knowledge of reproducing nature correctly. But on a second level, *disegno* means design, and is seen as *disegno della mente*, as an intellectual ability, related to *concetto*, *idea* and *inventione*. Now *disegno* is nothing less than the ability of *inventione di tutto l'universo* (Doni, after Kemp 1974, p. 225). Cellini identifies this double meaning by speaking of *disegno primo* as the intellectual ability to design, and *disegno secondo*, which deals with everything that can be represented with the aid of dots, lines and fields. (Kemp 1974, p. 231)

Federico Zuccari brought discussion of the term to a provisional conclusion at the Roman Accademia di San Luca, founded in 1593. He now makes a clear distinction between *disegno interneo* (which Cellini called *disegno primo*), which he sees as the ability to form *"a new world in one's self"*. (Zuccari, after Kemp 1974, p. 232) and *disegno esterno* (which Cellini called *disegno secondo*), which relates to the practical execution of *immagine ideale*. (Kemp 1974, p. 231 ff.)

A possible reason for this division of artistic work could, according to Kemp, be the artists' socioeconomic situation. Only a few of them were granted major commissions; when this happened, they concentrated on the design, and then called upon a large number of colleagues to help with the realization. On the other hand, artists who won very few commissions were forced to restrict themselves to design. Thus it was of interest to both groups to emphasize design.

Kemp describes two different ideas from that period of designing. Vasari sees design as active mediation between nature and art. The designer draws his ideas from the observation of nature, on the basis of his general judgement. Here Vasari is drawing on the ancient legend of the painter Zeuxis, who chose the most beautiful parts of the body from five selected models and used them for a painting of Helen. (after Kemp 1974, p. 229) But Zuccari sees design as a God-given creative activity. He says that nature can be imitated because it is driven by a spiritual principle, and art follows this same principle. Man should

"produce countless works of art, to a certain extent imitating God and competing with nature, and be able to create new paradises for himself with the aid of painting and sculpture". (Zuccari, after Kemp 1974, p. 232)

Kemp deals with the design and working practices of those days only peripherally. He also does not ask the obvious question of why the term *disegno* acquired two meanings, rather than creating a new term, especially as this double meaning has survived to the present day in some languages (English design, Portuguese desenho). It is in fact generally remarkable how many of the views developed at that time still apply. For example, the person who has invested the most intellectual work in a project is not seen as the author of a design; the author is the person who formulated the basic ideas and prescribed the direction the project should follow subsequently. Many people successfully put into practice the insight that qualified designers can practise their creative abilities in various artistic disciplines. But

Design for the Quinta da Malagureira development, schematic sketch of the silhouette of Évora, with a note on the illegal settlements, Álvaro Siza, sketchbook no. 23, Mai 1978

negativo:
clandestino: rede de ocupação aberta?
em vez de limitar essa rede —
limitar abertos p/ um sistema
sucessivas SOBREPOSTAS E
Retestar numa só { paisagem
aptidão solar
facilidade de
comunicação
valores culturais
pré-existentes
etc.

Indefinir de Évora: um plano ideal da burguesia esclarecida
que a evolução histórica torna obsoleta
A ruptura das soluções paternalistas
que fazer?
Auxiliar das forças de transformação
a dar mapas propostas
proposta

Zuccari's view that ultimately design means the ability and responsibility to *"form a new world in one's self"* (after Kemp 1974, p. 232) is no longer generally held. This is one reason for the often lamented short-sightedness and superficiality of many designs, and not just architectural ones.

Current definitions of design are often either circular (*"design is shaping"*) or simply replace the term with another one (*"designing means making decisions"*). Statements like *"design means ..."* are made by designers to express their view of design strikingly, but they are not definitions. This way of talking about design is often found in the accounts architecture practices publish about themselves. Among such one-dimensional definitions is that formulated by Jürgen Joedicke: an architectural design, in other words the result of designing, is *"the experimental and ultimately drawn solution of a building problem"*. (Joedicke 1976, p. 13) The author shows how unsatisfactory he finds it himself in the sentence that follows: *"Very different situations occur within a design process, and they require different resources"* – although he does not explain what these situations could be and what resources they require. Here at least the inadmissible limitation Joedicke is imposing is made clear, which cannot be said of Aicher's equally one-dimensional statement that *"designing means constructing models"*, an assertion based on a very general, science-based concept of the model.

The assumption that "designing means deciding" also forms the basis for more complex accounts of the design process. The Viennese architect Ottokar Uhl sees drawing up a draft as "deciding about the basic features of the project," and continues:

"In a rational design method, the complex overall decisions that are customary for an intuitive approach can be broken down – at least in principle – to the smallest unit of decisions between one of two things ("bit"), a unit in information theory" (Uhl 2003, p. 261)

Decisions are indispensable steps in a design process, but this applies to any reasonable activity. Equating design with decision-making neglects the creative element in favour of hierarchical argument. It is assumed that it is not the person devising the ideas who is designing, but the person who makes the decisions. But if decisions are to be made, there must be alternatives about which way they can be made. It is the quality of these alternatives that fundamentally determines the quality of the decisions to be taken. In any case, the necessity of making decisions should be sufficient reason for devising more sophisticated evaluation processes (Joedicke 1976, pp. 33–34) and thinking about fundamental decision theories. (Rittel, p. 245 ff.)

There is a second group of definitions that is already much more complex in its structure, but ultimately reflects nothing more than the personal approach to design taken by the particular authors. The German architect and theoretician Friedrich Ostendorf starts the foreword to the first volume of his *Sechs Bücher vom Bauen* (Six Books on Building) by lamenting that a great deal has been written about architecture *"in old and modern times,"* but never a book that talks seriously about design; never had *"one of the many architectural theorists come up with the idea of expressing himself on this theme clearly and in detail"*. Ostendorf goes on to say that if one were to ask (in 1913) a number of contemporary German architects what they understood design to be, they would all come up with a different answer, if they produced one that was comprehensible at all. (Ostendorf 1913, p. 2) For Ostendorf, design means *"formulating one or several or many ideas for the building in one's mind, on the basis of thorough thought about and processing of the building programme, including situation and spatial requirements"*. (loc. cit., p. 129) He feels that the essential criterion here is the clarity and simplicity of the design idea. He describes the design process – in a single paragraph – as formulating an idea *"in the mind of the building artist"*. This is then captured on paper as a sketch, and revised as the process continues. For Ostendorf the crucial criterion is that the design idea should first be thought through *"in the mind's eye"* and only recorded on paper as a second step. (loc. cit., p. 4, p. 129) Only in this way can one arrive at *"clear artistic ideas"*, as everything else comes into being *"in an inartistic and senseless way on paper"* and is *"absolutely impossible to grasp as an idea in its tangled complexity"*. (loc. cit., p. 4) Consequently, Ostendorf defines design as *"the search for the simplest appearance for a building programme"*, (loc. cit., p. 12) *"as only that which is simple and legitimate, and nothing that is convoluted and arbitrary, can be clearly grasped within the idea"*. (loc. cit., p. 129) Restriction to the plane of thought is intended to avoid complex and less striking designs. When he postulates that only this is real design, everything else is mere drawing (loc. cit., p. 129) he is confusing a criterion with the activity itself. Essentially Ostendorf is interested in disciplining design.

Architects like Günter Behnisch can make very little of Ostendorf's view. Behnisch sees designs as *"complex and complicated structures, influenced by countless forces from numerous disciplines"*, (Behnisch 1996, p. 30) developed in long-term design processes. He replaces Ostendorf's somewhat dramatic expression *"mind of the building artist"* with the dry words *"my head"*.

"I did not find advice of this kind helpful, maybe because such demands were not
sufficient for my head, or that I felt that the head alone could grasp architecture only
imperfectly, that there were also dimensions lying outside the realm of the rational,
or that I had recognized that we are not intended to be able to grasp many dimen-
sions of reality in our heads at once." (Behnisch 1996, p. 29)

The close link between such definitions of terms and personal ways of working is made clear, for example, by Ottokar Uhl who finds the term "architectural design" questionable in itself because it suggests isolation, intuition (in German, *Entwurf* suggests *"der grosse Wurf"*, the successful pitch, the big achievement), immediacy and a complete lack of effort. He says that the term "planning" could possible replace "architectural design", but would mean a methodically conducted decision-making process for preparing external actions. Uhl consequently demands that design and realization should not be seen as separate actions, but that planning and building should be considered as a continuous process. (Uhl 2003, p. 63) This view clearly reflects Uhl's own participatory planning and building practice, without making any major contribution to explaining what design is.

Within functionalistic discourse, the term "architectural design", which has something of an artistic ring to it, is frequently replaced by the seemingly more rational expression "planning". Planning, seen as merely technical design, dealing with a manageable set of quantifiable qualities, is well suited to formulation in terms of methodological procedures. For a functionalistic approach to architecture it would make sense to define procedures of this kind for the design as well. Otl Aicher criticizes the concept of planning, which he sees as a *"concretized, targeted projection method"* (Aicher 1991/1, p. 133), which simply extends general principles into the future as a chain of causality according to the respective planning logic. But as the world does not ultimately follow logical principles, he feels that planning should be replaced by the more economical method of cybernetical control, whose field of action is concrete reality within the perceptible environment. (Aicher 1991/1, p. 143)

Horst Rittel on the other hand describes planning as *"solving tricky or wicked problems,"* a description that, with some restrictions, also applies to larger design tasks. In contrast to *"tame"* problems, there are no definitive formulations of the task in hand for *"tricky"* problems (which elsewhere he also calls *"wicked"* problems), and no definitive solution either. The solutions are not right or wrong, but at best good or bad, usually just better or worse. He feels that there is neither a direct nor a final possibility of checking the quality of a solution, and furthermore there can only be one attempt at a solution – large public buildings for example are almost irreversible. So each *"wicked"* problem is unique. But he says that at the same time planners do not have the right to be wrong, on the contrary they are responsible for the consequences of their actions, which are often far-reaching. He continues that each *"wicked"* or *"tricky"* problem can be seen as a symptom of another problem, and one can never be sure of tackling a problem the right way or of seizing a problem by the roots rather than just curing a symptom. There are several or many explanations for this kind of problem, and the choice of explanation determines the nature of the solution to the problem. (Rittel 1992, p. 20 ff.)

Rittel makes a fundamental contribution to understanding design by describing how it differs categorically from the realms of technology and science, that concern themselves with clearly defined *"tame"* questions. He sums up the differences in the *"paradoxes of rationality"*: if rational behaviour is seen as an *"attempt to predict the consequences of intended actions,"* then one would arrive at an infinite series of consequences and consequences of consequences. The more time and energy devoted to investigating the consequences, the less there is left for concrete action. A model for describing consequences must contain itself, as it determines the consequences that should be considered. (loc. cit., p. 40 ff.) Thus Rittel sets out the boundaries of the concept of rational planning.

A third category is formed by definitions of design that are formulated so broadly that their constituent concepts cannot themselves be expressed in a conclusive definition. By way of example, we can cite Aicher's statement that design is *"making technical, constructive organization forms and implementing*

a programme in the form of an organization". (Aicher 1991/1, p. 101) He completes
and explains this technical sounding approach in the same text in this way:

"design is a process of intellectual ordering, clarification of connections, defining of
dependencies, creation of weightings and requires of the designer a special ability to
see and to fix analogies, connections and fields of reference." (Aicher 1991/1, p. 102)

This description too fails to consider large areas of design activity, emphasizing intellectual abilities but neglecting creative production.

The question "What is design?" turns out to be a fundamental one, to
which there is no conclusive answer, something Flusser would call a "riddle
to be deciphered" – in contrast to a soluble problem. It would certainly be a
worthwhile task to examine the use of individual terms more carefully in
relation to certain persons or discourses, but this would be primarily of
philological interest, rather than of interest for design theory. In the following section, the lack of precision in the term will be seen as a characteristic
whose meaning is to be deciphered as far as possible.

The term "design" relates to three fundamental areas of activity that are
sometimes simply identified by the terms "seeing, thinking, doing". Further
differentiation of these terms helps us analyse it more precisely, but
describes it rather than defining it. An attempt is made to explore design as
an activity, to make it accessible, comprehensible, open to experience, not so
much reflecting on the meaning of the term, but on the activity itself.

AICHER AND FLUSSER: *NEGATION* AND *TRANSCENDENCE*

Otl Aicher's and Vilém Flusser's published work on design theory con-
verges in the somewhat utopian and anti-academic belief in the possibility of
liberation through new, radical approaches to design thinking and activity.
They think in completely different ways, but refer to common core elements.
They correct and complement each other in essential points and when considered together point to the beginnings of a comprehensive design theory.

Both Aicher and Flusser question Modernism from its very roots. While
Aicher, however fragmentarily and unsystematically, addresses a broad
spectrum of design-theoretical questions in his writings, developing realistic
ideas, Flusser's statements remain too general and abstract to offer any
chance for concrete analysis in many spheres. Aicher develops concrete
ideas, coherent in themselves, that are nevertheless also open to attack. Both

writers' works make an important contribution to design discourse. Both men are discussed in detail in the chapters on theory (Aicher, see p. 209), and on tools and gesture (Flusser, see p. 88, 105). Their basic attitude to design is discussed below.

Both Aicher's call to see the *"world as design"* (Aicher 1991/2) and Flusser's desire to find fresh hope moving *"from Subject to Project"* (Flusser 1994) are rooted in the emancipative canon of Modernism. For both of them, this is thwarted by the experience of "apparatuses" that have become uncontrollable for both individuals and society. This is a topos that appears even in the early 20th century in Franz Kafka or Kurt Tucholsky, and was developed by writers like Max Horkheimer and Theodor Adorno in relation to the culture industry. But while Aicher proclaimed *the world* as an object to be designed, Flusser sees *himself* as a subject to be designed.

Comparing the two positions reveals a fundamental difference in the way the two authors think: Aicher tends to respond negatively to subject areas he finds problematical, but is unable to overcome these problems intellectually. He remains in their thrall simply because he rejects certain positions so vehemently. Flusser on the other hand overcomes difficulties by moving to higher planes of contemplation, and so can make contradictions work for him productively by turning them into something he sees as positive. Thus for example Aicher's radical criticism of the digital leads him to conclusions that are similar to Flusser's. While Flusser acknowledges that digitalism is unstoppable, and looks for ways of dealing with it positively alongside its negative consequences, Aicher rejects everything digital in principle. The same applies to his rejection of art with reference to Modernism. The fact that he makes the criterion of functionality an absolute, his self-sufficient thinking, the general claim to a *"world as design"*, but also his dogmatic language and impatience with other ideas seem to make him captive within a way of thinking that is opposed to his own claims about his political and cultural position.

Flusser also addresses the problem of theory that has become an instrument of power, the cause of which he sees in the need to provide explanation derived from the natural

Otl Aicher: *Entwurf der Moderne* (Designing Modernity). Arch+ no. 98, 1989

sciences and which is not appropriate for many questions. He then develops another concept of theory: theory is no longer to explain, but to analyse meanings, not remove problems from the world, but to describe possibilities, not shut off, but to open up.

This example makes it clear: something that is fully acceptable as a designer's personal approach, even if it becomes idiosyncratic, turns into a restrictive ideology if it is combined with a claim to general validity. Here it is essential to distinguish between *general* and *special* design theory. Formulating individual design approaches has fundamentally different aims from a theory that has the right to claim *general* validity. Designers have to reach a single solution that can hold its own in competition, and they should also develop an identifiable way of working. To achieve this, they have to make precise, concrete suggestions, and convey these convincingly, backed up by consistent arguments. Hence in many cases, essentially for rhetorical rather than objective reasons, they negate everything that questions their personal approach to a solution. They are then no longer conducting an open discussion, but making an authoritarian gesture by demanding that their own ideas be accepted without reservation. But a general design theory should aim to indicate a broad spectrum of design possibilities.

Two questions are fundamental for any design theory: how do forms emerge? And from what do they derive their meaning? Flusser describes how artificial forms created by people emerge from addressing the material through gestures of making that are ultimately based on arbitrary decisions. Form and meaning are connected in this process, but without being mutually dependent. There can therefore be no compelling logic explaining how forms and their meanings emerge. On the other hand Aicher's approach of

rationalizing design processes describes the attempt to restrict the proportion of arbitrariness in order to make design decisions more rational and easier to understand. Flusser realizes from a position of concrete powerlessness that there are certain forms he cannot change himself, but that he can manipulate their meaning. Aicher describes designing a concrete world on a small scale

"… the artistic task of endowing with form, which always selects, cuts away, renounces: no form without refusal."
(Adorno 1970, p. 216) Photograph: Stephanie Meyer, 2002

Vilém Flusser: *Virtuelle Räume* – Simultane Welten (Virtual Rooms – Simultaneous Worlds). Arch+ no. 111, 1992

as a strategy of survival in a society dominated by apparatuses. Here both abandon an obsession with a common and authoritative future for us all, offering instead a picture of a world in which isolated individuals communicate with each other freely. They are looking for the open, non-repressive society that they each had re-established for themselves on several occasions, either by withdrawing or by emigrating from a society that had become repressive.

Aicher's thinking turns out to be that of a craft designer who strives for a concrete "good" and "correct" form, which he derives from its function. He does this through clarity and negation, and these also become his preferred intellectual strategies. On each occasion he looks only for a single solution, but a realistic and convincing one, reaching it by a process of selection and negation of all other possible solutions. But Flusser's question is: how can I as an individual lend meaning to my personal gestures? He views this as a central aspect of designing that as an intellectual act has no or only limited practical impact on the world, indicating instead possible changes *symbolically*. In his last, unfinished work *Vom Subjekt zum Projekt (From Subject to Project*, 1994) he tries to rethink design fundamentally by addressing areas not normally accessible to designers, either because they are taboo or because they are obscured by customary practices. Here Flusser is arguing as a philosopher opening up new areas of intellectual possibility without having to be particularly concrete about it. He is a designer here in the more profound sense of the concept, thinking a long way into the future without knowing precisely what it is supposed to look like. In his search for gestures that confer meaning by going beyond fulfilling existing functional programmes, he finds truth in aesthetic appearance. Meaning can emerge from form, but also from quite different factors. By asking how he can endow his gestures and actions with future meaning he is trying to transcend concrete givens.

Ways of designing

All I ask is method, never mind what method. Denis Diderot (1751, keyword Encyclopédie)

We learn to design and give form to things by doing so. But what are we doing when we design? Design developed out of the anticipative consideration of making something. Designing means devising a form for an object without having that actual object in front of you. Giving form or shape to something relates to a concrete object that exists and can be worked on directly. By comparison, designing relates to the future form of an object that can be depicted only in an abstract or reduced form when it is being designed. Given the lack of any direct feedback through trial and error, designing therefore differs from the artistic work of painters or sculptors as well as from the working method of craftsmen, who as a rule are all able to manipulate their artefacts directly. Essentially this is a question of scale and the complexity of the object to be made. A characteristic of architectural design is the great distance in terms of both space and time between the design and the realization of what has been designed. There is always something uncertain, daring, utopian about designs. Designers have the responsibility of recognizing the requirements and consequence of a design and ensuring that they are considered in the design itself.

The possibilities, but also the consequences of design are now more fundamental and far-reaching than ever before. But above all, designs have acquired a scale and a degree of complexity that the question arises as to whether they are still manageable. In his analysis of the "apparatus", Vilém Flusser has identified the paradox that the meaning of every design decision can be precisely its own opposite on other levels of consideration. In the early 21st century we live mainly in worlds that were made and shaped by human beings, but they were not necessarily designed, at least not in a sense that recognizes and considers the requirements and consequences of a design.

Ways through a landscape (on the banks of the River Douro, west of Oporto)

PERCEPTION AND THOUGHT

Perception is the first and at the same time the fundamental step in any design work. It arises from the sum of the observations made as an individual, as a single person relying on his or her own individual sensibility. The perception of something real as well as the perception of something that has just been designed is based on the ability to perceive a place, a situation, a building, but also a project in all its different phases of development, with all one's senses. The sum of the architectural situations we perceive creates a stock of memories, and we draw on these when designing.

In August 1963, the 74-year-old Le Corbusier, looking back on a life rich in experience as an architect, product designer, urban planner, painter and writer, in brief, as a designer in the broadest sense, noted in one of his famous sketchbooks: *"La clef, c'est: regarder... regarder, observer, voir, imaginer, inventer, créer."* ("The key is looking ... looking, observing, seeing, imagining, inventing, creating"). (Le Corbusier, after Croset 1987, p. 4) Perception is fundamental to designing. Conversely, designing turns out to be a specific training in perception that sensitizes designers to certain phenomena and leads to an enhanced ability to perceive. Our sensual organs translate visual, acoustic, tactile stimulation into electrochemical signals that the brain processes as meaningful information. The processing and interpretation of these signals is a fundamental creative process, the deliberate disruption of which can be used to stimulate the imagination, a process that Leonardo da Vinci was already aware of and used. The tricks and dodges he described would now be called creative techniques and illustrate how closely perception and creative thinking are connected. In this context, Leonardo mentions a *"new kind of speculative invention which though apparently trifling and almost laughable is nevertheless of great utility in assisting the genius to find variety for composition"*. This *"invention"* involved *"looking attentively at old and smeared walls, or stones and veined marble of various colours"*:

"You may fancy that you see in them several compositions, landscapes, battles, figures in quick motion, strange countenances, and dresses with an infinity of other objects." (Leonardo 2005, p. 62)

The fact that Leonardo took advantage of these possibilities is confirmed elsewhere by his admission: *"I have already seen shapes in the clouds and on walls that stimulated me to beautiful inventions of the most various things."* (after Chastel 1987, p. 386)

Façade using the principle of optical diaphragms, Institut du Monde Arabe, Paris, Jean Nouvel, 1981–1987

Human perception operates in the field of tension between what is identified by the saying "One sees what one knows" and the question: "How can we see and recognize something that we do not yet know?" All perception takes place against the background of what is already known. New information is compared with existing memories, and classified among them. Seeing something really new requires perception in the form of patient observation, and this is a creative act that needs time and concentration. All our senses are involved in this, our ability to recognize and remember, as well as our expectations, permanent impressions and prejudices.

All design tools are both means of perception and also means of expression, a connection that the architect El Lissitzky illustrates succinctly with a photogram (*Self-portrait: The Constructor*, c. 1924) by overlapping head, hand, eye, compass and circle against a millimetre grid. In an autobiographical note under the heading *Eyes*, Lissitzky suggests how his *self-portrait* should be viewed:

"Lenses and eye-pieces, precision instruments and reflex cameras, cinemato graphs which magnify or hold split seconds, Roentgen and X, Y, Z rays have all combined to place in my forehead 20, 2,000, 2,000,000 very sharp, polished searching eyes."
(after Lissitzky-Küppers 1967, p. 325)

The essential function of design tools is to make internal ideas perceptible for the designers themselves and for others, and thus to make them an object for possible reflection. One of the ways in which design tools can work is by reducing a complex state of affairs to a few manageable aspects that can easily be manipulated. Each and every design tool influences perception and design thinking in a characteristic way through this way of working.

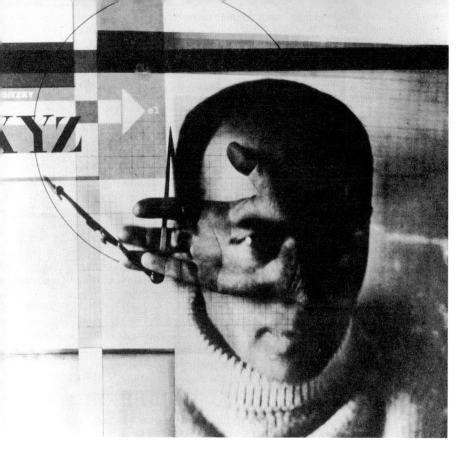

El Lissitzky: Self-portrait, *the constructor*, 1924

The mental processing of information provided by perception and memory is certainly the part of design thinking that is most difficult to grasp. It involves both rationality and emotion, it is characterized by personal memory and imagination, and happens in the form of conscious and unconscious mental processes. Edward de Bono's insights are particularly revealing in this context. In his book *Lateral Thinking* (1970) he describes the contrast between logical and intuitive-creative thinking. Starting with an analysis of the dominant perception processes, he identifies a kind of logical-analytical *("vertical")* thinking that is predominant in Western culture, whose counterpart is intuitive-creative *("lateral")* thinking. He says that the latter is particularly suitable for generating ideas and solving problems. This view, which was considered somewhat esoteric at first, has been confirmed by research by neurologists like Sperry (1968, 1973) and Eccles (1973).

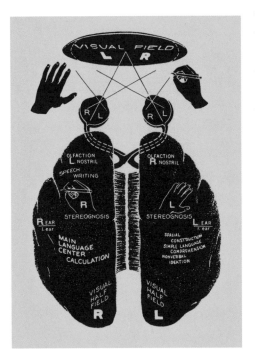

The specialization of different areas of the brain for certain functions has been thoroughly researched since the discoveries by Broca, who located a "language centre" in the left hemisphere (after Linke 1999, p. 54) and Wernicke, who discovered that the upper temporal gyri are essential for the understanding of language. (after Eccles 1973, p. 258) The term "centres" is no longer used today; instead the organization of the brain is seen as a complex interwoven arrangement of linked systems that accommodate individual functions. The location of most language functions in the left hemisphere applies to 98 % of all people, regardless of whether they are left or right-handed. (Eccles 1973, p. 259) But the essential spatial organizers are located in the parietal lobe of the right half of the brain. (Linke, p. 76) Johanna Sattler sums up the fundamental difference between the way the two hemispheres function by saying that the left hemisphere of the human brain

Roger W. Sperry: the lateral distribution of functions in a surgically separated human brain

(which controls the right-hand side of the body in terms of sensors and motors) deals with analytical, logical-linguistic thinking and operates in a linear fashion, i.e. with one mental step following another, while the right-hand hemisphere prefers visual-spatial, synthesizing and holistic thinking, which is highly connective and functions in simultaneous mental steps. (Sattler 1998, pp. 33–42)

This distinction is to be found in the work of a number of authors who characterize the two ways of thinking with different pairs of concepts. (e.g. Eccles 1973, p. 275 f., Edwards 1979, p. 39 f., Sattler 1998, pp. 33–42) Western culture traditionally tends to be dominated by linear-analytical, verbal thinking from the left hemisphere, while the visual-spatial thinking of the right hemisphere is more important for architectural design. Perhaps the most impressive plea for this kind of thinking comes from Rudolf Arnheim in his book *Visual Thinking* (Arnheim 1969). A similar approach is taken by the writer Italo

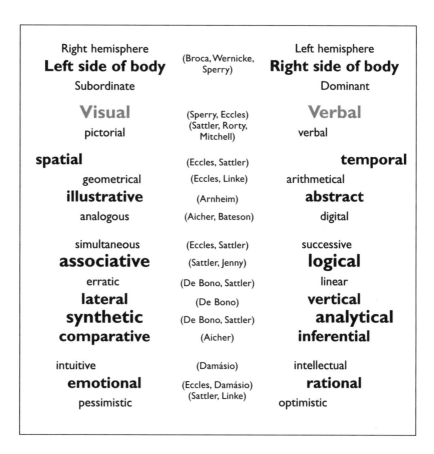

Right hemisphere **Left side of body** Subordinate	(Broca, Wernicke, Sperry)	Left hemisphere **Right side of body** Dominant
Visual pictorial	(Sperry, Eccles) (Sattler, Rorty, Mitchell)	**Verbal** verbal
spatial	(Eccles, Sattler)	**temporal**
geometrical	(Eccles, Linke)	arithmetical
illustrative	(Arnheim)	**abstract**
analogous	(Aicher, Bateson)	digital
simultaneous	(Eccles, Sattler)	successive
associative	(Sattler, Jenny)	**logical**
erratic	(De Bono, Sattler)	linear
lateral	(De Bono)	**vertical**
synthetic	(De Bono, Sattler)	**analytical**
comparative	(Aicher)	**inferential**
intuitive	(Damásio)	intellectual
emotional	(Eccles, Damásio) (Sattler, Linke)	**rational**
pessimistic		optimistic

Various authors allocate pairs of terms that describe the two complementary ways of thinking; the terms overlap in a common field.

Calvino in his lecture on *Visibility* (Calvino 1988, chap. 4) and Otl Aicher, who argues for *analogous thinking* and inveighs against *digital thinking*, (Aicher 1991/1, pp. 34–52) as does Peter Jenny, who defends associative, pictorial thinking as a necessary extension of linear thinking. Jenny argues that we should take the process of learning to think in images just as much for granted as we do the process of learning to read and write. (Jenny 1996, p. 220, p. 228)

It is not surprising that the two ways of thinking are seen as competing with each other and evaluated very differently in individual fields of study. For example, architects and fine artists like to condemn verbal thinking as "grey theory". Cultures that consistently reject images are thus suppressing the visual-spatial thought of the right hemisphere in favour of the linguistic-linear thought of the left hemisphere. They rate order, abstraction and hierarchy very highly, and resist anything comparative, associative and emotional. But it seems to make better sense to avoid this confrontation and see the two ways of thinking as complementary, and to use the possibilities of mutual suggestion and stimulation on the one hand and reflection and observation on the other. One approach would be, for example, to assess the result of a rational calculation holistically and emotionally, or to analyse the outcome of a pictorial synthesis by linguistic means. In design, this can be controlled by systematically changing tools.

DESIGNING AS A PROCESS

Architectural design developed from building, and was and is closely linked with the processes of building. For architects it represents the mental preparation for producing a building. One of the major difficulties of designing lies in understanding what the designed object will mean in reality.

Designers are therefore often driven by the desire to leave decisions about the design as late as possible, so that they can apply large quantities of information to making them. Designing is a process of approaching concrete reality laboriously and gradually: working from the large to the small scale, starting with the abstract and becoming more and more concrete. The term process is derived from the Latin *procedere*, literally continuous operation (Onions 1996, p. 712) and we associate it with something difficult and protracted, brought under control by a gradual, methodical and rational approach in which certain procedures have to be followed as in a court of law, so that the interests of all those involved are accommodated.

Many approaches to describing the process of design are also attempts to structure design processes according to specific examples. An important step was made when designing was no longer perceived just as a mysterious creative act, but as a development process that can be grasped rationally, at least within certain limits. The understanding of the term design has since shifted from that of the unquestionable creative "act of genius" to a sense of developing something. Industrial products such as cars, aircraft or computers are *developed* in long-term processes, not designed. Even Mies van der Rohe preferred to use the term "development":

"We do not produce designs. We consider what could be done, and we then try to develop it, and then we accept it. We always develop from a critical point of view." (after Blaser 1977, p. 14)

Aicher describes the design method in Norman Foster's office in terms that are also more appropriate to gradual development than design. The most elaborate part consists of

"reaching the distillate of the best possible solution in trials, experiments and studies, in numerous iterative cycles of investigation and evaluation using models and prototypes [...] with the help of one's own work and consultation with others". (Aicher 1991/I, p. 101)

Design processes can be described in terms of sequences of different forms depending on the level of observation. Horst Rittel's diagrams show four basic possibilities for structuring the design process. He calls designing an *"iterative process of generating variety and reducing variety"*. (Rittel 1992, p. 75 ff.) The individual iterative steps could be seen as a circular, constantly recurring sequence of the work stages described above, which take the form of a spiral curve. Rittel suggests that idealizing the design process as a *linear sequence* would describe how a "great master" works, who already knows in advance what is to be done, and essentially no longer has to involve himself in the design adventure. He has already solved comparable design problems successfully, and can simply work his way along a tried and tested design path step by step. Rittel's *testing* or *scanning* describes an approach in which the first solution that happens to occur to the designer is used as an attempt to master a design problem. If further work shows that this approach is not going to produce the desired result, then the designer goes back to the beginning and tries a different route to the solution. Rittel calls the formation of alternatives *the systematic production of several alternative approaches* to a solution and the selection of the best one using an evaluation filter that covers all relevant aspects. It can also be done by *forming alternatives in a multi-step process*. In order to eliminate as many nonsensical alternatives as possible from the outset, Rittel recommends working with constraints (self-imposed limitations) for this process, which help to cut down the variety of possible design solutions to a sensible and manageable number.

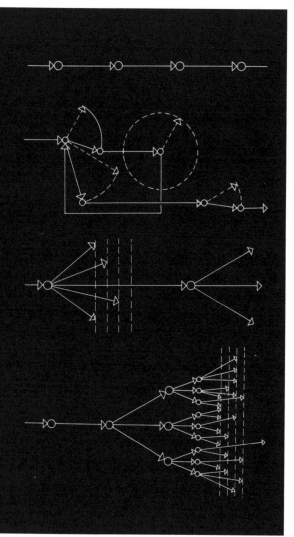

Horst Rittel: design processes of generating variety and reducing variety
a) linear sequence
b) testing or scanning
c) systematic production of several alternative approaches
d) forming alternatives in a multi-step process

The sequences of events that Rittel describes are essentially simple and self-explanatory. His analysis raises them to a level of abstraction that permits systematic comparison. However, more appropriate to the complexity of design processes is the image of a spiral searching movement that Marshall McLuhan uses in his writings on media theory. McLuhan criticizes the contradiction between the usual linear approaches to dealing with objects and the objects themselves, which are not linear, on the contrary:

"all these subsist together, and act and react upon one another at the same time. [...] The entire message is then traced and retraced, again and again, on the rounds of a concentric spiral with seeming redundancy. [...] But the concentric with its endless intersection of planes is necessary for insight. In fact, it is the technique of insight, that is necessary for studying media, since no medium has its meaning or existence alone, but only in constant interplay with other media." (McLuhan 1964, p. 28 ff.)

Applied to designing, this means taking each design problem and considering in what medium or combination of media it can best be processed. The architect Konrad Wachsmann developed comparable ideas as many as ten years earlier in his seminars at the Institute of Design in Chicago and as part of the Salzburg Summer Academy. From 1951 onwards, Wachsmann conducted experiments in team design, systematically alternating between the technical and the personal perspective for devising a design. He describes this way of working as

"a team-work system in which work is conducted on a problem selected by the group, using a combination of basic skills, more advanced studies and research, using direct experiments and subsequent development work". (Wachsmann 1959, p. 204)

Wachsmann says that the design team, which corresponds with a seminar group, should *"ideally [have] 18 to 24 members, and is divided up into working groups each with three participants".* (loc. cit.) Each group of three works on a particular aspect of the brief for a particular period of time from its own specialist perspective *"in an interplay between found information, laboratory experiments, continuous development work on the model and at the drawing board, and in internal discussions among themselves".* (loc. cit.) The result is then presented to the whole team for discussion. After each discussion, the work is passed on to the next group, until each group has worked on each design approach once, from its own point of view. At the end of the design phase the results of the work are revised for presentation. This procedure may well be very

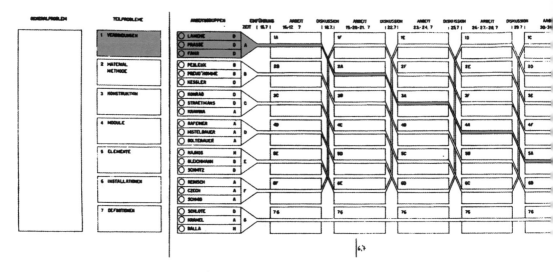

Structure of an experimental team design process, Konrad Wachsmann, 1959

suitable for breaking down fixed ways of thinking and for initiating interdisciplinary projects as part of experimental design exercises, but the amount of time and effort needed and the rigidity of this method would be difficult to apply in architecture practices.

The German regulations for architects' and engineers' fees (Honorarordnung für Architekten und Ingenieure, HOAI) is indeed based on an idea of design as a process. It divides the design and building sequence into nine working phases. Each phase is described verbally, pictorially and in the form of fee calculations. By prescribing certain results for certain design phases (for example, a set of design drawings at a particular scale) but not others (for example building working models, which counts as a special service), it is standardizing the process of design in a form that leaves little room for innovation. Deductive work from the large to the small scale is certainly appropriate for most building briefs, provided that conventional building methods are employed. But developing technically or aesthetically innovative (or even merely industrially prefabricated) buildings is more likely to be based on detail or on developing new combinations of materials. What is more, the actual design phases account for only 18% of the full fee (WP 2: preliminary planning 7%, WP 3: design planning 11%), which leaves little scope for devising truly innovative ideas.

Structure of a traditional design process, Heino Engel, 2003

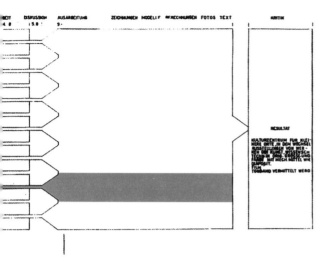

SCHEMATIC PLAN FOR THE SEQUENCES OF A DESIGN PROCESS

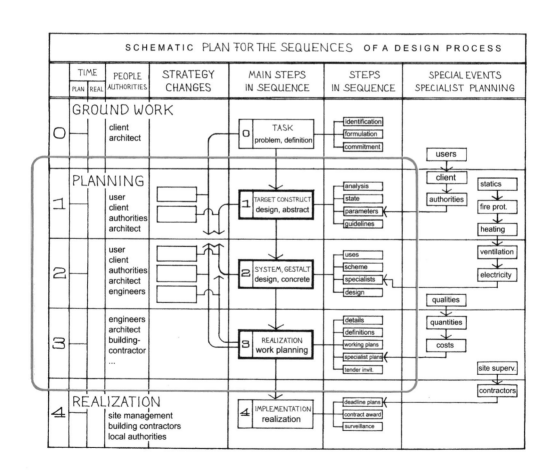

The various dimensions of designing can be presented as a sequence of comprehensible steps in decision-making to differing degrees. The more holistic, innovative or personal a design is, the less it can be predetermined. From this last point of view, the above-mentioned presentations seem like abstract half-truths and idealized positions that fail to connect with the essence of design. There are crucial moments when the design process does not move in a straight line or from the large to the small, and also not in a spiral, but simultaneously, and not infrequently in unpredictable, chaotic quantum leaps. Only technical, engineering-based design, managing and project controlling tends to follow more generally applicable rules and can therefore be summed up better in terms of methodical steps.

Even outside of this differentiation, the attempt to break designing down into a more or less linear sequence of rationally comprehensible decision-making steps will also founder when faced with the complexity of design briefs. Günter Behnisch describes the design of a building as a *"complex and complicated structure, influenced by countless forces from countless disciplines."* He compares this structure to a *"gearbox with thirty to a hundred gearwheels, indivisibly enmeshed"*. If just one of these wheels is turned, the whole structure will move. It is in motion throughout the planning and building period, which means that the appearance of the building is constantly changing. Realizing the building fixes the structure in a particular state, and if one were to go on designing, other solutions would arise. (Behnisch 1996, p. 30)

Complex designs can be evaluated only simultaneously, not consecutively. Otl Aicher explains in this context that a design decision does not mature in a straight line, but by considering a field, by comparing a whole variety of values; connections are being created, and a balanced judgement has to be made, not a balance sheet. (Aicher 1991/2, p. 161) As a rule, several design factors overlap in every design decision, and a choice has to be made about what is more or less appropriate from the chosen point of view, a touch better or worse, a tiny bit more aesthetic or less appealing, as well as what consequences this decision may have for other areas of the design. Numerous attempts have been made at systematizing and rationalizing the evaluation of projects and buildings. (e.g. Rittel 1992, Musso et al. 1981, Weiss 1975, Sanoff 1970) But the decision as to which factors should be included in such an evaluation, and how the various aspects are weighted, cannot be summed up in points or percentages. The choice of the standards to be followed and of the

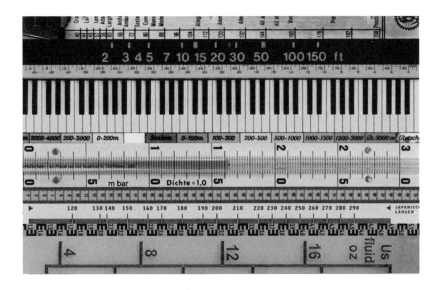

Juli Gudehus: *Precision work* (detail)

arguments that will ultimately carry the greatest force in reaching a decision
has to be made again and again for each individual case.

However rational a description of designing as a process may seem at
first, this representation remains less than satisfying. Processes can be differentiated between those that are strongly determined, weakly determined
and undetermined. (Bense 1998, p. 423). Strongly determined processes can be
described so precisely step by step that they can be repeated or understood
by others if they follow this description. This includes design processes for
technically defined objects which, for example, can be "calculated and
designed" in engineering terms. The solution of architectural design problems, which as a rule fall into Rittel's category of "wicked" problems, must
be described as weakly determined processes that can be fixed only vaguely
in advance. They can be described in retrospect, but this description either
remains general and imprecise, or becomes so specialized and detailed, that
it is difficult to apply to other problems and cannot be repeated with any
sure promise of success.

DESIGNING AS AN INDIVIDUAL ACT

In ideal terms, design could be described in two opposite ways: as a linear or spiral searching movement, in the course of which all the development steps of a design process are worked on in a logical sequence, or as working simultaneously on all aspects of a design. Whilst the second notion appears more suitable due to the range of complex and mutually interdependent factors involved, it is naturally bounded by our limited ability to do, or think about, several things at once. Alvar Aalto's synoptic working methods, as described below, perhaps comes closest to this ideal. (see p. 121 f.)

All design processes culminate in concrete design acts. There is nothing very mysterious about the act itself; we are all familiar with the situation from our own work. We see a problem, try to solve it, are dissatisfied with the solution, try again, set up variants, compare possibilities, until an acceptable solution is found. The designer's entire knowledge and skill are realized at that singular moment when someone makes a sketch, changes a model or formulates an idea. Only at higher levels of consideration can designing be represented as a continuous process. The smallest step in the design

Álvaro Siza, sketchbook no. 300, Nov. 1989

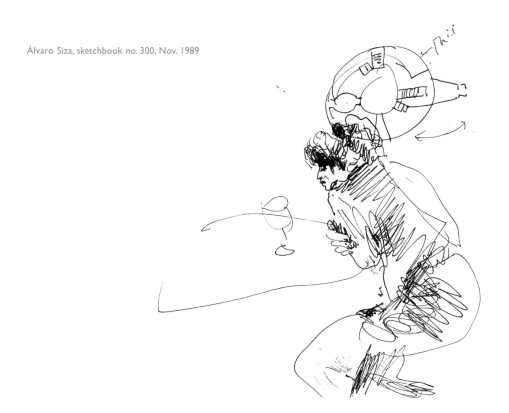

process, which designers can break down no further, is the individual act of designing in which all their knowledge and skill comes together at once and they are present as a full person, with all their senses, all their abilities, all their experience and all their cultural characteristics. This act of designing can be a moment of inspiration, but it can also be an idea that was devised over a particular period of time, it can be a gesture, a thought, a word, a sentence, a conversation, an observation, a judgement, a mouse click. It can be an act of perception, an act of thought, of linguistic or gestural expression or of criticism, or, very probably, all these things at once.

Emotions rank very highly in design, especially in the act of designing. Their importance can be measured by the fact that in certain situations, when no solution for a problem seems to be on the horizon despite intensive work, design seems extraordinarily oppressive emotionally, while at other moments it can make people particularly happy. In the context of design, Günter Behnisch speaks of a "creative process that is often painful even today". (Behnisch 1986, p. 31) In his study of some particularly creative people's biographies, Howard Gardner discovered that periods of heightened creative exertion are often accompanied by phases of depression, leading to mental and psychological breakdown in all seven of the cases he examined (Freud, Einstein, Picasso, Stravinsky, Eliot, Graham, Gandhi). (Gardner 1993, p. 436) And close relationships with one or more people who understood what they were doing and supported them were important for all seven subjects in these creative breakthrough phases. (loc. cit., p. 438, p. 455 ff.)

Since ancient times, designing has been seen as related to emotional elements, and the idea of creativity is lined with emotions. Looking at melancholy as part of the theory of the four temperaments, Aristotle asks:

"Why is it that all men who have become outstanding in philosophy statesmanship, poetry or the arts are melancholic, and some to such an exent that they are infected by the diseases arising from black bile?" (Problems, XXX, 1)

The gesture of melancholy, the bowed head resting on a hand, expresses both reflection and mourning. Albrecht Dürer's famous copperplate engraving *Melencolia I* shows this temperament personified as a female angel sitting on a stone step, surrounded by tools which could be seen as attributes of design. The figure is resting her head, with its wreath of little leaves, on her left hand, her right hand is resting on a closed book and is holding a

compass inattentively; its hinge is shifted somewhat to the right, and is placed just above the centre of the picture. Her face is in deep shade. But the angel's expression is not downhearted or depressed, as might be expected. In fact a slight smile is playing round her lips, and the raised eyes are looking with interest and expectancy at something that seems to be not far beyond the left-hand edge of the picture.

Dürer brings an abundance of detailed and highly artfully and precisely drawn items together in his picture to create a mysteriousallegorical symbol, using a draughtsman's resources to show the irreducible complexity and complex simultaneity that can be felt by a person exposing him or herself to the totality of human existence in the world. Overwhelmed by contradictory, mysterious and alarming phenomena, and at the same time incapable of resisting its fascination, the seated angel lets the hand holding the compasses drop.

Among the many interpretations of Dürer's engraving, (Schuster 1991) two are particularly interesting in relation to this book: firstly, the interpretation as a programmatic image of artistic activity, (Schuster 2005, p. 101) that a series of tools are used as attributes, and secondly the interpretation as representing a person committed to creativity with a *"melancholy emotional structure"* who *"is subject to an abundance of psychological tensions as a requirement and as a tribute to his or her virtue"*. (loc. cit., p. 100) The following chapter (see p. 85) shows that the woodcut of Virgil Solis that Walther Ryff published – first as the frontispiece for the book *Von der geometrischen Messung* (On geometric measurements, Nuremberg 1547) and then in his German translation of Vitruvius *Ten books on architecture: Vitruvius Teutsch* (Nuremberg 1548) – is conceived as a kind of counter-image or antithesis to Dürer's engraving.

Another example of the iconological combination of melancholy and creativity is an engraving that Andreas Vesalius published in 1543 in *De Humani Corporis Fabrica* (On the fabric of the human body, Basel 1743, p. 164). It shows a skeleton leaning in a thoughtful-melancholy pose on the top slab of a tomb and with its hand on a skull that has been placed on the slab. The sentence *"Vivitur ingenio, caetera mortis erunt"* (Creativity survives, everything else belongs to death) is engraved on the front of the tomb in somewhat clumsy capitals. The author of the picture had made an effort to represent all the "tools" that belong to the body, and also identified them meticulously with letters and numbers, thus forming a link with the legend, where

Albrecht Dürer: *Melencolia I*, 1514, copperplate engraving, 23.7 × 18.7 cm, Staatliche Museen zu Berlin, Kupferstichkabinett, inv. no. 352–1902

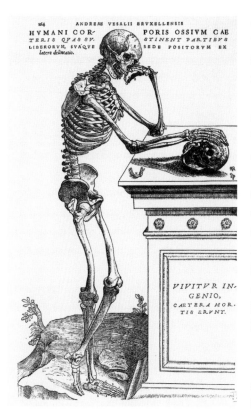

HVMANI COR-   PORIS OSSIVM CAE
TERIS QVAS SV-   STINENT PARTIBVS
LIBERORVM, SVAQVE   SEDE POSITORVM EX
latere delineatio.

VIVITVR IN-
GENIO,
CÆTERA MOR-
TIS ERVNT.

Andreas Vesalius: Human skeleton, from: *De Humani Corporis Fabrica*, Basel 1543, p. 164

all the bones are listed and described individually. At the same time the skeleton's reflective and melancholy pose refers to man's intellectual capacities as his actual tools.

By contrast Vitrivius, in his description of design, emphasizes the positive emotions when speaking of a *"feeling of happiness"* accompanying *"solving dark problems"*. (Vitruvius, I 2, 2) Elsewhere he recounts the anecdote about Archimedes, who leaps out of the bathtub *"in a transport of joy"* shouting the Greek words *"Eureka! Eureka!"* (I found it! I found it!), and *"rushed home naked"* because he had just had such a wonderful idea. (Vitruvius IX, preface, 10) The contemporary term heuristics, the *"theory of ways of interpretation"*, literally the means serving to find out (Onions 1996, p. 439) also refers to this story.

In the 20th century, designing is still seen as being dependent on emotion, despite all the arguments about objectivity and functionality. Bruno Taut, for example, sees rational and intellectual elements as the basis of designing, but they have to be controlled and refined by *"feelings"*. Taut writes that when designing one has to wait *"until one stops thinking and actually only feels"*. (Taut 1936, p. 38 f.) He describes his approach to design as follows in his book *Architekturlehre* (Foundations of architectural design):

"First one thinks through all aspects of the thing in purely intellectual terms, the orientation, the situation in the landscape, in brief everything that influences the thing as a whole, and draws up a scheme. [...] Then, ideally at night, when one will not be disturbed, one concentrates one's feelings on the matter in hand, but without drawing at first. [...] One has to wait until what was hitherto just a scheme starts to fill up with life, until one stops thinking and actually is only feeling. [...] Something one calls the "idea" grows very unclearly in the emotions. The emotions are like a filter; they capture only the experiences and the knowledge that are useful for this new task. Then at last the hand starts to draw, almost automatically, or unconsciously. The mind is switched off." (Taut 1936, p. 38 f.)

But if this is the case, how can we talk about designing without introducing a sense of mystification? Is design, as one could conclude from this view, something emotional at its core, and thus irrational? Does emotional have to be equated with irrational, or can we talk about the intelligence of the emotions? Our thinking is best equipped to solve problems of great complexity with emotional decisions. This corresponds to the fact that we tend at first to feel rather than to analyse the complexity of both spatial and aesthetic experiences. Emotional evaluation is holistic, exposing itself to the totality of a situation. The brain processes far more information subconsciously than it does consciously. Decisions that we make "intuitively" or "emotionally" are based on things not consciously perceived and for which rational justifications are often sought after the event. In recent years these processes have been the subject of considerable research and have led to a reappraisal of the role of intuition and emotions as sources of inspiration. (Traufetter 2006)

Emotion represents the sum of experiences undergone in our consciousness. It encompasses expert knowledge, implicit knowledge from actions and a designer's general knowledge of the world and condenses these into a feeling that something is "better" or "worse", "more correct" or "less correct", a feeling that inherently appears inadequately justified. The emotions provide a necessary corrective for the rational, which can lead people astray, particularly in the field of design. Rational thought, being linear, tends to reduce a broad spectrum of relevant factors to a few that are manageable. A rational argument can seem perfectly conclusive, but yet follow a one-dimensional logic that fails to consider crucial factors and does not consider the complex interplay of the various levels of meaning within a design.

The Portuguese neurologist António Damásio found indications in his studies that emotions form the basis for everything that we think. People who have lost their ability to respond to things emotionally, who have lost their feelings, says Damásio, also lose the ability to plan ahead and act with an eye to the future. Given that their intelligence is otherwise intact, these people are no longer in a position to relate their actions to a wider context. (Damásio 1999) Designers need something that could be called an *éducation sentimentale*, which enables them to be aware of their emotions and interpret them correctly. Conversely, the many buildings that evoke only unpleasant feelings show how much emotion is neglected in training.

The simultaneity of different levels of action in one and the same act of designing makes it difficult to analyse further. The fact that designing is often mystified as something brilliant, intuitive and purely emotional is therefore not without reason. By comparison, the view of designing as a process discussed earlier orders its procedures chronologically and thus reflects the way in which our activity is tied to time. In the process it contradicts the simultaneity of the overlapping and interdependent aspects of a design problem. Both approaches sum up essential aspects of design, but contradict each other and each remains unsatisfactory in its own right. A third approach, combining the two approaches, sees design as a cycle of recurring steps. It breaks down the act of designing into its component parts, but also describes the temporal structure of design processes.

THE DESIGN CYCLE

The exhibition curator Jean-Christophe Ammann answers the question *"What does an artist actually do?"* with an explanation that essentially applies to all designers:

"He works on something whose end product he can discern only very vaguely. [...]
He has some idea, but he is constantly confronted with failure. For it is possible that
what is emerging does not fit in with his idea. He either changes what he is doing,
or he changes the idea. One can also say that doing constantly changes the idea,
because doing is more important than the idea." (Ammann 1998, p. 18)

The interplay of seeing, thinking and doing, the reflection of one in the other through perception and expression, forms the basis for all design activity. Both the act and the process of design can be described using the metaphor of a cycle – a cycle of inextricably interwoven thoughts and actions, broken down into a constantly recurring sequence of three areas of activity (A1–3) or six working steps (W1–6).

The "design cycle" starts with perceiving the task and situation (A1/W1), followed by their mental consideration which leads to a first idea of the object or building to be designed (A2/W2). These design ideas are first expressed through simple gestures or words, but later also with the aid of external tools (A3/W3). What has been expressed is then perceived again (A1'/W4) and compared with the initial idea. Both the idea and its expression are the subject of further consideration, they are criticized and subsequently changed (A2'/W5). These changed ideas are in turn expressed again (A3'/W6) and the cycle begins again. Step by step an ever more concrete, precise and more complex representation of what has been designed gradually emerges in spatial-pictorial and linguistic form.

This sequence of recurring steps is just as much a part of long-term design processes as the individual act of designing. The three named spheres of activity that characterize the "design cycle" – perception, mental consideration and the expression of inner ideas – can sometimes be distinguished very clearly in the consecutive working steps, but often they are so tightly interwoven that the individual elements can scarcely be isolated any longer and fuse into a single action – an act of designing. The design process in its turn is made up of countless large and small "design cycles". It is a continuous interplay of perception and expression, of working out "inner" ideas and presenting them "outwardly", of creativity and criticism.

Therefore a general theory of design must treat the five themes **perception, thinking, expression, design tools** and **criticism** on an equal footing. Such a theory should be portrayed in a form that does not constrain but opens things up, that does not determine and define but identifies possibilities, that does not proclaim "eternal" values but reflects the structures of value systems, that does not prescribe methods but supports the development of individual strategies, that does not argue solely from top to bottom but also from bottom to top. In the following section an attempt will be made to develop an appropriate framework with a view to examining the subject of design tools in more detail.

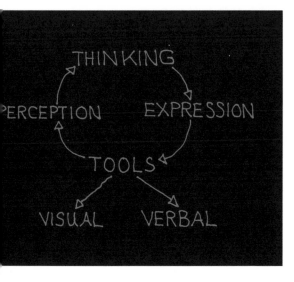

The design cycle

DESIGN TOOLS

Each tool must be used with the experience that created it.

Leonardo da Vinci (Codex Arundel, 191R)

81

Architectural design as a complex activity that is difficult to define can also be approached and described by means of the tools and cultural techniques deployed in the design process. Looking at it from this point of view helps achieve an appropriate degree of detachment from personal working methods, and makes it possible to see the fundamental relations between the individual activities. Starting with gesture and language as the primary design tools, the tools that developed from them can then be introduced: on the one hand, sketch, schematic outline, design drawing, perspective view and model as visual tools, and on the other description, criticism, theory, as well as calculations and computer program as verbal tools.

The design tool is such a central issue because ideas, thoughts and visions cannot be conveyed directly; they can be expressed only with the aid of "tools", "instruments" or "media". We have to communicate our ideas through gestures, by talking about them, drawing them, writing them down or presenting them in some other way. There is a danger with any of the possible "tools" that they could falsify our ideas. Each has their own rules and ways of working, their limitations and possibilities, and they always force the person using them to move in a particular direction. If people are not aware of this, the risk is that the tools will make themselves independent and push their users towards results that are a long way from their original ideas. Today's segmented design processes exacerbate this danger further. A design that may seem entirely convincing in a particular medium, i.e. con-

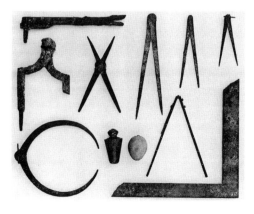

forms exactly to its rules, can turn out to be completely unsuitable in reality. Experienced designers know how to accommodate this discrepancy. They know the particular qualities of their tools well enough to be able to compensate for them where necessary.

Collection of Roman bronze tools from Pompeii

SYMBOLS OF CREATIVITY

Tools is the general terms for equipment used for working with materials. But what are the "tools" of design, and what are its "materials"? Medieval images show master builders and architects with items like compasses and set squares, which are to be read as attributes of their activities. What do these devices convey about the nature of design?

Tools have been understood as attributes of craftsmen and master builders from time immemorial. Ancient Roman tombstones and excavations in Pompeii show entire collections of appropriate tools, though they are more properly associated with building than design: yardstick, set square, plumb line, level and compasses, and also hammer and chisel. (Zimmer 1984, p. 265 ff.; Hambly 1988, p. 20, ill. 10)

The Babylonian ruler Gudea is portrayed seated, with the ground plan of a large building on his lap. This statue, called *"The Architect with the Plan"*, was created in Mesopotamia around 2125 BC; the drawing concerned is a ground plan on a reduced scale of the walls around the temple precinct, Gudea's "Holy City". (André-Salvini, in: Las Casas 1997, p. 74 f.) It shows a masonry structure with external abutments and six gates, each reinforced on both sides by projecting walls. What aids were available to Gudea and his architects?

Statue of the Babylonian ruler Gudea,
c. 2125 BC, and the plan on the statue's lap

Leonardo da Vinci: *Shower* of a variety of tools, Windsor Castle, The Royal Collection 12698

An allegorical drawing by Leonardo da Vinci illustrates one set of problems raised by the tools available. He depicts a threatening storm with tools of all kinds falling from the heavens, and with the caption: "*O miseria umana di quante cose per danari ti fai servo.*" (Oh human misery: for how many things do you enslave yourself for money.) (after Hermann-Fiore 2002, p. 332 f.) In the Enlightenment one of the greatest challenges faced was to manage and order the flood of tools, the respective activities, their effects and significance, taming the ever re-emerging chaos of possibilities. Albrecht Dürer's famous copperplate engraving *Melencolia I* (see p. 74) also shows a row of tools in the foreground that are clearly related to building and designing lying scattered and apparently useless on the ground. Only a few decades later, Walther Hermann Ryff (or Rivius; 1500–1548) and Virgil Solis (1514–1562) put forward a different image that contrasts markedly with these oppressive visions.

"*Vivitur ingenio, caetera mortis erunt*" (Creativity survives, everything else belongs to death) is the title of a woodcut by Virgil Solis (Röttinger 1914) that Ryff published twice as a frontispiece in Nuremberg: in 1547 in his book *Von der geometrischen Messung* (Of geometrical measurement) (after Grote 1966, p. 5) and a year later as title page for the second German edition of Vitruvius's *Ten books on architecture* (*Vitruvius Teutsch*, Nuremberg 1548, see p. 40), which Ryff translated, commented and illustrated. The picture shows a collection of equipment and tools that are associated not only with the work of master builders and architects but also with science, scattered around the floor: we see a level, various compasses and pincers, hammer, chisel, plane and saw, set square and gauge, books (as a reference to architectural theory?), two different levelling devices, a geometry textbook, bellows and crucible on a

Viuitur ingenio, cætera mortis erunt.

Aurum probatur igni, ingenium uero Mathematicis.

burning brazier, a bottle of chemicals, mallet and chisel, a ruler, pen and inkwell, paintbrush and palette, tweezers, two compasses and a clamp with plumb line. In the middle of the page, on a double plinth raised above this collection of equipment, stands a genius (symbolizing the architect?) barefoot and portrayed as a putto, holding a sponge or stone hanging on a cord in his left hand which points downward, and in his raised right hand two wings (as a symbol of inspiration?). The plinth and the little boy are in correct perspective, but the floor is tilted upwards into the plane of the picture, so that the figure is effectively framed by the tools it should actually be standing over, and is keeping his head above them only with difficulty.

Obviously Solis borrowed a number of pictorial elements unchanged from Dürer's engraving *Melencolia I*. But the structure and mood of the picture is entirely different: it appears as a pointed antithesis to Dürer's engraving. The personification of melancholy is omitted, and so are the bell, scales, hourglass and sundial as reminders of our mortality. The figure of the putto also suggests that Solis based his version on Dürer's engraving, as the shape of its body, clothing, face and hairstyle is very similar to its predecessor. But while Dürer's figure is sitting on a millstone writing on a slate, Solis places his putto dominant in the centre of the picture. Standing on a solid, cubic plinth, and holding up a pair of wings triumphantly in his right hand, he has clearly overcome all doubts and melancholy.

Against this background, Virgil Solis' woodcut published by Walther Ryff seems like an optimistic and now positive reinterpretation of creativity, which had previously been permeated with the idea of melancholy. Full of childlike happiness the boy, taking the wings of inspiration into his own hands and dominating the tools that are raised around him, is presented as symbolizing the architect in Ryff's translation of Vitruvius. Perhaps this is modern *Homo Faber's* first expression of optimism, throwing all caution to the winds. This optimism, as Dürer's picture reminds us, can be achieved only at the price of a degree of simplification that suppresses all the contradictory, puzzling and alarming aspects of design. Yet Solis' woodcut can also be seen as the starting-point for a view of architecture based on the tools, on the sense of making.

Soon after, the goldsmith and sculptor Benvenuto Cellini (1500–1571) posed the question of what objects can be considered as "design tools". He

Attributed to Virgil Solis: woodcut, published as frontispiece to the book *Von der geometrischen Messung* (Of geometrical measurement), Walther Ryff: Nuremberg 1547, and to Walther Ryff's translation of Vitruvius, *Vitruvius Teutsch*, Nuremberg 1548 (ill. p. 40)

Benvenuto Cellini: Diana Ephesia, design for the seal of the Accademia del Disegno in Florence (detail), c. 1564. London, British Museum

was an eminent member of the *Accademia [dell'Arte] del Disegno*, founded in Florence in 1561 by the architect, painter and art historian Giorgio Vasari (1511–1574) together with Agnolo Bronzino and Bartolomeo Ammanati. In a design for the seal of the newly-founded Accademia dating from c. 1564, Cellini suggests using an image of the many-breasted, all-nourishing goddess of nature Diana Ephesia to embody design. He understands disegno as the *"origin and beginning of all human activities"*. (Cellini, after Kemp 1974, p. 222) Quite casually, just below the middle of the page, Cellini introduces an alphabet in capital letters. A tool resembling its particular shape is allotted to each letter – a first, sketchy attempt to list and classify design tools, here consisting of tools for crafting and drawing.

The analogy Cellini draws between the shape of the letters and the shape of the tools suggests that the individual tools can be chosen in the same way as the letters of the alphabet. Designers have to learn how to use them properly in the same way as we use the ABC. Once proficient with their tools, designers can be just as expressive as writers who have a good command of the alphabet. If we stay with this image, we will soon see that the writer still needs a lot of other things before he can be creative: vocabulary, grammar and rhetoric, a capacity for invention and story-telling. At any rate, in the new Renaissance understanding, tools are no longer primarily used in man's struggle against nature, injuring and destroying it, but for creating *"a new, artificial world, which man and nature work on together"*. The art historian Horst Bredekamp sees Cellini's drawing as a *"snapshot of positively exuberant optimism about art and technology"*. (Bredekamp 2003, pp. 130, 137)

This drawing marks the first steps towards describing creative activities. The path leads us on to one of the major projects of the French Enlightenment: the *Encyclopédie, ou dictionnaire raisonné des sciences, des arts et des metiérs*, published from 1751 to 1771 by Denis Diderot and Jean-Baptiste le Rond d'Alembert in Paris; the first edition encompassed 17 volumes of text and 11 of plates. The aim of the enterprise was to present all the tools and working techniques known at the time, arranged by profession. Knowledge that until then had been a closely guarded professional secret in the guilds was thus systematically structured and made available to the public. The impressive work records the sum of technological knowledge of its day, in texts and elaborate, detailed illustrations, at a time when the art of the Baroque overlapped with the early days of the industrial revolution. Information about natural science is juxtaposed with explanations of technical processes from agriculture, craft and military warfare. Articles on wood, metal, chemistry, textiles, ceramics and glass are accompanied by representations of artistic techniques from architecture, fine art and music, writing and book printing. Tools are no longer seen as mere aids; from this point on they are the centre of attention.

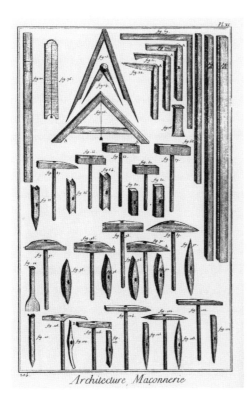

Architecture, Maçonnerie

Tools relating to Architecture, Maçonnerie (architecture and stonemasonry), from the *Encyclopédie* by Diderot and d'Alembert

All design is embedded in the entire sequence of actions involved in making. This was a key term for both Otl Aicher (cf. p. 212) and Vilém Flusser. It can be traced back via the Old Saxon verb *makon* and the English *to make* to the Greek *mag–* to knead, (Onions 1996, p. 547) which indicates a remarkable connection with the original model-making material, clay. Otl Aicher attributes a central role to making, but defines the term only cursorily, whereas Flusser analyses making in detail. Neither author relates it to some indifferent activity, as in colloquial phrases like "making do" or "making yourself unpopular", but understand it as concretely designing and making objects and thereby shaping reality. According to Flusser, the aim of all making is *"stamping form on the objectified world"*. He sees making as a particular working gesture, directed not at other people but at material. He starts by looking at the movements of our hands to analyse the gesture of making. (Flusser 1991, pp. 49–70) He defines making as the attempt to put theory into practice. This is achieved in his view *"when what should be has become objective and concrete, the object has become valuable and the value an object"*. (loc. cit., p. 57) The metaphorical dimension of his account is revealed when in this context Flusser speaks of the two hands as "theory" and "practice" having to be brought into agreement by the gesture of making. Flusser tries to sum up the infinitely complex procedure of making in simple images. Here the theme of thinking is almost completely ignored. But his metaphorical images show how much the process of thinking is shaped by the concrete movements of our hands, and supported by concepts that are shaped by these movements, abstracted, drawn off from them in the truest sense of the words.

In his systematic analysis, Flusser identifies a sequence of ten distinct active steps that are so submerged in everyday habit that they are scarcely perceived as being separate. For him, the gesture of making starts with a gesture of perception (1), described as a gesture of grasping and understanding that is active and in a very particular sense violent; it selects and isolates an object. This

Making as kneading: Pizza dough

is followed by a first step towards an evaluation gesture (2): a suitable form for this object is chosen, and an attempt is made to imprint this form or this value upon it, to "inform" it. This phase begins with the gesture of *Herstellung*, meaning both physical creation and the act of putting something somewhere (3); a gesture in which the object is detached from its context that has to be negated, and placed in an affirmed context. In the process it is possible to sense the resistance or the raw nature of the material. In the gesture of examination (4) the hands then penetrate the object and thus compel it to reveal its inner structures. They grasp how the object is to be changed, and they can now use the gesture of deciding (5) to determine what value and what form they want to impose upon it before starting with the gesture of production (6).

But given the resistance of the unshaped material, the hand finds itself compelled to adjust the form it wants to imprint upon the object. Flusser calls this *"constant reformulation of the form under counter-pressure from the object"* the gesture of creation (7): *"Creation means devising ideas during the gesture of making."* (loc. cit., p. 64) In contrast with the classic Platonic idea of eternal, unchangeable ideas, that can be realized only imperfectly, Flusser stresses *"that new ideas emerge in the midst of theory's struggle with the raw, resistant world"* (loc. cit., p. 65) It is not creative to impose prefabricated ideas on prepared material by force, as happens in the case of industrial production, nor to create virtual stereotypes in the laboratories without coming to terms with the raw material.

Flusser sees the gesture of creation as a struggle in which weak human hands are threatened with injury and destruction. In this case they can either give up, or reply with the gesture of tool-making (8). The hands withdraw temporarily from their resistant object to find another one that can serve as a simplified and more effective extension of them. However, preparing tools is in itself a gesture of making. According to Flusser, in order to make tools, one has to make other tools, ultimately resulting in a practically infinite recursive sequence of toolmaking. The danger is that by focussing attention on making tools and tools for tools, the original object of the gesture of making may be forgotten entirely, and consequently it may no longer be possible to tell an object from a person: everything becomes open to treatment. This, according to Flusser's critique, is the situation in today's industrial society.

In the gesture of realization (9) the hands, now provided with tools, return to their original object – provided they have not forgotten it. The product subsequently produced is thus shaped less by the hands than by the tool. The form that is finally realized is influenced by three factors: the form originally intended, the resistance of the object and the work done by the tool. But as the two hands – practice and theory – can never be made to agree completely, and so the work is never completed, the gesture of making is an infinite gesture. Flusser says that it does not come to an end until the hands withdraw from the object, open up and present their work. This can happen with a degree of resignation if it is apparent that every continuation of the gesture of making would be of no significance for the work. In contrast with the gesture of making, which differentiates, excludes, violates and changes, its conclusion in the gesture of handing over (10) changes this into a gesture of opening, of giving, of love for others.

Flusser's analysis shows how far designing and shaping – the gesture of creation – are tied into the context of multiple gestures of making. The possibilities and meanings inherent in creation are largely determined by this connection. The gesture of making can change the direction in which it is moving in any phase of the creative process, to the point of changing into its opposite. A simple change of direction for an individual gesture can appear as something else, something completely new. If the hands choose a different object, a different form, a different context, a different tool, a different course for the gesture of creation or the gesture of handing over, it is possible that a completely different piece of work will emerge, or the one that is coming into being will acquire a completely different meaning.

THE AMBIVALENCE OF TOOLS

The basic understanding that Flusser elucidates suggests that tools are *"everything that moves in gestures and thus express a freedom"*. (loc. cit., p. 222) Tools do not only shape our concrete actions, but also our thinking. *"Tools change our behaviour, and thus our thinking, feeling and wanting. They are experience models."* (Flusser 1989, p. 2) They are objects made to serve a particular purpose. The question: *"What is that and what can I make with it?"* is generally governed by how they have always been used in the case of traditional tools. According to Flusser, new tools are particularly fascinating precisely because, more than any other thing, they contain a hidden virtual potential, and because of their as yet not completely fixed form, we can liberate ourselves from the intentions of those who created the tools (Flusser 1991. p. 193 f.). By examining the conditions of expression and articulation, thus elaborating a theory of gestures, a theory of design, we can identify the limitations of our thinking in order to liberate ourselves from them.

"The oppressive dominance that tools exercise over our thinking takes place on many levels, and some of them are less obvious than others. We must not allow the tools to take the reins and ride us." (loc. cit., p. 102)

Flusser also says that tools are not instruments of freedom in every case. In the modern age, his analysis runs, tools no longer serve to solve problems, but start to become problematical in their own right. Once they become objects of research, and not just traditional models, but are made through scientific innovations, this leads to "bigger and more expensive" machines. These raise the question of who owns them and what they should do with them. Flusser says that in the course of the Industrial Revolution the relationship between man and machine was reversed. Man is no longer the constant and the machine the variable, but man has become an attribute of the machine, as one man can be replaced by another one in the course of the work. (loc. cit., p. 26 f.) Flusser also says that the pre-industrial relationship between man and tool is reversed, the new tools no longer function for man, but man functions for the machines. (Flusser 1998, p. 240) He also points out that the machine can be much more creative than a human being if it is programmed appropriately. It does not liberate man from work in order to leave him room for creative activity, but overtakes him in this sphere as well. (Flusser 1991, p. 28 ff.)

Tools become critical for Flusser when they manifest themselves as "apparatuses" that are difficult to comprehend fully, and which he defines as *"complexes of machines synchronized and coupled together in complex feedback systems"*. (loc. cit., p. 26) It is in dealing with these "apparatuses", says Flusser, that design becomes a central question of human existence. In his book *Vom Subjekt zum Projekt (From Subject to Project)* he develops the idea that we could overcome our *"subservient existence as subjects"* in designing, and start to *"recover from submissiveness and straighten into design"*. (Flusser 1994, p. 27) Flusser sets a new

Tools. Photograph: Christian Pieper, 2005

view of design against a pessimistic approach that sees the world dominated by industrial and state apparatuses that exist only for their own sake. Flusser asserts that hitherto we have changed thanks to our tools, yet without anticipating how we are changing: *"We are subject to our tools, even though we design them ourselves."* But he says that now we are in a position to design their "repercussions" on ourselves as well. (Flusser 1989, p. 3)

The ability to design the consequences and effects of the tools, machines and apparatuses that we have created has foundered hitherto on the limited

Flusser describes apparatuses as "opaque black boxes", taking the camera as an example.

scope of our imagination, on the tight boundaries within which we can think our way through complexity, and above all on the difficulties of predicting the behaviour of complex systems. As programmable apparatuses, today's computers allow a depth of processing that can reveal the consequences of a design decision much earlier, and through a user interface adapt these to our design abilities. They can simulate new tools and show us the "repercussions" of these tools before they become reality. Once we have discovered the structure of the apparatus, then there is hope of getting a grip on it. (Flusser 1993/2, p. 78 f.) If this succeeds then we are

"no longer subject to our design but we become conscious designers of the changes that this design is bringing about for us". (Flusser 1989, p. 6)

Hand-operated concrete mixing machine by Heinrich Strube and Co., c. 1900

"DESIGN TOOLS" AS A METAPHOR

"Design tools" are not tools in the same sense as a hammer or a screwdriver. The term (as defined more precisely on p. 104) is a metaphor, transferring the image of a hand tool to complex states of affairs. Using this metaphor causes a shift of perspective that makes it possible to consider certain connections between effect and significance "objectively", as if they were objects, in order to describe their qualities without being dominated by personal opinions, but from the point of view of the designer. The term "design tools" thus implies linguistic objectification. In a similar way to how Flusser describes the gesture of making, i.e. analysing not the making itself but its meaning in the form of gesture, we are not so much focussing on design per se as on certain connections, their effect and significance: on a complex structure of material and immaterial relationships between objects and the cultural techniques developed for their use.

In order to better understand the meaning of the metaphor of "design tools", we shall return to the craftsman's tools. A shoemaker has a large number of different tools, and he stores them in a precise order at his workplace. As a rule, these tools have two ends: the soft handle, often made of wood, which transfers the force of the hand into the tool, and the hard head, usually made of metal, which is used to work on the item concerned. Each tool's shape is adapted to the special job it has to do. But here certain tools are used in a way that is quite contrary to their usual function, for example when the wooden handle of a hammer is used to smooth a leather sole. Experienced craftsmen resist the suggestive effect of tools, consisting, as can often be seen in children, of working on everything with the particular tool that happens to be to hand.

An intimate and exclusive relationship, similar to the kind that many musicians develop with their instruments, is rarely to be seen in designers.

They tend to maintain an essentially objective relationship to their "design tools", especially as they use several as a rule, so that specific qualities can be exploited on the one hand and compensated for on the other. But the double value of tools expressed in the soft handle and the hard, metallic end is also

A cobbler's tools

found here, on a different level of meaning. Every design tool both acknowledges external circumstances (grasping and holding) and also expresses inner ideas (stamping internal ideas of design on a material support). Every design tool can be used descriptively, i.e. illustratively, to describe a given, or prescriptively, i.e. creating a design, to represent something new. The shift from the descriptive to the prescriptive mode can be freely decided by the designer: a copied detail can be declared to be a model for a new work in no time.

Each hand tool reduces the wide range of all possible movements to a few select movements, enabling us to deploy them more effectively. Design tools are both suitable for reducing complexity and also for creating complexity as the design process proceeds. But the mechanisms for reducing and creating complexity are different for each tool, and themselves problematical. It is particularly true that the question always arises as to whether one is actually dealing with a successful abstraction or just with a plain simplification whose consequences are being neglected. So the Swiss sociologist Lucius Burckhardt reproaches designers for solving problems *"intuitively"* by reducing their complications to *"so-called essentials"*. The sum of what is deemed inessential and gets lost in the course of this process is liable to create new and greater problems. (Burckhardt 2004, p. 26)

But the tension in the "design tools" metaphor in fact arises from the relationship between similarity and difference inherent in it. The concept suggests that inner images and ideas can be processed as directly as the material objects of a craft. Unlike simple tools, which follow simple mechanical principles that are easy to grasp and control, the effect of "design tools" is based on complex mechanisms for perceiving and thinking, and for expressing what has been thought out. Their primary role is not to work on material items, but to influence individual and collective inner ideas we have of designs, and to make it possible to represent them more or less materially. They are not equally direct, immediate and easy to control as hand tools, but create a less than transparent complex of different direct and indirect mechanisms. These follow the principles of geometry and abstraction, logic and meaning, and raise questions about the possibilities of representation and communication.

"The hammer forges the smith"– the way in which design tools strike back at the designer has not be addressed so far. The nature and qualities of the

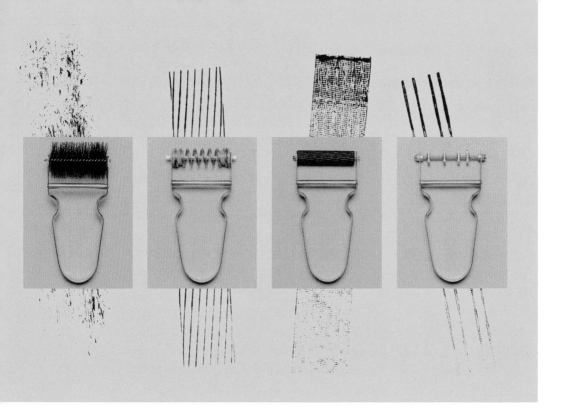

Peter Jenny redesigned Alfred Neweczeral's 1947 Rex peeler as a drawing tool.

design tools do not just make their mark on what has been designed, but prior to this also on the reflection about the design. The individual "design tools" have certain inherent structures and tendencies which, if they are not taken into consideration, are reflected in the form of characteristic deficits of the realized designs. The interplay between thinking and making is of fundamental significance to design. The structures and tendencies upon which the effect and use of the individual design tools are based have to be identified, to make it possible for readers to detach themselves gradually, as their awareness increases, from the spell, from the *"oppressive dominance"* (Flusser) exercised on our thinking by tools and machines organized as apparatuses. The use of digital technologies once again suggests an answer to the question of how we design, as both the boundaries of feasibility and the pathways of imposing material form that characterize the traditional design tools have been completely redrawn by the digitalization of those tools.

The earliest use of a term that could be translated as "design tool" is to be found in the Baroque period. The young architect Balthasar Neumann used the name *Instrumentum Architecturae* for a pair of proportional dividers he had *"invented and made"*; it enabled him to measure out the dimensions and proportions of the Tuscan, Doric, Ionic, Corinthian and composite column orders on any scale with dividers and transfer them to a design drawing. When fully open the two arms of the divider are the same length as the Nuremberg Shoe, i.e. 30.3 cm. (Hansmann 1999, p. 9 f.)

The term "tool" is repeatedly used in connection with design. For example, in his essay *The Tools of Art – Old and New* (1979) the art theorist Rudolf Arnheim discusses how the particular characteristics of each tool affect the result of artistic work. In their extensive analysis *Architectural Representation and the Perspective Hinge* (1997), Alberto Pérez Gómez and Louise Pelletier show that the *"tools of representation"* often influenced the conceptual development of a design. The volume *Bild – Schrift – Zahl* (Image – Text – Number, 2003), edited by Sybille Krämer and Horst Bredekamp, also addresses the relationship between culture and technique and the use of tools in a number of essays. Otl Aicher declares, without further explaining the term: *"the designer knows nothing. he has only his tools with which to approach a matter."* (Aicher 1991/2, p. 194) He explains the significance of models and criticism, discusses the advantages of the pencil and the disadvantages of the computer, reflects about the nature of photography, but it remains unclear whether and to what extent he sees these as design tools. Finally, in his Incomplete Manifesto for Growth, the designer Bruce Mau recommends:

"Make your own tools. Hybridize your tools in order to build unique things. Even simple tools that are your own can yield entirely new avenues of exploration. Remember, tools amplify our capacities, so even a small tool can make a big difference." (Mau 2000, p. 89)

Thrilled by his discovery of how effectively an upper thigh bone can be used as a club, a hominid throws the bone high in the air with a roar of triumph. The bone spins ever more slowly in slow motion and is then transformed by a match cut into a gigantic space ship, continuing the movement majestically in the earth's orbit. This key scene at the beginning of Stanley Kubrick's film *2001: A Space Odyssey*, dating from 1968, relates the discov-

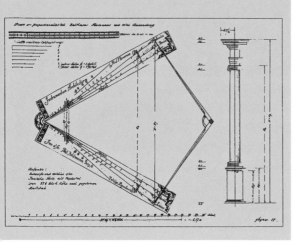

Balthasar Neumann: *Instrumentum Architecturae*,
Würzburg 1713, Mainfränkisches Museum

ery of the first tool (in the same instance used as a weapon) to the design of a space ship. Kubrick's match cut jumps over hundreds of thousands of years, and suggests that designing a journey in space is driven by the same primeval instincts as the use of a club. But above all Kubrick is addressing the close connection between tool and design. In a certain sense, tools are designs themselves: the hammer sketches out a powerful blow that can be precisely controlled; compasses and ruler sketch out circles and lines; linear perspective sketches out a particular way of perceiving space, and the reduced scale drawing sketches out the architect surveying the entire building site, emancipated from his daily drudgery. Buckminster Fuller, one of the most ingenious of 20th century designers, analyses tools as *"externalizations of originally integral functions"*. (Fuller 1969, p. 112) Shifting what were originally functions of the body outside of it, using non-living material, extends the boundaries of a tool's use until it eventually acquires independence as a machine.

"Tools do not introduce new principles but they greatly extend the range of conditions under which the discovered control principle may be effectively employed by man."
(Fuller 1969, p. 112)

But to what extent are the tools that have already been discussed "design tools"? It is true that the craft and drawing tools used in design are tools in the actual, direct sense, but they do not convey anything about our ideas of design. Conversely, a sketch or drawing is not a tool in the same, direct sense as the pencil used to create it.

The original, essentially endogenous, design "tools" are intellectual abilities: perception and memory, imaginative skills and a sense of form, the ability to think, inventiveness and judgement. But as the design process moves forward, design ideas develop in dialogue and constant interaction with their material manifestation. The design cycle, as we have seen, is a sequence of intimately entwined ideas and actions. It is possible to use the term design tools for all the aids that support the design process in any way: the above-mentioned intellectual and physical skills, just as much as the tools of the trade, for measuring and drawing, related to science and to art; tools in the more literal sense like pencil, compasses and ruler, and also in the extended sense like sketches, schematic outlines, design drawings and models, texts and calculations and not least tools in the figurative sense, the techniques, methods and strategies that form the basis for all these tools. But when defined so broadly, the meaning of the term can hardly be grasped.

Conversely, design tools like the sketch, design drawing, model or perspective view, design description or calculation can all be seen as media, the study of which is informed by the work of Marshall McLuhan, Vilém Flusser and Friedrich Kittler. But in the cycle of designing, the sender of a message is also its first recipient and critical assessor. In this way the message becomes the design, the medium a design tool. Seen from the point of view of designing, the media become tools, as they no longer primarily serve the purpose of communication, but above all the development of design ideas.

Tools in the more literal sense, like pencil, compasses and ruler, say next to nothing about the designs devised with their assistance. Therefore if we understand the medium-related, more or less material tools as "design tools", then it is reasonable to object that as a rule they are seen either as completed artistic works or as meaningless waste products of the design process. And yet in the design process, combined with the appropriate cultural techniques, they are the essential tools for developing, giving material form to and communicating design ideas.

If we use the formulation "more or less material" for these tools, this expresses a fundamental characteristic of design: intellectual ideas taking material form. The increasingly material quality of the design tools employed in the course of the design process is an essential prerequisite for the ability to gradually materialise design ideas. In the specific relationship between material quality and inner ideas, design tools are distinct from many other factors that influence design.

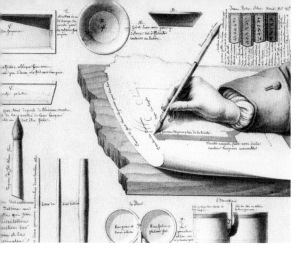

Jean-Jacques Lequeu: *Architecture Civile. Des instruments à l'usage du bon dessinateur*, 1782

The original tools for conveying design ideas are first of all gesture and language. Both express inner ideas, fleetingly but already physically, and in a way that can be documented. All the other design tools can be described as further developments and increasingly precise formulations of these two: the physical gesture becomes concrete via sketch, drawing, perspective and model, down to the full material manifestation of the complete building. But the spoken and written word creates, to use an expression by Joseph Beuys, the "social sculpture" that is the prerequisite for the emergence of buildings.

VISUAL AND VERBAL TOOLS

Design tools can be divided into two groups that complement each other. Tools that create images and form emerge from the physical gesture, and verbal tools from the written and spoken word. If these tools are arranged according to their complexity, then at the same time the emerging order follows their historical development, confirming McLuhan's thesis that any new medium contains the older one: the sketch captures the designer's first gestures, and these acquire geometrical precision in the initial plan; to-scale design drawings relate all the working plans needed for a building to each other, while a model in its turn sums up all the drawings as an object. A perspective view represents the spatial quality of the model, and becomes automatic in photographic form. Models and perspective drawings are objects of a comparable degree of complexity, but the model is much older than the perspective drawing as a design tool, and the geometrical operations used for creating a perspective drawing are clearly more complex than those needed for building a model. For this reason, the model should come before the perspective drawing in the sequence of design tools. Films and video recordings are created in their turn by creating a series of analogue or digital photographs.

The series of verbal tools follows the same principle: a sentence contains words, a descriptive text sentences. The text is then criticized, and several criticisms lead to a discussion whose results can be summed up in a theory. Formulae or algorithms can be derived from the theory, and these make it possible to calculate. Finally, a series of algorithms make up a program. Last of all, the computer brings both groups of tools together, the visual and the verbal, to create a meta-tool for design.

Visual tools that produce images make it possible to express inner ideas in a visual form, so that these can be looked at critically and conveyed to others, while the verbal design tools that produce texts are there to describe, analyse and criticize design ideas. Or put briefly: the visual tools are used primarily for devising form, and the verbal tools for developing the meaning of a design.

If the two series are placed side by side, some interesting parallels can be drawn: for example theory, which can be defined as the formalization of a perspective, stands alongside the visual tool of the perspective view. Photography, which can be described as an algorithm for creating perspectives that has become an apparatus, stands alongside the verbal algorithms. Schematic outline and design drawing as precise scale representations of a design correspond with description and criticism, whose job is to formulate scales (of criteria, of values) verbally.

The division into verbal and visual tools corresponds with two complementary ways of thinking: verbal, linear, logical thinking on the one hand and visual-spatial, concrete, simultaneous, associative thinking on the other. It also corresponds with the allocation of different thought structures to the two hemispheres of the human brain, as described by Eccles, Edwards and Sattler, among others, and the distinction between lateral and vertical thought structures made by de Bono, and also Aicher's division into analogous and digital thinking. (see p. 63)

simultaneous, comparative, associative, **visual**

emotional, spatial, lateral , analogous

verbal successive, rational, logical, rational,

temporal, vertical, digital

movement, action, staging **gesture**

dot, line, area **sketch**

schematic outline

elevation, ground plan, section,

detail, working plan **drawing**

module, exemplar, mould,

word concept, metaphor, neologism

sentence statement, phrase, text message

description letter, e-mail, minutes report,

building description, tender invitation

criticism distinction, evaluation,

contradiction, consultation, revision,

devastating assessment

sample, prototype, **model**

isometric drawing, axonometric drawing,

discussion dialogue, conversation,

building meeting, **dispute**, jury meeting

linear **perspective view**

light drawing, photogram, slide

collage, montage, **photograph**

still, adaptation

projector, clip **film, video**

beamer

theory hypothesis, acceptance, insight,

attempted explanation, discourse

algorithm equation, formula

calculation, model calculation

program sequence, process,

simulation, control

keyboard, screen, processor

hardware

saved data

software

computer

PC Notebook PDA internet mobile Server

The two groups of visual and verbal design tools

The following chapters will analyse the individual tools from three different points of view, which correspond to three fundamental planes of meaning that overlap in every design tool: the historical, the medium-related and its relation to design theory.

The development of tools and especially the time when they came into being are considered from a historical point of view, as the qualities of individual tools can often be identified most clearly in the early stages of their existence.

An analysis in terms of media theory is based on Marshall McLuhan's thesis that simpler, older media are always contained in the more complex, more recent medium (McLuhan 1964, p. 22). Design tools are now seen as media representing the subject matter of our thinking, starting with gestures and words and moving on to films, videos and computer programs as the most complex and hitherto most perfect representations. A series of questions arise: what aspects of a design are representative, in what way does it achieve this and what aspects does it not represent? What are the fundamental mechanisms by which a tool reduces and creates complexity?

From the point of view of media theory, each tool represents levels of meaning within a design that have to be determined more precisely. At the same time, each of the individual tools represents certain aspects of the world in the designer's work. Thus they offer the appropriate instruments for answering certain questions relating to these aspects and levels. The available tools and cultural techniques have to be used precisely and at the right moment, not to reduce the design question to ground plan, elevation and section, but to reflect about which problems can be worked on and solved when and in what medium. This approach can also help reinterpret many of the obstacles that crop up in the course of the design work, so that they do not just stimulate the designer's own work, but also help to justify it.

From the point of view of design theory, it is assumed that each of the design tools mentioned would be suitable, if used extensively enough, for representing a design in its entirety, and that all the tools are potentially contained within each other. The specific ways in which the individual tools function will be described with a view to their double aspect whereby each design tool serves to represent and to aid perception. What are the mechanisms by which the individual tools reduce the complexity of what is represented to a scale that the user can handle? And conversely, how do they make it possible to create complexity? What specific possibilities, opportunities and dangers are characteristic of the individual tools? In what respect are the cultural techniques corresponding to the individual tools suitable for influencing the form and/or meaning of a design? What is the "tendency", the "ideology" inherent in a tool? What, for example, makes a "good" sketch or drawing, or a "good" criticism?

Gesture

The concept of the tool can be defined to include everything
that moves in gestures and thus expresses a freedom. Vilém Flusser (1991, p. 222)

105   The gesture is the simplest and most primitive of all design tools, and
analysing it addresses all the fundamental questions of design. The gesture
provides an ideal example for examining fundamental questions: the relationship between inner ideas and what is actually expressed in a gesture, the
problems of designing form and of allocating meaning, and also the structure of the various levels of meaning. This section first explores Vilém
Flusser's view of the gesture and then applies this approach to design as a
whole.

   Flusser analyses a series of different gestures without formulating an
explicit design theory. But his study, subtitled *Versuch einer Phänomenologie*
(Attempt at a phenomenology) (Flusser 1991), contains key elements of a
methodical analysis of designing. In a series of essays, Flusser considers the
gesture as man's active being-in-the-world, something that characterizes all
"genuine" activities, activities that aim to express freedom. Flusser sees a
broad spectrum of human acts as gestures in this sense: *communicative ges-*
tures such as speaking, writing or telephoning, *working gestures* such as mak-

Vilém Flusser, gesticulating. Photograph: Michael Jörns, 1986

ing things or manufacturing tools, *interest-free gestures* that are an end in themselves like a lot of games, and ritual gestures that can be as everyday as smoking a pipe or shaving. (loc. cit., p. 223 ff.) These are all born of the fact that we are unable to express ourselves through thought alone, only through gestures and with the aid of tools. In the context of the *gesture of writing*, Flusser says:

"There is no thinking that would not be articulated by a gesture. Thinking before articulation is only virtual, in other words nothing. It realizes itself through the gesture. Strictly speaking one cannot think before making gestures." (loc. cit., p. 38 ff.)

Flusser develops his understanding of the concept, derived from the Latin gestae (literally: deeds), in several steps. At the beginning he defines gestures as *"body movements expressing an intention"*. (loc. cit., p. 7) These are deliberate movements (loc. cit., p. 235) for which there is no causal explanation, as causal explanations could not define the essence of a gesture: *"Why do some people smoke a pipe?"* He feels that the difference between cause and motive, between conditioned movement and gesture, suggests that causal explanations, however right they may be, miss what is meant by the question. (loc. cit., p. 161) He says that gesture is a symbolic movement, articulating and expressing meaning. Man uses the emotionally charged play of gesture, the *"symbolic representation of moods in gestures"* in an attempt to give meaning to his life and the world he lives in. (loc. cit., pp. 8–12) Thus works of art should be seen as *"frozen gestures"*.

So, he continues, a mood represented by a gesture can be true, but also untrue. In order to determine the truth of gestures, Flusser asserts that they should not be judged by ethical or epistemological criteria, but by aesthetic

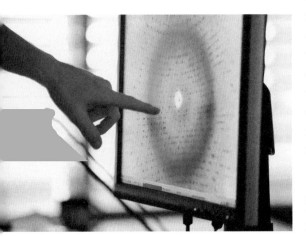

ones: the question is not whether a gesture represents truth or a lie directly, but the extent to which whatever it represents is truth or kitsch. A measure for this is the degree to which the mood is able to move the viewer. However, as Flusser notes, without a theory for interpreting gestures, it is not possible to make generalized judgements about this, and so it remains a matter

Photograph taken at the shooting of the film *Designing Truth* by Hinrich Sachs. Photograph: Ralf C. Stradtmann, 2005

of de gustibus non est disputandum, there's no accounting for tastes; something that one person may see as kitsch could be perfectly suited to another. (loc. cit., p. 12 ff.) Given this problem of objective differentiation, Flusser finally defines the gesture as *"a movement through which freedom is expressed, in order to reveal or conceal the gesticulator for others."* (loc. cit., p. 220 f.)

Seen as a "free" movement, the gesture is *"reaching from the present into the future"*, and can therefore only be adequately explained in terms of its meaning, its future. So for Flusser it must essentially be analysed in terms of meaning, as if deciphering an enigma or solving a puzzle. Problems are analysed in order to make them comprehensible, and therefore open to solution. But enigmas are analysed in order to penetrate them more deeply, to experience them more richly. (loc. cit., p. 90 f.)

This distinction is fundamental to the analysis of design. Flusser demonstrates this by taking the gesture of painting as an example. Analysing painting does not address this gesture from the outside, but itself becomes an element of the gesture under analysis. And even in the gesture of painting itself it is possible to observe a plane of meaning on which it is analysing itself critically. Hence the gesture of painting is

"not just reaching from the present into the future, but also anticipating the future into the present, and throwing that back to the future: constantly checking and reforming its own meaning." (loc. cit., p. 92)

Observing a gesture of this kind thus reveals the concrete phenomenon of freedom: "having meaning", "giving meaning", "changing the world" and "being there for others" are formulations that Flusser sees to express the same state of affairs: being free, really living. (loc. cit., p. 98) Just how closely gesticulating is related to designing is shown in statements such as the following:

"The gesture of painting as an interpretative movement is not "work" in itself, but a design for work. And yet the interpretative movement aims at changing the world, and brings this about as a consequence." (loc. cit., p. 97)

All design is expressed and articulated in gestures as well, so Flusser's study of gestures can be seen as a contribution to basic design research. It is also true of design that like every gesture, it is not subject to direct causality as understood by science. Nevertheless, Flusser feels that it is useful and desirable to formulate a design theory. His thinking on gestures can be summed up and applied to the field of design like this: we design without having a theory of design, indeed without being aware of the lack of such a theory, as our implicit knowledge of how to act is sufficient to meet the demands of practice. But a theory of this kind would allow us to *"step outside the gesture of design"*, to make our design a more conscious act and to change our behaviour with that in mind. A theory of this kind would not be intended to explain direct causal circumstances, but to describe and interpret design gestures and the tools we use to execute them. It would be an instrumental, tool-oriented theory, a theory that does not formulate rules and norms, but describes options. Its aim would be to discover the possible, often hidden semantic contexts determining the value of a gesture executed with certain tools. It would help to establish the factors influencing the value and meaning of design acts, thus creating an orientation instrument that would make it possible to design in a different, more deliberate way.

STARTING FROM GESTURES

In the posthumous collection *Vermischte Bemerkungen* (Culture and Value) the philosopher (and architect) Ludwig Wittgenstein speaks of the *"impression one gets from good architecture, that it expresses a thought."* And he continues: *"Architecture is a gesture. Not every purposive movement of the human body is a gesture. And no more is every building designed for a purpose architecture."* (Wittgenstein 1980, p. 22, p. 42) But how does an idea come to be expressed in architecture? And to what extent can we use gestures, or the cultural technique of gesticulating, as a design tool?

Gestures as expressive movements: the violinist Julia von Hasselbach. Photograph: Christian Pieper, 2006

Gestures in the sense of bodily movements that aim to express something form the basis of all design. Both everyday and design gestures fulfil a certain purpose, but point beyond this by the way they do it. This other, which even everyday gestures are intended to express, is closely related to what we mean by design. Something concrete, a handshake, a drawing, indicates future fulfilment: a promise kept, a new building. The English synonym for gestus is action, going back to the Latin gesticulare, meaning both giving attitude and carriage. (Onions 1996, p. 396) As such this term has always contained the idea of creativity. The sign languages that have evolved from gestures show how closely gesture is related to language. Unlike a merely instrumental act, in which the end is not form, but simply to fulfil an everyday purpose (like cutting a stone), and unlike ritual, which is essentially concerned with the formally correct execution of actions creating meaning (e.g. baptizing someone), a gesture definitely expresses the mood and attitude at the moment someone makes it.

What makes a gesture, a design so convincing that the idea it contains can be realized in future? Every gesture contains complex superimposed layers of meaning in a more or less tense relationship with each other, whether the gesture is one of casual everyday conversation, an actor's theatrical gesture, the designer's gesture, seeking form and meaning, or the architectonic gesture expressed in a building. The gesticulator's intentions (1) overlap with the ideas actually expressed (2) and with the way they are endowed with form (3), which in its turn is read in relation to the conventions (4). Each gesture conveys a meaning pointing to a future state of affairs (5) that as a rule is doubted by the observer (6) to whom the gesture is addressed. The temporal (7) and spatial (8) context provide an additional framework within which the gesture is read as appropriate or inappropriate. The ways these eight planes relate to each other join to form a level of meaning that determines whether we perceive the gesture as coherent or contradictory. A gesture has succeeded if the observer not only understands what it is expressing, but accepts that it is credible.

In relation to expressive movements by the body as a whole, an individual gesture is already an abstraction. It is precisely at the beginning of the design process, when the aim is to develop a design approach from the specific features of a location, that it is important to experience a situation physically. It is only the body's senses and movements that make spatial experience possible in all its complexity. When we observe the body's movements, sensations and reactions to a space or a place, the body and its senses becomes an instrument of perception. It becomes an expressive tool only when we are able to address all the countless superimposed sensory impressions, to filter out the significant ones and to derive movements from them. One of the earliest design forms involves developing a design idea on the spot from one's own movements, working on a natural scale when walking, so to speak. This process is present in city foundation rituals from classical antiquity as well as in contemporary site inspections. In this context, design becomes physical sensations of space projected on to a particular place. When Le Corbusier bases a design on the promenade architecturale, he is developing his spatial ideas from the movement sequences the building offers its users. By translating physical movements into ideas of space and architecture he is getting away from a static, object-related view of architecture.

The designer Peter Jenny, who teaches at the Swiss Federal Institute of Technology in Zurich, demonstrates in his exercises what an inexhaustible formal repertoire is contained simply in the hands and the space between the two hands: *"We are literally reaching into a sketchpad full of visual finds."* (Jenny 1996, p. 39) But gestures and body movements are not fully finished designs. Whether the movements used to actually make an object can be regarded as gestures or just instrumental processes is governed by whether they convey a meaning beyond the object's mere purpose. If they lead directly to its actual shaping and creation, as is the case for some kinds of craft and art, then design and manufacture are identical. This is not the case if the movements represent an object that is to be manufactured later, or by other people, i.e. they anticipate it in a simplified form. The first essentially spontaneous and intuitive attempts make an idea perceptible for the first time, both for the person gesturing as well as for those who are watching. Shifting inner ideas into the outside world makes it essential to articulate what has been thought out, thus shaping our awareness of it in a new and different way. It establishes critical distance and reflection and marks the beginning of the design cycle.

36 gestures. Photographs: Axel Buether, 2004–2005

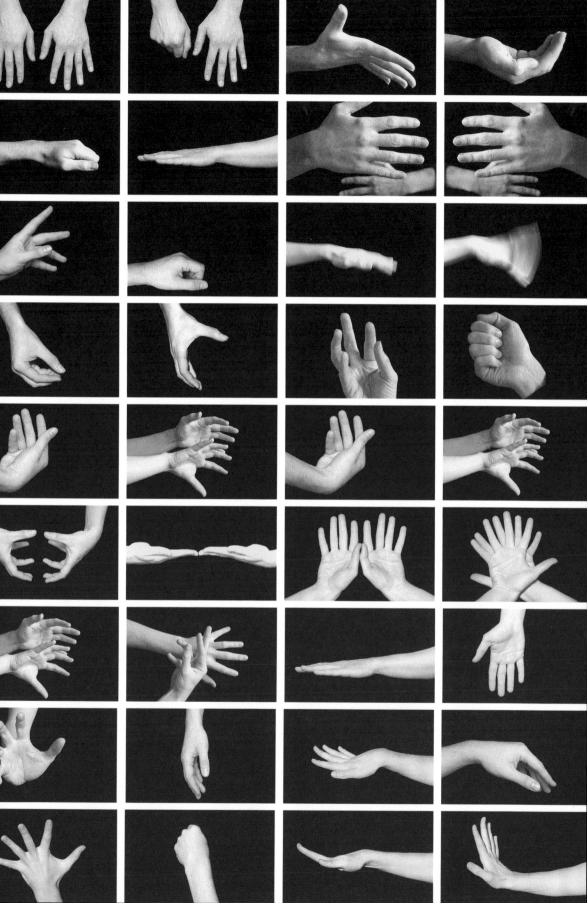

Sketch

Creation must take place between the pen and the paper.

Gertrude Stein (1935, after Bergeijk 1998, p. 49)

113

In its origin, the sketch is nothing other than a gesture that has been abstracted and fixed. In the sketch both the temporal and the spatial dimension of the gesture's motion have to be translated on to a two-dimensional plane in the form of dots, lines and surfaces. A pencil and a piece of paper make it possible to present, "with rapidly executed gestures", inner images, most of which would be forgotten after a few minutes, to the designer him- or herself or to a second viewer, thus capturing and remembering them. Sketches, whether they are pictorial or verbal, are extremely close to the original idea, which makes them particularly valuable to designers. But it is not just this: shifting the inner image outwards into an "expanded working memory" turns the image into an object from which one can distance oneself again, in order to consider it "objectively", examine it, criticize it and subsequently work on it again. What is the difference between a sketch and a drawing? The keyword drawing covers all two-dimensional images consisting mainly of lines, whether they are sketches, preliminary drawings or working drawings, perspectives or other graphic images. (Koschatzky 1977, p. 304 ff.) It is hard to pin down the term sketch precisely, it covers a broad spectrum of expressive graphic possibilities extending from a quick note to an ambitious artistic drawing. So artists call a freehand sketch a drawing if the format is somewhat larger, while as a rule architects distinguish between the small, imprecise rapid freehand sketch and a geometrically precise plan or preparatory drawing, made with compasses, ruler and set-square (or with a computer and plotter), usually in a large format.

Tobias Hammel: Sketch for *House of Yagaah III*, pencil, black felt pen on cardboard, 29 x 23.5 cm

Even though sketching may sometimes seem unassuming and casual, it is often the most important tool for many designers. Architects like Norman Foster or Álvaro Siza fill up hundreds of sketchbooks or pads with *"personal scribbles and jottings"* (Foster 1993, p. 5) in the course of their lives, using them to flesh out their ideas, then handing over the working out of precise drawings, models and calculations to their colleagues, or to specialists.

The sketch is the intimate medium, largely kept from the eyes of a critical public, in which design ideas – left plain and unprotected at first – are developed and shown to the designer's close friends and colleagues. This applies to all phases of the design process. Sketches are made during early discussions with the client, at site visits, as a response to designs that have already been worked out more precisely or in dialogue with engineers and builders on the building site.

PARCHMENT AND PAPER

Sketches can be drawn or scratched with a sharp object on any flat surface that happens to be available. The speed and ease of this gesture – the term comes from the Italian word schizzo and means a brief account or description, literally, jab (Onions 1996, p. 1996) – requires materials that are both readily available and sufficiently durable. The lack of cheap and at the same time non-perishable drawing surfaces may be a reason why no sketches have survived from the pre-Renaissance period.

One famous exception is Villard de Honnecourt's 13th century portfolio of drawings in the French Bibliothèque Nationale. It contains 325 individual sketches drawn in ink on both sides of 33 pages of fine parchment, often with short explanations. These consist mainly of views and ground plans from existing buildings, drawings of figures and ornaments, but also design sketches and technical drawings. (Hahnloser 1935, Binding 1993)

Freehand design sketches have survived in large numbers only since periods when paper became a cheap and durable material. It remains to be established to what extent qualitative changes in design thinking in the Renaissance were driven by the emergence of new drawing materials. If sketches by an artist like Leonardo da Vinci or Michelangelo are compared with freehand drawing in the Middle Ages, we are struck by a new intellectual freedom and openness, as well as the precision of the drawing, which is

Sheet 29 from Villard de Honnecourt's Portfolio,
13th century. Paris, Bibliothèque Nationale

also a characteristic of medieval miniatures and book illuminations. Things are being looked at in a completely new way. To our eye, spoiled by perspective and photography, the medieval way of drawing sometimes looks flat and formulaic, but we are still astonished today by the vivid clarity of this work. Drawing and sketching is now at the service of researching reality, trying out new ideas, representing proportions, details and spatial connections precisely. Michelangelo explains the fundamental importance of drawing and sketching as a design tool in a conversation with the Portuguese painter and writer Francesco de Hollanda. His words give us a sense of how enthusiastic the designers of his day were about these new possibilities:

"Drawing, which in other words can be called designing, is the source and epitome of painting, sculpture, architecture and of every other kind of painting. It is the root of every science. Anyone who is master of this great art should acknowledge that he has incomparable power at his service. He will be able to create forms greater than any tower in this world." (from de Hollanda 1550, p. 59)

Rapid elaborations of formal relationships that break off as fragments as soon as the draughtsman thinks of something new; exploratory variations of ideas; rapid changes of presentation forms and of drawing device and a lack of concern about the aesthetic effect of a page distinguish design sketches from art sketches. Naïve viewers often feel sketches like this are inept and unprofessional, which can have an entirely liberating effect. Erich Mendelsohn reports that as a young student he

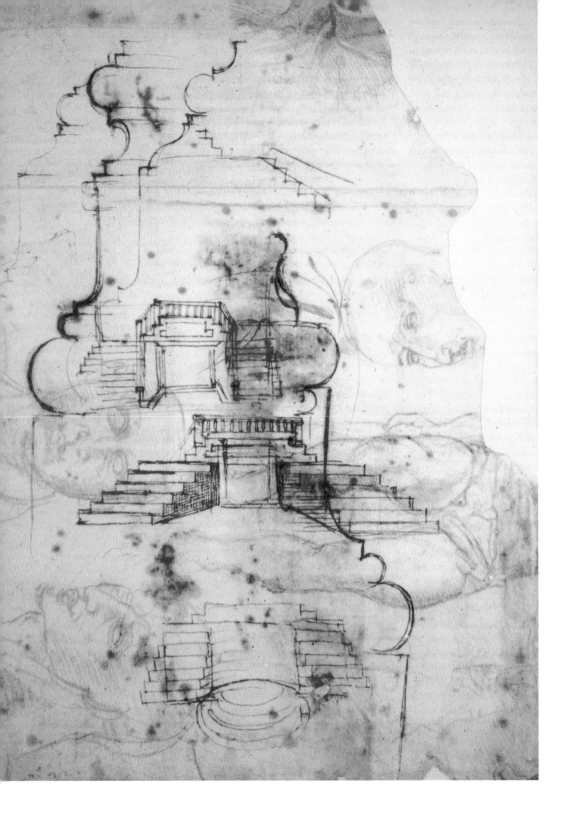

"flicked through Michelangelo's sketchbooks in Rome: pilasters, capitals and all that kind of thing: all scribbles. It was a revelation to me. [...] If Michelangelo can do it, so can I." (after Posener 2004, p. 364)

Because they are largely indeterminate, sketches can be entirely meaningless to outsiders. Precisely because they are so fundamentally random, individual designers must develop a high level of discipline and particular skills when using this tool themselves. Sketching does not become a communicable cultural technique until it is consciously used as a design tool, until the high degree of freedom it affords is so contained by a personal choice of expressive devices that third parties can also discern not only personal handwriting but also reflective treatment, individual expressiveness and ultimately individual thinking. This requires the ability to read one's own sketches and decode their various levels of meaning. One paradox of this tool lies in the fact that in order to be useful as an expressive device it needs a certain lack of inhibition, but also practice and discipline if it is to become recognizable as personal expression.

CREATIVE IMPRECISION

The most important qualities of this design tool are that it should be rapid, imprecise, open and direct. They are interdependent. A fleeting thought can be recorded directly in a sketch, without further aids. Often sketching is the first step towards the materialisation of an idea. This can happen quickly because the resources used are simple, but the result is less precise than other means of representing things. In the early stages of the design process a certain lack of precision makes it possible to articulate ideas experimentally without needing to have a precise solution in mind. Designers are often accused of unduly generalized and careless thinking because of this inclination towards imprecision. But it is essential to the design process. Günter Behnisch explains that *"thoughts that we did not yet know we had can emerge from imprecise sketches."* (Behnisch 1987, p. 40) It is the ambivalence of the sketch that opens up space for the imagination. Behnisch talks about

"apparently slovenly sketches, very imprecise, in which one [...] suddenly saw things shining out through several layers of tracing paper [...] things one had not drawn, they simply came about [...]" (Behnisch 1996, p. 29)

Design sketches by Michelangelo, c. 1525. Florence, Casa Buonarroti, 92 A (recto)

The ability of our perceptive faculties to create an image rich with information from only a few hints is an automatic feature of subjective creativity. One way of triggering it is by making sketches that indicate something with very few lines.

The rapid nature of sketching makes it possible to change very nimbly between different presentation methods and to combine them at will. All the other design tools also offer sketching modes, in other words the ability to use them rapidly, imprecisely yet allusively and in a simple, reduced form. The ground plan, elevation and section as a quick exploration of variants, alongside it the obsessive elaboration of a particular detail; axonometric views drawn from a model or perspectives that examine how the designer's own body relates to a particular space. This can be used to provide rapid illustrations in a discussion, and include sketched-out texts and calculations. Thus the sketch becomes a special design tool, containing all the others within a meta-plane. This tool creates complexity through imprecision, through superimposition, by creating connections, variants and sequences of sketches, through hints and by intensifying atmosphere. Thus the sketch is an excellent device for developing the imagination. Its agility means that success can be achieved rapidly, and helps towards handling forms effortlessly, and three-dimensional thinking in particular.

Like every design tool, a sketch can be both descriptive, i.e. illustrative, describing something that is already there, or prescriptive, i.e. creative, used to represent something new. The interplay between perception and expression corresponds with the two complementary modes of design thinking.

How does sketching affect our own perceptions? It guides and intensifies them, especially when dealing with existing forms and spaces. Descriptive, acquisitive sketching compels us to engage more deeply than simply absorbing a global impression of an object or a spatial situation, especially as this comes about largely because of pre-shaped mental pictures and less through sensory expressions. We have to look so precisely, detail by detail, that we can reproduce them in drawing. Just as we pay better attention if we take notes during a lecture, sketching sharpens our eye when we are observing a spatial situation. Sketching is therefore a particular way of training our perceptive skills. The simplicity of the tool compels us to reduce to essentials. On a second plane, it draws our attention to something that is not or cannot

A

B

C

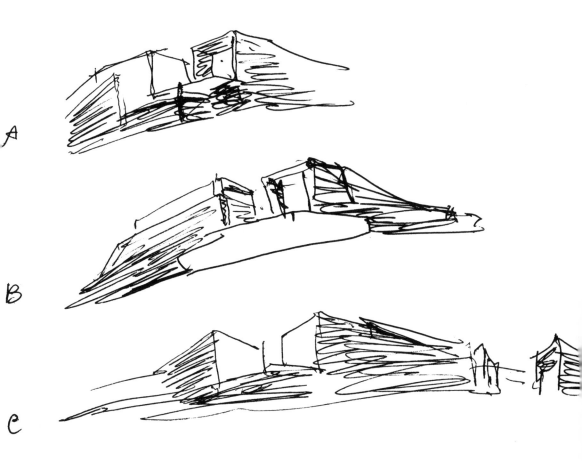

Design sketch for the Schilderswijk West apartment block, The Hague, variants A, B, C,
Álvaro Siza, single sheet, December 1985

be represented, to the things that are left out and the way the abstraction highlights what is already there, to deliberate "falsifications" and distortions.

Both acquisitive and creative sketching mean translating a spatial idea or a spatial impression into a two-dimensional one, thus consciously or subconsciously carrying out an abstraction process that a camera would handle automatically. This can happen in various ways. The time dimension can become the movement of a line, or be presented as a superimposition or as a sequence of individual sketches. The spatial dimension can also be represented as individual overlapping forms, as a combination of ground plans, views and sections, as an isometric drawing or a perspective.

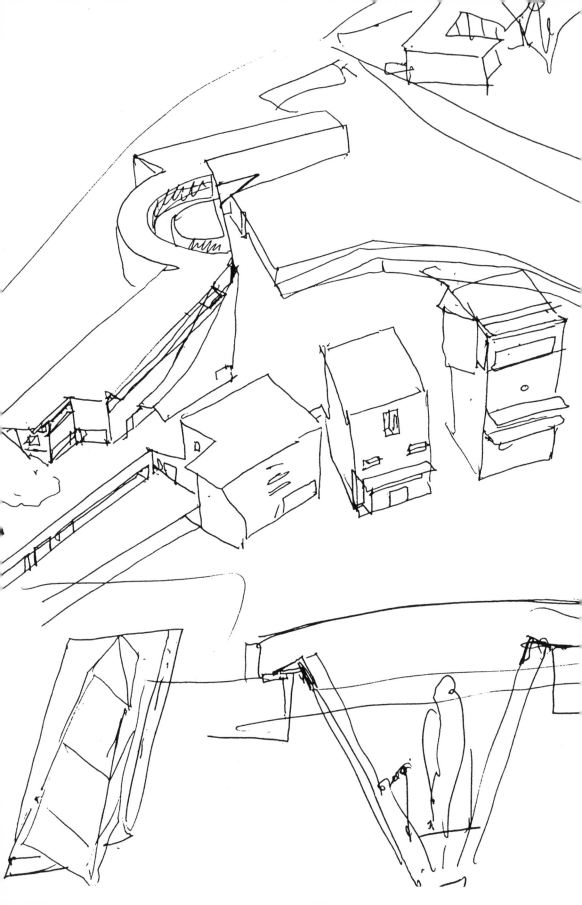

Creative sketching requires speed and agility, while acquisitive sketching requires a slowing down and intensification of perception processes. If it is deliberately used as a means of observation it opens up stretches of time in which perception becomes possible not just as reproduction of what is known, but as a creative process. By identifying hitherto unknown structures, new forms and unexpected connections, passive reception becomes active, creative observation. What are we shown when we draw or look at our sketches?

VISUAL-SPATIAL THINKING

The example of sketching makes it clear how little creative design thinking needs language or concepts when forms are to be developed. In a much-quoted text dating from 1947, Alvar Aalto describes his approach to design as deliberately switching from logical-verbal to intuitive-pictorial thinking. He says that first of all he addresses the numerous, often contradictory demands made by a design commission intensively, so that he can then distance himself and find a solution in another mode of thought by painting or sketching:

"I forget the whole maze of problems for a while, as soon as the feel of the assignment and the innumerable demands it involves have sunk into my subconscious. I then move to a method of working that is very much like abstract art. I simply draw by instinct, not architectural synthesis, but what are sometimes quite childlike compositions, and in this way, on an abstract basis, the main idea gradually takes shape, a kind of universal substance that helps me to bring the numerous contradictory components into harmony." (Aalto 1947, from Schildt 1998, p. 108)

The psychologist Edward de Bono identifies two different and complementary ways of thinking in the human brain in his book *Lateral Thinking* (1970), in a very similar way to Aalto. Starting with an analysis of dominant perception processes, he identifies a logical-analytical way of *("vertical")* thinking that is predominant in Western culture, complemented by intuitive-creative *("lateral")* thinking. The latter is particularly suitable for generating ideas and problem-solving. Bono describes sketching by designers as a technique that is particularly suited to and supportive of intuitive and generative *("lateral")* thinking. (De Bono 1970, p. 100 ff., p. 246 ff.)

Design sketch for the new faculty of architecture at Oporto University (FAUP), top view of the various buildings. Álvaro Siza, sketchbook 252, June 1987

Insights from research into the function of the brain (e.g. Sperry 1968, 1873, Eccles 1973, Damásio 1994) confirm Bono's approach. The two human cerebral hemispheres are dominated by different, but complementary, thought patterns. The left hemisphere handles language and time, and it is dominated by linear, sequential, logical-analytical, rational thought processes. The right hemisphere handles spatial and visual matters, and is dominated by non-linear, simultaneous, intuitive-synthetic, emotional thought processes (Edwards 1999, p. 56 ff.). To put it briefly, the left hemisphere thinks in a verbal logic, the right hemisphere thinks in a visual logic, or in Aicher's terms: in a digital vs. an analogous logic.

A number of teaching methods have been developed on the basis of these insights, aiming to use the different thought structures in the two hemispheres effectively. The drawing teacher Betty Edwards suggests using certain forms of sketching to change from the linguistic-rational to the visual-emotional mode of thought. She describes exercises like drawing facial profiles freehand in mirror-image, or drawing portraits upside-down. She says that sketching exercises of this kind suppress the input of the otherwise dominant left hemisphere, so that the other one can develop its spatial-visual abilities more fully (Edwards 1999, p. 80 ff.).

Different reasonings lead Aalto, de Bono and Edwards to similar results. For them all, sketching is a favourite means for changing consciously from the verbal-logical to the visual-spatial mode of thinking.

Numerous publications have appeared in recent years featuring design and travel sketches by well-known architects that allow us to look over the author's shoulders as they draw (see bibliography). In most cases only aesthetically successful sketches are published presenting an idealized picture that has limited use as an example for other designers. The countless unassuming, searching, only half-convincing, failed and rejected sketches, which in fact represent the majority of daily work in many cases, are very rarely printed. This also applies to the myth of the *"first sketch"*, which is usually preceded by numerous *"preliminary sketches"*. Erich Mendelsohn, who set particular store by his *"first sketches"*, tried out a number of variants before committing himself, distinguishing between *"preliminary sketches"* and the *"first design sketch"* (Mendelsohn 1930, p. 150). Hans Scharoun's famous *"Urskizze"* (lit. "primal sketch") of the Philharmonie in Berlin was drawn after three weeks in closed conference; it too was anything but a *"first sketch"*. (Wisniewski 1991, p. 10 ff.)

Sketches help to direct the attention of third parties to particular aspects of a design. We do not perceive architecture simply as what it is, but also as what its authors intend it to be. Even if the difference is as great as that between Aldo Rossi's atmospheric sketches and the lucidity of his completed buildings, the sketches are powerful enough to confer a very different, far-reaching significance on the simple reality of what has actually been realized. In this case they illustrate a poetical Utopia that has not been realized, which thus becomes part of this architecture's cultural dimension.

Experiments in digitalizing this tool have met with little success. The normal drawing programs are too precise and thus too slow and information-poor. High-resolution graphics tablets with flat screens that respond to the pressure of a stylus are a digital form of sketching paper. They make it possible to input more precisely and rapidly than with a mouse and keyboard. They are effective tools in combination with drawing and image-processing programs, though considerably more expensive than pencil and paper. Certainly digital intervention loses the simplicity and directness of freehand sketches on paper. Specialized sketching programs offering menus with a selection of "personal" handwritings can only simulate what a freehand sketch really achieves. But the rapidity of the sketch can be achieved digitally in a variety of other ways, using photographs, photomontages and sketch models as 3D presentations.

Language

*He predicted the future form of this shapeless heap of masonry
and beams that lay about us.* Paul Valéry (1921, p. 65)

125   The spoken word as the first material manifestation of our inner ideas is
certainly the most ephemeral of all design tools. It is closer to the fleeting
thought than to the physical gesture and its primary record, the sketch.
However, linguistic design ideas are not codified in forms, but in the sounds
of the voice, in words and sentences. Thus language as a design tool operates on a different plane of abstraction from the sketch. The *logos* supports
logical thinking, rationality and calculation, social interaction, the attribution
of meaning, theory and criticism.

Vitruvius counts the emergence of language from gestures and the
sounds of breathing among the historical prerequisites for the emergence of
architecture. (Vitruvius, II 1.1) He sees language as a basis for architecture in
two respects: a society that builds and for which building can take place was
first constituted through speaking, and Vitruvius insists that the architect
must be a fluent writer *"so that he may strengthen his own memory by reading
what has been written in the field".* (Vitruvius I, 4) Adolf Loos also sees the lin-

guistic element as one of the fundamentals
of architecture when he defines the architect
as a *"mason who has learnt Latin"*, and
explains: *"Good architecture, how something is
to be built, can be written."* (Loos 1924, p. 210)

But it would be hasty to assume that this
is allotting equal status to verbal and visual
design tools. Ludwig Wittgenstein pointed
out the fundamental difference between
zeigen (showing) and *sagen* (saying): there are
things that cannot be expressed clearly in
language, but that can be shown. They *show*
themselves between the lines of a text, but
more clearly in works of art, in a drawing or
a building. Wittgenstein also places the

Letterpress type. Photograph: Christian Pieper, 2005

spheres of ethics and aesthetics, crucial for architecture, in this category. (Wittgenstein 1921, Propositions 6.421, 6.522)

The fact that all design tools originally belonged together in the *"de-signing"* of inner ideas becomes clear when looking back at the first written texts by the old high cultures: they consisted of signs, i.e. sketches of ideographic characters from which hieroglyphs and the alphabets we are familiar with developed later. This original unity is still echoed even in late medieval sources, when the Latin word *designatio* can mean description as well as drawing and model. Likewise, the Italian term *desegno* could originally mean description as well as drawing. (Binding 1993, p. 187 ff.) The German verb *reißen* in the sense of drawing (as in *Reissbrett*, drawing board, for example) is derived from the same root as the verb *to write* in English. (Onions 1996, p. 1015)

Verbal *"de-signing"* has become more and more sophisticated in the course of history. A whole variety of different kinds of texts have emerged from the first description of buildings and the early days of architectural history via the orally transmitted secret knowledge of the ancient and medieval stonemasons' guilds to state building regulations, and they have acquired completely different meanings as design tools. Even the scientific engineering calculations that started to come into being in the 18th century can be considered as texts in the sense of linking concepts that follow strict mathematical logic. In the computer age, the original unity of design tools can also be seen in the drawing programs (that are themselves also generated from text).

TRAINING AND PRACTICE

It is fairly unusual for architects to see language as a design tool. Regardless of the diversity and meaning of linguistic forms of expression in their daily work, architects like misusing the saying ascribed to Goethe *"Bilde, Künstler! Rede nicht!"* (Create, artist! Do not talk!) – either to justify an aversion to language and theory that is typical of the profession or simply to shut each other up by quoting the classical writer. In fact these words have had their original meaning reversed by not being quoted in full. They form the first line of a motto that Goethe placed before the "Art" section in the 1815 edition of his works: *"Bilde, Künstler! Rede nicht! / Nur ein Hauch sei dein Gedicht"* is how the complete two-liner goes (Create artist, do not talk! Your poem is but a breath.) Goethe is addressing lyric poets like himself with his succinct challenge to abandon talking, in other words rhetoric, and to make a poem a carefully-formed trace of a structure.

In design education, linguistic modes of expression are neglected, at least in German higher education institutions, while in the Anglo-Saxon countries in particular more attention is paid to discussion in essays. Architects are not infrequently surprised in their early professional years to find out what a major part the verbal element of their work plays. Conversations and discussions in the office, working meetings, conferences and negotiations with the various people involved in the project; telephone calls, e-mails and letters, minutes; formulating descriptions of buildings, tendering requirements and contracts make up a large proportion of the work of a designing and building architect. Public presentation and discussion of ideas, concepts and designs is a standard situation in both degree courses and professional practice, where success depends on the speaker's oratory abilities.

But what does it mean to understand and use the forms of expression described above as tools in the design process, to recognize their creative potential and make them useful when designing? Formulating the task in hand is one of the first verbal design steps at the beginning of any piece of design work. It describes the problems to be solved, the resources available to do this, the demands made on the solution and the criteria to be used to judge them. Every design problem can be defined in a different way, and the chosen definition determines the directions to be taken and the requirements on which the search for solutions is based. The critical reflection of a design task set by third parties and the reformulation of that problem can

often open the way to innovative approaches. Hence every problem as posed should be constantly interrogated by those working on it, and tested for consistency and reasonableness. A modification or a complete reformulation of a design problem can be a first step towards solving it, for example by developing a fresh perspective, a previously unconsidered but particularly appropriate approach to the problem. This can happen simply because of the words chosen for

Writing. Photograph: Stefanie Meyer, 2002

describing the task in hand. There is a difference between designing a "wardrobe" or a "mobile container system for storing textiles", between "building a house" or "constructing a *machine à habiter*".

Design often demands things or connections to be named for which everyday language has no terms. Or a state of affairs has to be described in such a way that it is perceived differently from the norm. For this reason designers develop their own terms, like every profession, their jargon and technical language. Language's general tendency to be normative, abstract, to generalize, to be conventional and ultimately conservative means that in this context any banning of images is a reflex resistance to anything new. While a photographer has only to press the shutter release on his camera to capture something that has not been seen previously, and a draughtsman with his pencil or a modelmaker with his lump of clay can make new forms visible in a trice, designers also need ways of naming things that are new, still unknown, not yet named, things that have only just developed. To this end they use language in a particular way that can be disturbing for outsiders, following several strategies. The most immediate is extending the meaning of concepts, as Alberti does for example with the Latin term *velum*, which actually means cloth or sail, but which he applied to the gridded veil he used to help him draw perspectives from nature. (see p. 163 f.) One example of *newly* coined terms is the word Dymaxion, which Buckminster Fuller often used. Waldo Warren, a *"merchandising namesmith"* who had made a name for himself by coining the term radio to take the place of wireless, was looking for a term to characterize Fuller's ideas. Warren took the words *dynamic and maximum* and put them together to form *Dy(namic)Maxi(mum)on*. Fuller used this coinage as a kind of trademark, applying it to many of his projects and concepts, such as the *Dymaxion House*, the *Dymaxion Car* or the *Dymaxion Chronofiles*. (Krausse 1999, p. 132) Fuller himself was responsible for the term tensegrity, formed from tensile and integrity, applying it to structures made up of compression and tension ties whose forces were dissipated largely by tensile stresses. (Krausse 2001, pp. 240–256)

CREATING METAPHORS, INTERPRETING, ABSTRACTING

Creating metaphors is another strategy for naming previously unknown things. Here a familiar expression is detached from its usual area of applicability and transferred into a new, hitherto strange sphere and related to different expression. Metaphors are understood on the basis of a previously unnoticed similarity between the two areas. But it needs this tension between similarity and difference to open up new and surprising perspectives and create the power of suggestion that is the key feature of innovative metaphors. Le Corbusier combines the spheres of housing and industry in his *machine à habiter* metaphor, thus suggesting that housing can be designed as rationally and effectively on the same basis as an industrial production plant. The creative tension contained in this metaphor, to which generations of architects have succumbed, arises from an image that introduces polemic by neglecting the aesthetic, emotional and prestigious aspects of housing. In the metaphor *Stadtkrone* (City Crown), Bruno Taut combines the decorative, honorific, valuable but also hierarchical aspects of the crown with the urban notion of an elevated city centre.

Referring to Earl MacCormac and his book *A Cognitive Theory of Metaphor* (1985), the philosopher Hans Lenk sees the metaphor as a way of creating new meanings, without which *"[n]ew ways of thinking and new expressions for those thoughts cannot emerge"* so that *"neither knowledge nor language can grow"* (MacCormac, p. 206). Lenk identifies a fundamental pattern of creative processes in the development and use of innovative metaphors, valid not only in the linguistic sphere, but artistically as well. He therefore suggests

Johann David Steingruber, *Architectonisches Alphabet*, 1773

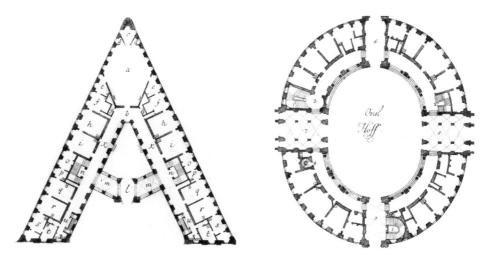

that MacCormac's theory of metaphor, originally applied only to language, should be extended to a general theory of creative action. In order to define his concept of a creatively continuous principle going beyond the linguistic sphere, Lenk links the terms creativity and metaphor to coin the *"creataphor"*, which he defines as

"metaphors embracing perspectives, bridging layers, or metaphors that leap to create and maintain tension, playing in a stimulating way between similarities and dis-similarities". (Lenk 2000, p. 279 ff.)

Just as sketching makes us look at and represent a form or a space accurately, writing a text forces us to clarify our thoughts, order them logically and test them for correctness. Describing a building makes us identify and name its form, structure, qualities and hidden associations. The word text – derived from the Latin *textus*, which literally means "tissue", and is traceable back to the verb *texere*, which means both "to weave" and "to plait" (Onions 1996, p. 913) – probably comes from the same root *tek* – as the Greek *tekton*, used to define the craftsman and the master builder. In the meaning of the common root *tek-*, (translated as to shape, to make), we find a reference to the concept of making which Otl Aicher and Vilém Flusser valued so highly in their design thinking. (see p. 88, 212)

Translating a design idea from the visual to the verbal sphere demands a radical change of perspective. Formal logic is now replaced by linguistic logic. This requires the interpretation and abstraction of a design idea, which should then be described in generally comprehensible terms. This triggers cognitive processes that sometimes surprise the writers themselves, because they are compelled to make themselves aware of circumstances that they would not have considered otherwise. It is precisely when a text has grown vigorously over some length, and the writer begins to wonder whether a design idea really has been captured that surprising insights can occur. While pictorial thought sometimes tends to fix a certain idea, a certain inner picture, in a situation like this, the switch to verbal thinking can help to break down fixed ideas and overcome them by taking a new perspective.

The Brazilian architect Oscar Niemeyer is one example of someone who uses writing as a form of self-interrogation in which the medium of language is deployed to check the conclusiveness and comprehensibility of an architectural concept. Before concluding the first studies for a project he adds a textual commentary to it which provides a *"necessary description"* of his concept. He says that for him this works as a *"prova"* – in Portuguese this word means both examination and proof – of his design. If he cannot find sufficient arguments, and is unable to explain his ideas convincingly with the help of the text, he knows that the design is not yet good enough. (Niemeyer 1993, p. 9, p. 43)

Once a concept has been formulated, then it can be "worked on" with another linguistic design tool, by subjecting it to criticism (see p. 198 ff). This means changing the perspective again, distancing oneself from the empathetic description of what has been designed and questioning it in a spirit of doubt. The interplay of positive description and negative questioning produces dialogues, conversations and discussions in the course of the design

Fashion designer Isabella Blow. Photograph: Pascal Chevallier, WIB

And God saw that it was good.

Then God said, «Let us make man

in our image, in our likeness,

and let them rule over every beast.»

So God created male

and female

and created him in the image of God.

And God blessed them

and said to them, «Be fruitful

and increase in number;

fill the earth and subdue it.

Rule over every beast.»

Then God said, «I give you

every plant and fruit. They will be yours for food.

And to all the beasts, I have given every green plant.»

And it was so.

God saw all that

he had made, and it was very good.

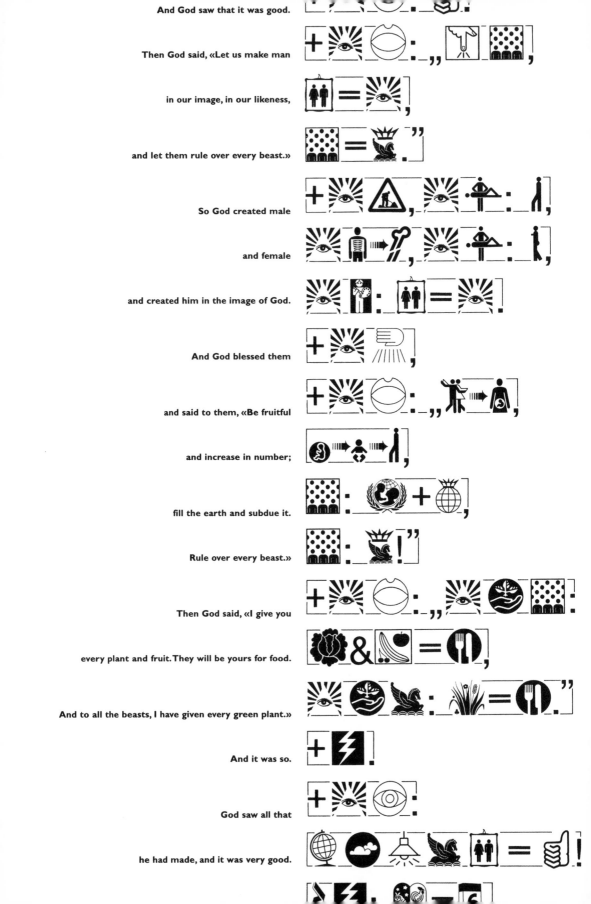

process. Ever since Socrates, situations of this kind have been seen as particularly suited to producing new insights. Socrates developed his method, also known as the "art of midwifery", with the aim of showing his pupils the limitations of their knowledge. He systematically asked questions in order to bring out the ideas his pupils were pregnant with, and to test whether they were *"a false phantom"*, or something with *"true instinct with life and truth"*. *"I cannot myself give birth to wisdom,"* Plato has him say in one of his dialogues, but *"the many admirable truths [his pupils] bring to birth have been discovered by themselves from within."* (Plato, Theaetetus, 150 c,d)

This chapter has by no means discussed the verbal design tools exhaustively. Two other chapters are devoted to examining the linguistic tools of criticism and those of criteria and value systems. The chapters on calculation and computers will discuss the extent to which engineering calculations and digital programs can be used as design tools in the sense of complex, rationally shaped texts. The last chapter of the book will take Otl Aicher's writings on design theory as an example of how theory can be deployed as a verbal design tool.

Juli Gudehus: *Genesis* (detail), 1992

Design drawing

But drawing [il disegno] is so outstanding that it not only explores
Nature's works, but produces infinitely more than nature [...]
and from this we conclude that drawing is not only a science but a deity,
whose name should be duly commemorated, a deity which repeats all the visible
works of God the highest. Leonardo da Vinci (after Maiorino 1992, p. 90)

Can we still understand what Leonardo da Vinci meant by these words? The Christian idea of an almighty God as the creator of the world presented the designers of Leonardo's day with a problem: they were creating something new as well, but were ordinary human beings entitled to do this? When he credits drawing with creating something new (and in this case he is using it to mean the lines – and not the paint – that provide the outlines for the bodies in painting), he shifts the problem of creativity away from the person to the tool, *"a deity which repeats all the visible works of God the highest".* In this way he avoids presenting himself as creative – and thus divine.

GEOMETRY AND ABSTRACTION

We now take reduced-scale, geometrically precise design drawings so much for granted as a design tool that we are scarcely aware of their function as such. But what principles are they following when they *"teach the master builder to create a building that is pleasing to the eye,"* as Leonardo puts it in another place? (after Chastel 1990, p. 136) The drawing, called *forma* in Latin, *disegno* in Italian, changes the relationship between designer and designed in many respects. By making the object that is depicted smaller, it increases the draughtsman's ability to manipulate it to the same extent. If the ground plan of a cathedral is reduced to the size of a hand, it is not only easy to gain a complete impression of it, but also to modify it according to the draughtsman's ideas. Reducing the size of the object that is being worked on makes it into a toy, and the designer into an all-seeing, powerful creator. When the draughtsman draws what seems essential to him, he analyses the object drawn at the same time, and decides what factors his design work should relate to. As each abstraction makes the drawing less vivid, many can only be read by experts. As with writing, drawings need to be interpreted. But at the same time drawing is a fiction that allows the draughtsman to allocate any meaning he wishes to a line.

The geometrical precision that drawing allows cannot be achieved by any other design tool. Vitruvius succinctly remarks: *"The difficult issues of symmetry are resolved by geometric principles and with geometrical methods."* (Vitruvius I,4) This suggests that drawing makes it possible to check the proportions and the geometrical structure of the design precisely. That is why it is still the most important design tool for many people. The question of whether *disegno* or *colore* is the most important element in painting, much discussed in

 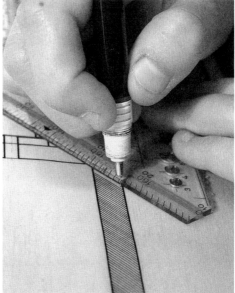

Drawing. Photograph: Marianne Kristen, 2002

15th and 16th century art theory, was never a matter of debate in architecture. The control it permits, as mentioned above, promoted drawing to the status of the preferred medium for academic training. If this is also linked with a view of architecture determined by regularity and right angles, it can become the design tool that dominates everything else, as at the École des Beaux-Arts in the 19th century.

Experts take this medium so much for granted that they often forget how rarely laymen are able to read ground plans or sections. Verbal or written explanations certainly make drawings more intelligible, but laymen cannot usually imagine three-dimensional effects and connections on the basis of two-dimensional diagrams. They are also not familiar with the technical conventions, unspoken because they are taken for granted, according to which drawings are created and read. Laymen are usually able to read perspective drawings better, but the statements such drawings make are less transparent to understanding.

Accurate drawing can also be used as a device for perceptual analysis. Just as writing a text demands clear thinking, with ideas placed in a logical order and checked for correctness, drawing requires a shape or a space to be measured out and presented precisely. It forces the draughtsman to be disciplined about structuring and reducing what is seen, and establishing

Tobias Hammel: *House of Yagaah III*, pencil, Indian ink, acrylic on cardboard, 17.05 m x 2.7 m, exhibition, Berlin 2006

hierarchies within it. But designing with the aid of drawings, ground plans, elevations and sections can also over-emphasise the role played by sets of graphic rules. Plan graphics quickly become a point of argument when architectural decisions are being discussed. But graphic and spatial laws rarely correspond precisely. *"Are the drawing and the project the same thing?"* asks the Portuguese artist Joaquim Vieira, who teaches in the architecture faculty at Porto University, and then shows how greatly the one can differ from the other. (Vieira 1995, p. 38 ff.)

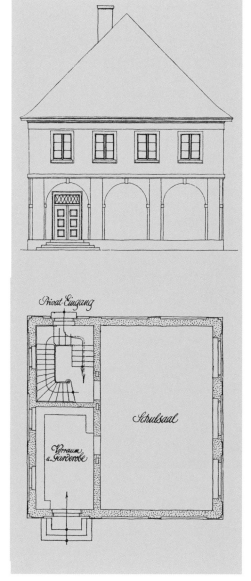

Drawing's most important modes of operation are geometry and abstraction. But there are limits to the clarity and rationality so valued by academic classicism that are not noticeable at first glance. This medium has a graphic logic of its own. Something that looks sound and impressive as a drawing may very well not be like that in reality. Only architecture that bases all its elements on the Cartesian system of three perpendicular axes can be represented without distortion in ground plans, elevations and sections. In addition, the reduction to two dimensions removes a fundamental aspect of architecture: space. The consequence of this is that a structure that has been considered in terms of space rather than graphically often seems shapeless as a drawing; the three-dimensional qualities of a design are difficult to convey in a two-dimensional drawing.

Drawing ground plans, elevations and sections is still based on the assumptions of Euclidian geometry. Buckminster Fuller, the architect of the geodesic domes, questioned these assumptions in his studies of the geometry of the sphere:

Design for a school building, ground plan and elevation, Friedrich Ostendorf, 1913

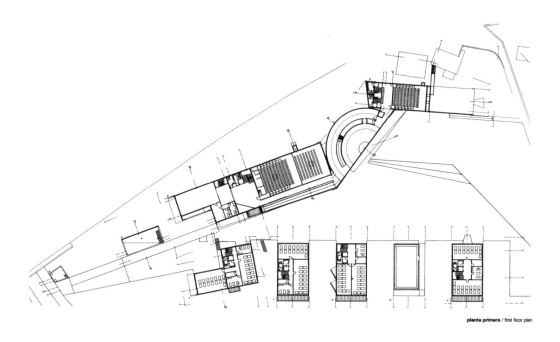

planta primera / first floor plan

Faculty of architecture at Oporto University (FAUP), ground plan, Álvaro Siza, 1986–1995

"In his theories on construction and proof Euclid restricted himself to three tools –
ruler, compasses and pen. But he in fact used a fourth tool, without taking it into
account, and that was the surface on to which he inscribed his diagrammatic constructions." (Fuller 1944, p. 175)

So the starting-point for Euclid's proofs is "in the special and abstract realm of
an imaginary planar geometry". If geometry is translated literally as "measuring the earth", then according to Fuller Euclid's conditions make sense only
if one works on the basis that knowledge about the spherical nature of the
earth had been lost in his day. (Fuller 1944, p. 175)

There are quite a few architectural failures that can be ascribed to the
seductive lure of drawing. The removal of the third dimension combined
with a reduction in scale and increased clarity makes drawing such an effective tool that handling it can be difficult. The more abstract a drawing
becomes, the more ways there are of interpreting it, and the more difficult it

also becomes to predict how the building will work in reality. One fundamental difficulty of using any tool is its inherent tendency towards abstraction and oversimplification. This produces problems of the kind that Vilém Flusser is addressing here:

Geometry versus nature: beach promenade near Oporto, Manuel de Solà-Morales, 2000–2001

"But hands equipped with tools do not have the sensual quality of bare hands. They cannot distinguish a person from an object. [...] So the danger in the tool-making gesture lies in forgetting the original object and thus the difference between an object and a person as well." (Flusser 1991, p. 68)

Ground plans drawn on clay tablets, with measurements in cuneiform script, have survived even from the days of Babylon. (Pevsner 1966, p. 622) We are also familiar with architectural drawings on papyrus from Egypt, organized on a strict grid. It is not known what part these played in the design process. The working drawings from ancient Greece previously mentioned have survived. It is assumed that these came into being as detailed plans based on an over-all plan on a reduced scale, presumably drawn on parchment. All that survived in Rome too were working drawings in real scale on stone, of the Pantheon pediment, for example; there is only written evidence of drawings on parchment. Fragments of ancient plans on marble have also been found in Rome, but these were made for presentational purposes, not as part of the design process (Hesberg 1984, p. 120 ff.).

Vitruvius makes it clear how highly drawing was thought of in the ancient world in his description of a master builder's basic knowledge: he must *"have knowledge of draughtsmanship so that he can more easily illustrate examples at will to represent the appearance of the work he proposes"*. (Vitruvius, I,4) Vitruvius makes a distinction between three different kinds of architectural drawing in the following:

"Ichnografia *is the skilled use, to scale of compass and rule, by means of which the on-site layout of the design is achieved.*
Orthografia *is a frontal image, one drawn to scale, rendered according to the layout for the future work.*
Scaenografia *is the shaded rendering of the front and the receding sides as the latter converge on a point."* (Vitruvius I, 2,2)

Even though these techniques have been in use in Europe since antiquity, the early Middle Ages, when Vitrivius text was by no means unknown, adopted a different, more direct approach to its design practice. There are reports of drawings on wax tablets, and some schematic ground plans on parchment have survived, but they do not seem to have been very important in design terms. Design was mainly carried out using drawings on a natural scale scratched on to the floor or walls, with existing buildings of the same type serving as a pattern and model. This changed only from the first half of the 13th century, when drawings, first of all in the form of drawings on a reduced scale, started to be used more frequently again. (Binding 1993, p. 172)

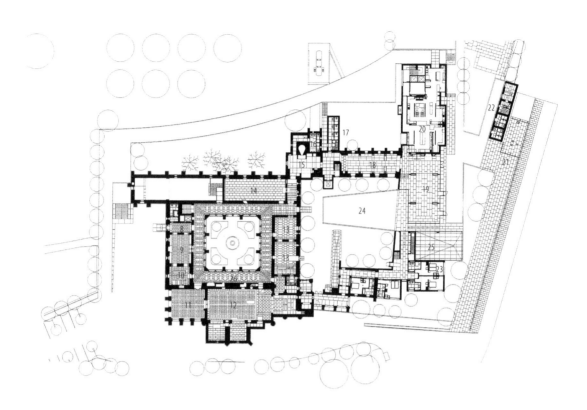

Ground plan of a medieval monastery with modern extension. Arraiolos, Pousada dos Loios, José Paulo dos Santos, 1993–1999

The profound changes that led from medieval to modern thinking can also be seen in the newly developed design tools from the beginning of the early Italian Renaissance. This seminal change was marked, among many other things, by a fundamental transformation in the way design was seen, manifested in the development and use of new design tools. Sketch, drawing, perspective and model came into being in the form in which they are still used today in the first half of the 14th century, in northern Italy. A new way of perceiving things was developed, no longer driven by prescribed "eternally valid ideas", but by direct sensual experience. And it was also at this time that public discussion and criticism of prestigious church and state building projects started to emerge again.

A prerequisite of this development was the replacement of feudal society by an early form of mercantile bourgeoisie that started to establish itself in the northern Italian cities. In the course of this, the technical administration of the masons' craft associations moved out of the clergy's hands to the guilds. Building became a public matter, with the consequence that more and more laymen were involved in decision-making. This in its turn compelled the designers, who now came from the fine arts rather than the building trade, to find much more vivid ways of presenting things than they had before. The symbolic medieval way of looking at things, now seen as formulaic, was replaced by illustration methods that came much closer to reality. Artistic and technical competitions were institutionalized as a decision-making device.

"It was for the building of the Duomo in Florence that 'open' competitions seem to have made people realize for the first time what artistic potential could be stimulated and used in this way." (Lepik 1995, p. 12)

The first competition for this building project was held in 1355, to determine the shape of the pillars in the nave. A competition for the overall form of the cathedral was held in 1367. The competition for the building of the dome, won by Filippo Brunelleschi, was held after 1417, followed by invitations to tender for the form of the lantern (1436), the façade (1490) and the dome gallery (1500) (Lepik 1995, p. 13).

The media switch that took place at this time – from a life-size drawing to a reduced scale drawing and to perspective, from prototype and template to model, also on a reduced scale – did not only lead to building and designing being more separated from each other, but it also meant that people who had been trained in a quite different way were responsible for the designs: goldsmiths (Brunelleschi), painters and artists (Michelangelo) who had mastered what were then new media, replaced the stonemasons organized in guilds.

DESIGNING OR DRAWING

Drawing, seen as the classical design tool as it were, works with geometrical-mathematical abstraction: designing – for a draughtsman – means imposing geometry. The process of representing a project with mathematical precision, drawing as the "language of the engineer", is rational and functional, not an atmospheric painting. The idea is objectivized and can be criticized using rational arguments, and so the drawing became the most popular academic tool for the classical Beaux-Arts tradition as well as for rational technical training. Its disadvantage is a high degree of abstraction; it is hard to make out spatial relations. Le Corbusier devoted a whole chapter to these problems in Vers une Architecture, using the polemical title *"L'Illusion des Plans"*. (Le Corbusier 1963) Le Corbusier does expressly accept design based on the ground plan, as this determines the organization and structure of the building, but vehemently criticizes the act that ground plans are designed according to the aesthetic requirements of the Beaux-Arts tradition. He takes the town plan of Karlsruhe as an example, which he calls the *"most lamentable failure of an intention, the perfect 'knock-out'"*:

"The star remains only on paper, a poor consolation. Illusion. The illusion of fine plans. From any point in the town, you can never see more than three windows of the castle, and they always seem the same ones; the most humblest everyday house would produce as much effect. From the castel, you can never look down more than a single street at a time, and any street in any small market town would have a similar effect." (Le Corbusier 1963, p. 184)

Jean Prouvé, originally trained as a smith, preferred designing in a workshop in his own practice, and also criticizes academic design practice relying entirely on drawing as a design tool. Many of his designs emerged directly from work on prototypes determined by the material and by the efficiency of the devices and machines available. It was only when a form had been found that drawings were prepared retrospectively, as a record. In a conversation, he says he feels sorry for young architects who, because they work exclusively with abstract drawing, are deprived of the important stimulus provided by realizing a project:

"There they discovered what actual architectural inspiration can be, that the lines they drew on Monday can be realized on Tuesday. They knew at once what they would actually see. But now young architects mainly draw things that are not built at all. Do you not think that this is fatal for their minds and spirits?" (Prouvé 2001, p. 29)

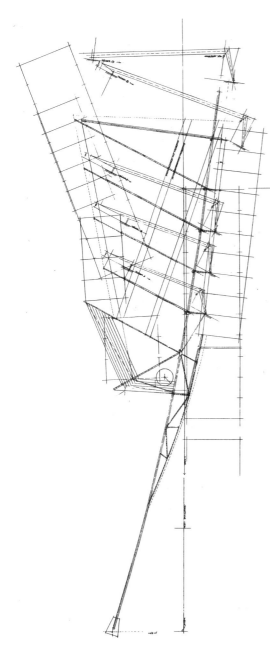

The specific resistance that drawing as a design tool confronts the designer with lies on the one hand in the confinement to simple geometrical constructions, as only these make it possible to construct and convey a form precisely, and on the other hand in the limited number of drawings that can be prepared for a project. Ostendorf's criticism of drawing has already been mentioned. He says that it leads to developing something *"on paper in an inartistic and meaningless way"* that *"simply cannot be grasped as an idea in its confused complexity"*. (Ostendorf 1913, p. 4) When we look at today's working drawings, prepared according to the conventions and rules of drawing regulations, packed so full of information, like a pattern chart, that it is impossible to discern an intelligible form, it is easy to understand Ostendorf's argument. But then he fails to point out that only that which is portrayed parallel to the plane of the two-dimensional drawing appears undistorted. A normal set of drawings, made up of ground plans, elevations and sections, makes anything that does not correspond with the three axes of Cartesian space seem distorted or even nonsensical. It is therefore entirely justified for Ana Leonor Rodrigues to describe drawing as a design tool that *"imposes order on architectural thinking"*. (Rodrigues 2002) The question is whether we are content with this order. Peter Eisenman draws a radical conclusion from this:

Geometry of the Hysolar Institute building, Stuttgart University, Günter Behnisch und Partner, 1987

"Anything that you can draw that does not relate to the three-dimensional reality must be drawn on a computer. [...] plans, sections and elevations return one to the space of vision, to projective space. That's why I no longer draw." (Eisenman 1992, p. 108)

DIGITALIZATION OF DRAWING

Eisenman continues to pursue this idea elsewhere by saying that only things one already has some idea about can be drawn by hand. However, he feels that images can be created digitally that one has never seen or had in one's mind before (Eisenman 1992). Digitalization translates all representations of a design into a uniform code, but one that can be read only by machines. The boundaries between the different ways of representing ideas are becoming more permeable. This means that it is possible to link the individual presentation modes and bring them together in a common data base. Once this base has been established, little additional effort is needed to switch from one way of representing things to another, presenting the design simultaneously as a perspective, ground plan and section or as a room finishing schedule and quantity survey at the same time, automatically, so to speak.

Long before PCs began to appear in architecture practices the mainframe computers of the 1960s were used by universities and local authorities for undertaking calculations, for example, to draw up site plans and for determining shapes. For example, a mainframe computer at Stuttgart University was used to determine the shape of the roof structure for the Munich Olympic Stadium (Nerdinger 2005, p. 267). In the early 1980s, when the first PCs started to appear in universities and architecture practices, they were usually not able to cope with graphic design. However, only ten years later computers, monitors and plotters replaced drawing boards in many architecture practices.

Scarcely any other design tool has changed so much as a result of digitalization as the drawing. The traditional two-dimensional drawing has literally acquired any number of extra dimensions. Transparent sketching paper has become layers and links that can be faded in and out, pencil and ink lines become areas of colour that can be structured at will, the torment of scraping and hatching disappears, and so does meditation about a delicate pencil

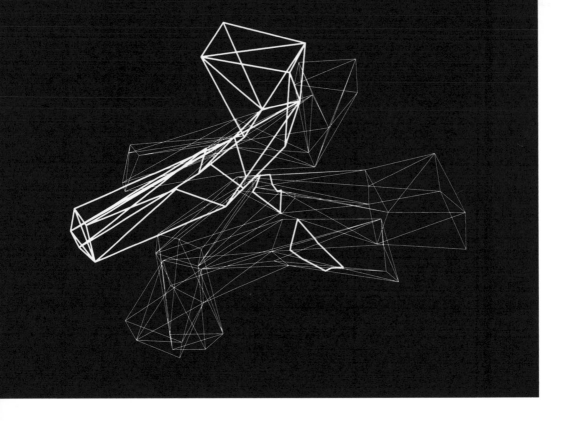

Wire geometry diagram for the IUHEI library, Geneva, Peter Eisenman, 1996

drawing. The simple drawing becomes a complex, polydimensional data structure that can be linked with other data at will and presented in a whole variety of ways – as a ground plan, section, elevation or perspective, as a moving 3D model that the mouse can "walk about in", as a video or mechanically produced model on a freely chosen scale, but also as a room finishing schedule, quantity survey, loadbearing or climate simulation; or as a cost analysis and tendering list. Something that was *one* project in the mind of the person who created the design, presented in different ways with the aid of the various design tools, now comes together again as *one* digital data structure.

The three-dimensional computer model has replaced the conventional drawings of ground plan, section and façade as a database for this poly-dimensional structure. Just as drawings, models or calculations represent a design idea only in terms of the possibilities afforded by the particular medium, this database too is an imperfect representation only, though on a higher plane, as it can be presented in various media. Complex geometrical connections no longer have to be laid down in absolute dimensions, but can be given as parameters, so that it is sufficient to change one of them to produce a new form. Representation by parameters opens up a great deal of new scope for designers, as variants can be drawn up with much less effort and very much more quickly. But on the other hand it means that conceptual questions have to be addressed more intensively in order to be able to program parametric models at all. And the elements of the drawing themselves change their quality when working to parameters: the previously neutral line becomes a vector, with direction, size and intensity (Eisenman 2005, p. 226).

While the limitations of the first drawing programs forced one to use the simplest possible geometry (which is probably a reason for the "boxes", the simple, rhomboid building volumes of computer-designed architecture's first decade), the PC soon became a prerequisite for designing complex geometrical structures. The present second decade of computer-designed and generated architecture is characterized by a counter-movement using freer forms. The architecture journalist Hanno Rauterberg calls this *"digital Modernism"*: architecture no longer only drawn on the computer, but using parametric algorithms to generate forms and geometries that could not be represented previously, leading to envelopes and spaces that were formerly considered impossible to build. (Rauterberg 2005, p. 54)

Inner courtyard in a bank, Berlin, Pariser Platz, Frank Gehry, 1994–1999

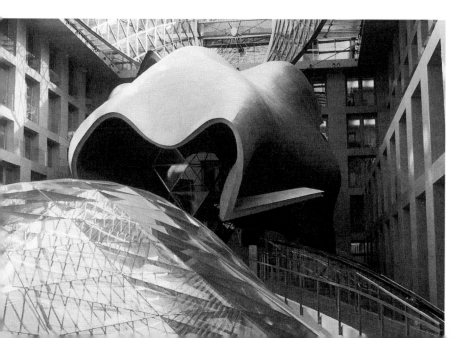

The obviously hand-made nature of traditional drawing is suppressed by digitalization in favour of representation devices that can lay claim to be more professional and at the same time more objective because of their perfection and the amount of detail they offer. As they look less (hand)made, they also seem less artificial and arbitrary. As they increase in perfection, they increasingly acquire the natural and convincing quality of photographs. Expressing individuality and formulating a personal, recognizable way of drawing and representing ideas has possibly become obsolete at this level.

Model

Models are traps for capturing the world. Vilém Flusser (1993/2, p. 14)

149

The architectural model can be used for a large number of purposes, which makes it a highly effective, but also problematical design tool. It appears in forms extending from toys to burial objects, from souvenirs and artistic sculptures to religious objects. The latent fetishist character of the model inherent in such manifestations contrasts with its pragmatic applications: it is just as well suited to scientific experiments as it is to designing structures and buildings. It offers the most direct approach to dealing with spatial, structural and sculptural questions. Seen as a design tool, the model makes it possible *"to think with one's hands"*, as it were, and at the same time to work conceptually. As a vivid means of communication, models help to bridge the gulf between laymen and experts.

If we see design as a gradual approach to built reality, then models, samples and prototypes are the tools closest to three-dimensional, material reality. Samples make it possible to compare building materials and the ways in which they can be handled, and then to make choices. Prototypes are parts of a building completed as an experiment, and their dimensions can extend

Max Bill looking at a model of the Swiss Pavilion for the Venice Biennale.
Photograph: Ernst Scheidegger, 1951

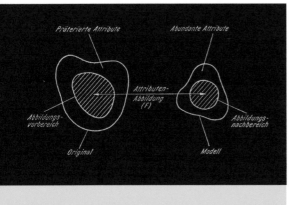

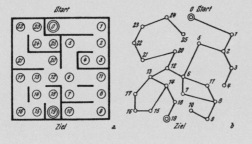

Top: diagram for the representation of model and original,
bottom left: labyrinth drawing as original,
right: graph model for the labyrinth drawing,
Herbert Stachowiak, 1973

to trial structures. Both are clearly defined ways of presenting ideas, constructed life-size, and with the materials intended for the actual project. But our linguistic usage is not so clear-cut in its implications when it comes to the concept of the model.

The words *model, modulation, modem* and *mode* all come from the same linguistic root "*m.d.*", which originally means "*measure*". (Flusser 1993/2, p. 62) Derived from the Latin *modellus*, small measure, and from the Italian *modello*, example, we use the word model for two kinds of things today: three-dimensional, simplified and reduced-scale representations of an object that both serve to develop its form, like a drawing, or objects as specimens which serve as a pattern for a piece of work that is to be produced. One and the same object can have two fundamentally different meanings: a representation of a mental image, or an example for something that is to be made.

The ambiguity of the concept is not a chance piece of linguistic imprecision. The possibility it contains of an arbitrary yet fleeting change of meaning – from the vague image of a design idea to a definite pattern for a concrete building, worked out in detail and sometimes seeming very real – is a modus operandi common to all design tools. But in the case of the model this shift of meaning from the vague to the concrete bridges a comparatively large difference, and so we can see it as a particularly effective tool.

Vitruvius absolutely refused to work on models because they meant that a great deal could be represented that could not be realized in reality (Vitruvius X 16,3 ff.) – an argument that would mean rejecting all representation – but Leon Battista Alberti did accord them some value. He uses two Latin terms to define architectural models: "*modulus et exemplar*". Instead of choosing the expression *modello*, which was already current in his day, in the sense of the pattern that was to be followed precisely, he introduced a pair of concepts that explain the ambiguity of this concept. *Modulus* actually identifies the scale or the recurrent basic dimensions (module), and exemplar the example or pattern. By using these expressions invoking Vitruvius, Alberti is emphasizing, as Werner Oechslin has shown, first the *"theoretical side, the conceptual and intellectual nature of architecture"*, and secondly the pattern function of the model. (Oechslin 1995, p. 40 ff.)

When Otl Aicher states categorically *"designing means constructing models"*, he does not mean any of the model concepts discussed so far. He sees a model first and foremost, excluding any idea of a three-dimensional object, as *"a construction made up of statements, concepts and conceptual operations"*. (Aicher 1991/2, p. 195) Here he is alluding to a model concept as used in the sciences. The scientist Herbert Stachowiak describes this in his General Model Theory on the basis of three characteristics:

Illustration: *Models are always models of something, representations of natural or artificial originals that could be models themselves.*

Abbreviation: *Models generally do not record all the attributes of the original they represent, but only those that seem relevant to the particular model-maker and/or model user.*

Pragmatics: *Models are not unambiguously assigned to their originals per se. They are made for a particular user, within a given period and for a particular purpose.*

(Stachowiak 1973, p. 131 ff.)

RELATIONSHIP WITH REALITY

The architectural model shares the mechanisms of abstraction and scale reduction with the drawing. Beyond this it offers the three-dimensional quality of its representation, which gives it its particular vividness, and the possibility of choosing the materials for making it freely – unlike samples and prototypes, which are made of the same material as the finished object.

Models can show buildings using simple, soft materials, and it is their difference from the real building materials that shows the theoretical range of this design tool. This is also clear in the difference between a model intended to show an idea, or intended as a working or presentation model.

We would put the former together spontaneously from anything that came to hand, and give it new meaning, as in a child's game – a pocket calculator becomes a model railway station "in no time" – but for working models we choose cheap, soft materials like wax, clay or plaster, and later cardboard, glue and balsa wood as well, all of which are easy to work with. Whereas abstract models illustrating ideas and imprecise working models restrict themselves to the essential lines of a design, presentation models are made with a great deal of time and effort from materials that are difficult to work like wood, plastic and metal, and worked out in detail. Combining all these approaches – abstraction, reduction, changes of material and meaning – permits observations and experiments, but also manipulations that go well beyond the possibilities of drawing. The greater precision and ease of reproduction of the drawing is being increasingly cancelled out by modern model building methods using computer-controlled precision milling. Various planes of meaning can overlap in one and the same model in a way that makes it into an object onto which a whole variety of different ideas can be projected. Its apparent closeness to reality makes the model into a means of communication that seems convincing at first glance, but whose ambiguity is often neglected.

The capacity of models of different sizes for conveying an image is not linear, but exponential: a model on the scale of one to two is certainly "half the size" it is in reality, but it has only an eighth of the volume. At a scale of one to one hundred the volume is only a millionth of the true size. So the spatial quality of architectural models is subject to a particularly high degree of abstraction.

Frei Otto analysed the problem of scale more precisely. If models are used for loading experiments, which was a method used for dimensioning structural elements before the development of structural calculation procedures, different exponential ratios have to be used according to the structural system. Furthermore, the theory of mechanics of materials state that in order to establish the load-bearing capacity the per-unit *"overall load in the model"* must equal *"that load in the realized design"*. (Otto 1989, p. 209)

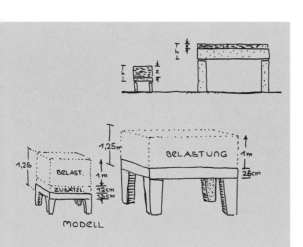

"An object of the same material and equal shape breaks at the same load." Load experiments using a model, Frei Otto, 1989

As the spans in the model are already proportionally reduced by the reduction in scale, loading experiments should not reduce the overall load per unit area by the same scale as the dimensions of the structural elements. *"An object in the same material of equal shape breaks at the same load."* (loc. cit.) For this reason, the load in the model should even be increased where necessary to compensate for the lesser self-weight of the structural elements. As Frei Otto has shown, a lack of familiarity with these relationships can lead to serious miscalculations. This may explain why so many architects are sceptical about this particular design tool. The deceptively convincing nature of models can easily mislead one into ignoring their essentially fictitious representational character as well as their inherent high degree of abstraction.

When design models built to defined scales were used for the first time in the early Renaissance, these were properly speaking "prototypes on a reduced scale", as they were not made in cheaper materials, or materials that were easier to work, but actually built from bricks. These first models originated in Florence as preliminary studies for building the cathedral dome. Their function did not relate to design alone: Filippo Brunelleschi also used them to test the building methods and load-bearing capacity of his design. (Lepik 1995, p. 84 ff.) Competitions and public debate meant that these presentations had to be vivid: model and perspective were developed almost simultaneously, as forms for "discursive" tools that are also comprehensible and accessible to laymen.

The ambiguity of the model, its toy-like and fetish aspects, the combination of vividness and good load-bearing capacity make it a particularly seductive medium. Even the Italian Renaissance architect and theoretician Vincenzo Scamozzi compared models with young birds whose genus was as yet scarcely discernible, but which could grow into eagles or ravens. From this he concludes that *"it is easy to deceive the client under the cover of the model"* (from Oechslin 1995, p. 48) Alberti also points out:

"The presentation of models that have been coloured and lewdly dressed with the allurement of painting is the mark of no architect intent on conveying the facts; rather it is that of a conceited one, striving to attract and seduce the eye of the beholder." (Alberti 1485, p. 34)

Alberti's next demand is still valid today:

"Better then that the models are not accurately finished, refined and highly decorated,
but plain and simple so that they demonstrate the ingenuity of him who conceived the
idea, and not the skill of the one who fabricated the model." (Alberti 1485, p. 33/34)

This is to be taken all the more seriously as Alberti sees the model as an important instrument for predicting the consequences of design decisions:

"For this reason I will always commend the time-honoured custom practice by the
best builders, of preparing not only drawings and sketches but also models of wood
or any other material. This will enable us to weigh up repeatedly and examine, with
the advice of experts, the work as a whole and the individual dimensions of all the
parts." (loc. cit., p. 33/34)

"The model is lying!" or "The perspective is distorting!" or "The film is manipulative!" are reproaches that designers still hear today. As we have already seen in the analysis of the gesture, we are confronted here with a fundamental problem that applies for all design. Design is "lies" to a certain extent – in the sense that it is representing something that does not yet exist in reality and that may or may not be open to realization. In this fundamental respect, design is different from creative work on a concrete object.

THE IMPORTANCE OF MATERIALS

Jim Drobnick calls Peter Eisenman's early work *"cardboard architecture"*. (Eisenman 1995, p. 320) Günter Behnisch too constantly pointed out how much the material used for the model helps to shape the design. If a soft, formless material like clay or plaster is used, he feels that it creates a different formal language from the use of slender rods, for example:

"Every planning step has its own materials and techniques. [...] Cardboard models
give rise to stodgy, flat, incorporeal buildings: wooden blocks produce wooden block
architecture, and plasticine produces relatively free plastic structures."
(Behnisch 1987, p. 40)

In fact it is scarcely possible to prove such direct effects. It is true that every material shows recognizable tendencies, but there is no inevitable link between building or model-building material and formal language. On the contrary, some designers feel challenged to wrest an expressive quality different from the expected one out of a particular material. They see it as an artistic challenge to work against its specific resistance, for example by trying to make stone look soft or plaster look hard. But it is certainly appropriate to seek out a suitable model-making material for every design task. Behnisch reports:

"The design for the Olympic Park in Munich was developed largely using a sand model. This sand was the closest we could get to the deep gravel we had to work with on site; it had acquired very little shape from its own structures, so was open to landscape designs." (Behnisch 1987, p. 40)

Clay as the first and archetypal model-making material – fired clay models have survived from prehistoric times – indicates the original meaning of the central concept of making that is so important for both Otl Aicher and Vilém Flusser, and its etymological origin in kneading. (see p. 88) This malleable material still influences the idea that some architects have of design. Álvaro Siza does not use clay for model-making as a rule, but explains that when designing he imagines his buildings are made of a lump of clay, and

Dome and extensions for the Duomo in Florence, working model in wood on a scale of 1:60, Filippo Brunelleschi and Lorenzo Ghiberti, c. 1420

Faculty of architecture at Oporto University (FAUP), working model on a scale of 1:50 (detail), finnboard and adhesive tape, Álvaro Siza, 1986–1995

that he shapes this and adapts it to the various conditions until the final form is established. Michelangelo used clay models to design the dome of St. Peter's; it was only when the form was fixed that the wooden model, still in existence today, was constructed to present his design to Pope Paul IV. (Evers 1995, p. 385, p. 391)

In current architecture training, clay or similar easily shaped materials like plasticine or wax tend to be neglected for model-making, but this material plays an important part in designing car bodies. Here a special clay mixed with plastics is used, as this has better drying and shrinkage qualities than pure clay.

In contrast with clay, which is formless and thus permits any form, industrially prefabricated semi-finished products like light- or heavy-weight cardboard and wooden or metal rods have a certain geometry inscribed in them from the outset. This geometry is just as subliminally present in the surfaces and lines of cut cardboard illustrating the structural behaviour of concrete

Competition model for the Grounds and buildings for the Munich Olympics, Günter Behnisch und Partner, 1967. Photograph: Ewald Glasmann

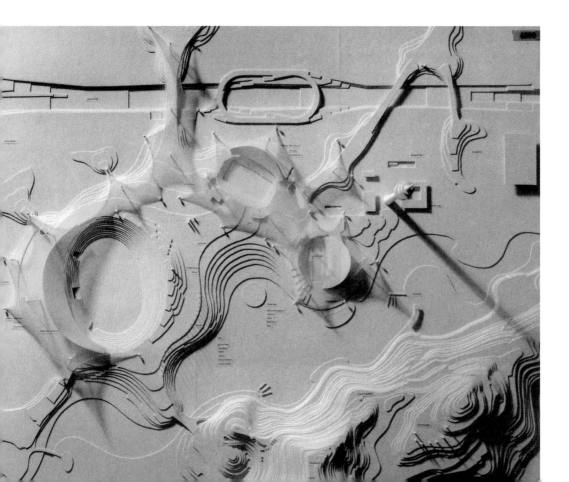

slabs as it is in the lines of the rods representing timber beams or steel gird-
ers. Glass is a material that is particularly difficult to represent in models, as
its sheen and reflective qualities, its differing degrees of translucency and
colouring in light and counter-light are difficult to achieve with model-mak-

Ancient models in fired clay, used as a burial object

ing materials. The resistance that the selected materials offer to the designer
can be seen as a source of discipline, but also as a constraint – a self-
imposed limitation that inhibits yet at the same time stimulates the designer's creativity and has to be overcome, as if in sport.

Sensing the resistance of a particular material and overcoming it is a sensual experience that is naturally experienced differently for every material.
The ability to "crawl into a model" in one's mind in order to imagine the
model's full-size potential can be enhanced by building oneself as a "model"
on the same scale as the one present or – astonishingly – by looking at models through a sheet of white paper with a peephole in it.

Feeling and understanding, perceiving with the fingers and thinking with
the scalpel make it possible to get to know the qualities of the materials
directly, to explore their formal language, but also to assess the load-bearing
capacity of a structure or anticipate difficulties in joining elements together
at an early stage.

Life-size clay models are used when designing car bodywork.

Given the complexity of these questions, it is once again clear that it is entirely reasonable to see model-making, scorned by many people as mechanical and banal, as an intellectual discipline, in the spirit of Alberti. It was taught as such by the Dutch model-maker Paul Verberne, for example, who worked in Israel. For him cutting material is a symbolic act he equates with writing. He feels that model-making means finding out *"how material-isations of space in a model can interfere with your thinking about space when you build a house"*. (after Schaerf 2002, p. 125)

Digitalizing models and model-making loses the sensual experience of material and space, and with that the experience of the directness with which half-finished models can be manipulated. As long as they remain

Model-making. Photograph: Stephanie Meyer, 2002

digital, 3D models are visible on the screen only as single, flat perspectives. They can be selected at will, but they do not convey any real impression of space. If the appropriate CNC mills and 3D printers are available for *Rapid Prototyping*, digitalizing model-making confers a high degree of precision. The coupling of a Personal Computer with a *Personal Fabricator*, a device that produces three-dimensional objects as rapidly, reliably and at reasonable costs as plotters do with drawings, is still a vision for the future.

Perspective view

...the purpose of geography is to provide a view of the whole.

Claudius Ptolemaeus (after Edgerton 1975, S. 101)

160   We take perspective illustrations so much for granted today that one often
       hears the need expressed to resist the dominance of linear perspective
       (Rudolf Arnheim). What does linear perspective achieve as a design tool?
       Many architects see it even more than the model as a way of presenting the
       completed design, and not as a tool for devising it. It is certainly too simple
       to assume that it is a realistic mode of three-dimensional representation
       whose problems lie only in ensuring that all the points in the construction
       will still fit on the drawing board. Other architects see perspective–in the
       form of rapidly made small sketches, or large scale drawings–as their most
       important working tool. Their question would be another: how does perspec-
       tive show the designer his design? What new factors does it introduce, which
       elements of architecture does it reinforce, and which does it undermine?

       Every design tool, according to the way in which it works, means that
       some aspects are emphasized and others neglected. A drawing asks for scale
       and geometry, a perspective requires an individual observer and reflects the
       three-dimensional effect of a design. As it makes the drawn area into pictor-
       ial space, and thus represents the primal image of virtual space, it functions
       entirely differently from architectural drawing, which is restricted to two
       dimensions. The story of its rediscovery contains numerous indications of
       how important it is as a design tool.

       The Latin term *perspectiva (ars)*, literally translated as *"the art of looking
       through"*, was generally used in the Middle Ages to define optics, the *"theory of
       seeing"* that was studied at all major universities. It was only after the mid 15th
       century that it started to be used in its current sense for depictions of illusory
       space. (Edgerton 1975, p. 59) This geometrically comprehensible representation of
       spaces and three-dimensional objects on a flat pictorial surface developed dur-
       ing the transition period from the medieval Aristotelian idea of space to mod-
       ern space: the transition from the idea of a finite space characterized by places
       with different qualities and in which there are no voids to space understood as
       a *"continuum of infinite dimensions [...], as a motionless void ready to accept matter,"* as
       the Jewish philosopher Chasdai Crescas put it c. 1400. (after Gosztonyi 1976, p. 197)

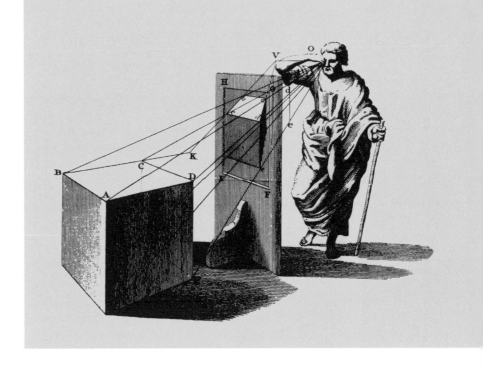

The principles of perspective projection, from: Daniel Fournier: *A Treatise on the Theory of Perspective*, 1761

THE DISCOVERY OF THE WORLD

The (re-?)discovery of linear perspective is attributed to the Florentine master goldsmith and architect Filippo Brunelleschi, who conducted two experiments in representing three-dimensional space in perspective on a two-dimensional plane in the years 1425/26. Here he was able to fall back on artistic and optical experiments made in the course of the 14th century. Painters like Lorenzo Ghiberti and Jan van Eyck had come very close to solving the problem. They had already used vanishing points in their paintings, though several of them, arranged on a common axis. Edgerton assumes that when preparing his experiments, Brunelleschi took advice from a Florentine scholar called Toscanelli, who later also encouraged Christopher Columbus to embark on his great journey across the Atlantic. This shows the profound change that the new ideas of space were triggering, not just in art, but in many other areas. In fact,

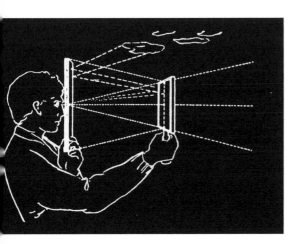

Brunelleschi's experiment: a perspective drawing is viewed in a mirror through a hole in the centre of the drawing.

Brunelleschi's experiments looked quite simple. Standing in the doorway of the Duomo in Florence, he painted a central-perspective view of the baptistery on a square panel, but added silver mirror foil in place of the sky. In order to be able to compare the original and the copy with each other accurately, he drilled a small hole in his painting at eye level. Looking through this hole, it was now possible to see a painted perspective copy in another mirror, with the real sky and its clouds reflected above it. He painted a second picture of the Palazzo Vecchio, which he shows in an oblique view, as a perspective with two vanishing points.

Leon Battista Alberti finally described the theoretical bases of linear central perspective in his book *De Pictura/Della Pittura (On Painting)* in 1435/6. Starting with the idea of a "visual pyramid" made up of sight rays, with its apex in the viewer's eye, Alberti defined perspective as a *"section through the visual triangle"*. The apex of the pyramid is reflected in the perspective vanishing point. The central ray, or *"the Prince of Rays"*, as Alberti calls it elsewhere, is the only ray that runs unbroken from the viewer's eye to the vanishing point. The horizontal drawn through the vanishing point becomes the picture space horizon. The centre of vision, *"the apex of the pyramid within the eye of the viewer"* is shown in side view in an explanatory drawing, and here it becomes the centre of projection in the construction. The *"section through the visual triangle"* becomes the perspective plane, and its position between the object portrayed and the centre of projection can be chosen at will. The positions of the horizontal divisions can now be read at the points where it intersected the sight rays.

But Alberti goes even further. In the *Libro Secondo of Della Pittura* he describes a second, simple and pragmatic aid for drawing perspectives, also based on the definition of the image as a "section through the sight pyramid". This makes it possible to draw perspectives from nature and thus to test the "theory" of their geometrical construction empirically. Alberti calls this simple device velo or *velum* (Lat. cloth, sail), and adds that among his circle of friends he usually called this the "section plane" (Lat. *"intercisio"*). Alberti describes this aid, first published in a picture by Albrecht Dürer, as follows:

"It is like this: a veil loosely woven of fine thread, dyed whatever colour you please, divided up by thicker threads into as many parallel square sections as you like, and stretched on a frame. I set this up between the eye and the object to be represented, so the visual pyramid passes through the loose weave of the veil." (Alberti 1540, para. 31)

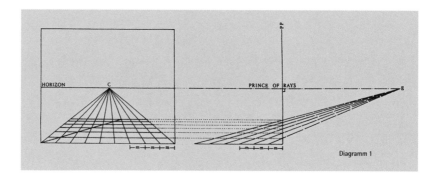

HORIZON   C   PRINCE OF RAYS   E

Diagramm 1

Alberti's method for constructing a perspective of a floor with a square tile pattern

Through simple measurement, the forms and lines from the grid woven into the semi-transparent veil can be transferred to the drawing surface, which has the same grid drawn on it. This is a useful aid for seeing perspective foreshortening and distortions. Seen obliquely, a rectangle becomes shortened in perspective to an irregular parallelogram, a trapezoid, and a circle becomes an ellipse. Our visual perception is structured in such a way that we do in fact see a trapezoid or an ellipse, but perceive it as a rectangle or parallelogram at first. This becomes clear when children or untrained adults try to draw a three-dimensional situation. The *velum* is an aid that makes it easy to detach oneself from the perceived form and master the difficulties inherent in tricking our perceptual apparatus and recognizing perspective foreshortening and distortions as such. Conversely, the ability to read a perspective three-dimensional illusion is not a gift of nature, but has to be learned. Children until the age of 8 to 12 and adults with certain backgrounds are not in a position to recognize the three-dimensional illusion of a perspective. (Gosztonyi, p. 809) The velum is still used for teaching drawing today. A simplified version of the principle is the practice, used by many draughtsmen, of measuring and sighting with a pencil in an outstretched hand. This method means that angles and proportions can be assessed without difficulty, and transferred to the drawing. (Edwards 1979, chap. 8)

Central perspective is a key discovery of the modern age. It formulated generally valid, empirically sound rules that allowed anyone applying them to depict three-dimensional situations. Seeing in perspective became the basis of a completely new understanding of space and landscape that shaped the art, architecture and science of subsequent centuries.

The principle of perspective already contains all the essential elements of photography, with the exception of the photochemical imaging process. In combination with the woodcuts that were starting to appear in Germany after 1400 and the technique of copperplate engraving developed around 1440, perspective presentation became a widely cultivated pictorial medium. (Klotz 1997, p. 182 ff.) In the engravings and paintings of the 17th and 18th centuries, the images had already achieved a degree of precision in representing

Albrecht Dürer (workshop): *Draughtsman drawing a recumbent woman*, 1538, showing how the velum is used.

light and space, structure and proportion, that is scarcely inferior to photographs, at least as far as architecture is concerned. Before Talbot and Daguerre invented photography, images were still created by hand, but even Leonardo da Vinci had used a predecessor of the photographic camera, the Camera Obscura, as an aid. Seen in this light, the invention of photography was merely a further step towards automating the imaging process which has progressed via cinematography to the modern video camera.

Perspective integrates the geometrical information from ground plan, elevation and section and translates it into a vivid three-dimensional image. It follows precise rules that anyone can understand. The most important innovation introduced by perspective is that it represents spatial situations with all elements relating to a uniform three-dimensional system.

"The strength of a grid-network measuring system lies in its ability to provide an abstract image of the space governed by an immutable framework of horizontal and vertical coordinates." (Edgerton 1975, p. 103)

As a tool for rationalizing space, it paves the way for the Cartesian system of three coordinate axes arranged perpendicular to one other and intersecting at a single point. As a geometrical instrument, perspective creates an illusion of depth that makes it possible to represent the continuity and infinity of space. The aim formulated in the Ptolemaic projection method of showing the whole world can be realized by perspective.

In order to be able to perceive this spatial illusion, the viewer must ignore the drawn or painted surface of the image, and he must stand at the point intended. Care must be taken *"that no objects in a painting can appear like real objects, if it is not viewed from a certain distance"*. (Alberti 1540, para. 19) The viewer is rewarded for this by the impression of being included in the picture space, the sense that he is standing on the same ground as the scenery depicted. Perspective, like no other medium, establishes a direct link between the space depicted and the viewer's body. It creates a picture space characterized by a suction, a dynamic movement into the depth of the space. Precision in depicting three-dimensional situations is combined here with a shortening of all the lines that do not lie parallel with the picture plane, and that can make even the calmest space look dynamic.

The spatial dynamic of perspective indicates that our experience of space is linked with movement, and with this invocation of movement in space, perspective points to the other, to areas that are not depicted in the selected detail. This promotes a holistic view of the world that also relates to a subjective observer's individual point of view. Here details can be presented in a special way, because perspective views show the different planes of depth within a space with the same sharpness of focus on a single plane, and do

this even in cases where neither the eye nor photography could bring this off. And yet perspective, unlike drawing or isometric views, tends towards a holistic effect including the context. Its dual function, with theoretical-mathematical image construction on the one hand and a practical-artistic depiction of spatial contexts on the other, makes it possible to achieve powerful realism as well as completely illusory portrayals. The actual excitement of perspective derives from the question of the extent to which something depicted realistically is true or untrue in reality.

This duality enshrines the medium's great possibilities, as well as its dangers. Every tool has its advantages and disadvantages, but things are rather more complicated in the case of perspective, which Erwin Panofsky called a *"two-edged sword"*. (Panofsky 1924) Drawings like ground plans, elevations or sections follow an unambiguous reference structure that always creates images of a building in the same way. But perspective's relationship with the image is determined by three factors: first by the choice of the viewer's position (centre of projection), then by the direction in which the viewer is looking, which defines the position of the vanishing point, and finally by the choice of the distance point, which fixes the distances between centre of projection, picture plane and the object depicted. All three operations are not immediately comprehensible to the viewer of the completed picture, but greatly influence the way it is presented. Shifting the distance point leads, similarly to altering the focal length of a lens, to a different field angle and also a different impression of spatial depth. It is rare for a perspective to correspond with the human visual angle of 180° in a horizontal and 120° in a vertical direction. Then there is the choice of time of day, which determines the incident light and the position of any people who may be included. Perspective forces the viewer to see a situation from the same viewing angle and distance as its author selected, at the same time, and in the same light. It is thus a design for a piece of precisely determined perception.

This fourfold "inscrutability" of perspective needs to be borne in mind all the more as its geometrical principle also forms the basis for photography, film and video, and thus our most important visual communication media. Like all these media forms, perspective is a highly expressive medium that depicts the world with "scientific" precision, but for precisely the same reason can convey convincing illusions. Its synthesis creates images with a high

Giovanni Battista Piranesi: *Carceri d'Invenzione*, plate XIII, *The Well*, second version, c. 1761 (detail)

degree of complexity that can no longer be seen as a geometrical construction by the viewer, and thus are not read analytically and rationally. They are instead viewed as images that our perceptual apparatus processes holistically and emotionally. Such images can be extremely powerful because they are so vivid and have such a direct emotional impact.

PERSPECTIVE AS AN ATTITUDE

This multiple range of options makes perspective a highly flexible tool that has served a variety of purposes since its invention. The Renaissance emphasized its rational, objective, static character, but the artists of the Baroque period did precisely the opposite. They made particular use of the

Upper hall in the Neue Nationalgalerie Berlin, seen diagonally and parallel to the grid

illusory possibilities afforded by the medium, its dynamic quality, its emotional content. The strict perspective grid, adopting the Cartesian idea of space, and the ensuing precise spatial perceptions formed the backdrop against which its Baroque spatial concepts first became conceivable.

A perspective can depict a single view only. It is thus bound to one of the basic conditions of human existence, and compels its author to address the viewer and his location. The artist has a free choice between a worm's-eye, normal or bird's-eye view, but this choice has consequences: it defines the viewer's relationship with the situation as represented, it allocates him a role. In a bird's-eye view he becomes monarch of all he surveys, in total command of the situation, and in a worm's-eye view a defenceless admirer of it. A normal view makes him, according to viewing position, an uninvolved onlooker or the protagonist to whom the whole situation relates. But above all it can show the space from the point of view of the individual user. Here the relative nature of any chosen viewpoint can still be discerned.

Perspective's realism makes it possible to depict Utopias, but it questions them at the same time. Every perspective claims to relate to the reality of the visual space, and even the most Utopian presentation is measured against this relationship with reality in terms of plausibility. The way perspective depicts its

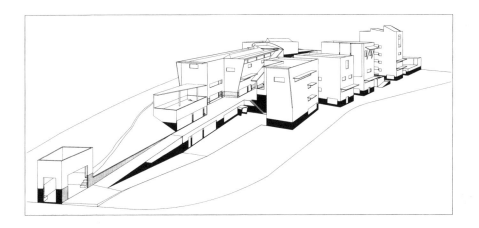

New faculty of architecture at Oporto University, perspective view, Álvaro Siza, 1986–1995

subjects may range from abstract to photorealistic, but a perspective's degree of abstraction, unlike that of drawing, remains fundamentally recognizable because of its relation to reality. Drawing works on the basis of the abstract line, but perspective works with concrete visual perception. So drawings that are kept abstract seem much more natural than highly abstract perspectives. Unlike drawing, which is abstract from the outset, perspective, which works on a concrete basis, makes every abstraction into a problem. So any abstract element will always appear stronger in a drawing than in a perspective.

We can discern clear tendencies in perspective both as a means of perception and as a representational tool. Architecture is known as "perspectivist" if its design is clearly dominated by the use of perspective – whether in the form of sketches, constructed drawings or photomontages – and when it addresses the elements this tool reinforces. Just like photography, film and video, perspective tends to be concrete rather than abstract, dynamic rather than static, spatial rather than surface-bound, contextual rather than object-related, aimed at the individual rather than the general viewer, realistic rather than Utopian, holistic, complex and emotional in its perceptions rather than analytical, rational and inclined to simplify. So it is not surprising that perspective was denigrated and resisted from all directions that run counter to these tendencies. Perspective was subject to many attacks by classical Modernism in the first half of the 20th century. Rejected as a tool of humanism and absolutism, decried as subjective and irrational, it was (and is) sometimes forbidden even by architects. In painting, the dominance of the perspective view was questioned by artists including Cézanne, and subsequently by Picasso and Braque:

"Scientific perspective is nothing but eye-fooling illusionism [...] which makes it impossible for an artist to convey a full experience of space, since it forces the objects in a picture to disappear away from the beholder instead of bringing them within his reach, as painting should." (Braque, after Richardson 1964)

The De Stijl and Bauhaus architects preferred axonometry and isometry, which seemed more objective, as they change only the angles in the solids depicted, without any perspective distortion of length. But we should exam-

A room that challenges our way of viewing perspective: staircase in the foyer of the Casa da Música in Oporto, OMA / Rem Koolhaas, 1999–2005

ine the extent to which we have this same a-perspectivist modernist thinking to thank for an undue number of autistic designs that do not consider either the built neighbourhood or the natural environs; they still shape our modern towns, and not just on the outskirts. Discussion within Postmodernism led to a new assessment of perspective introduced by the works of Samuel Edgerton (1975) and David C. Lindberg (1976). This is a position that Otl Aicher again criticized vehemently:

"it was a misapprehension with dire consequences to believe that the eye sees like a camera, to believe we live in a world of perspective. the consequence was the comprehension of the world as a sum of surfaces, as a full shot that offers me nothing but views. the consequence was a culture of the façade, of prestige, of show, of outward effect." (Aicher 1986, p. 16)

Certainly perspective ceased to be the dominant principle behind the creation of images early in the 20th century, but in the form of technically produced images – photographs, films, television pictures, videos, computer animations – it is now more than ever the undisputed basis of our visual communication. The high degree of manipulability inherent in perspectives justifies their being rejected in many contexts.

One piece of resistance this tool confronts designers with is the rigidity of the viewpoint, which once chosen restricts and confines both the viewer and the author of a perspective. Digitalization has made perspectives considerably easier to create. Many different viewing angles can be tried out rapidly using digital 3D models. Designers are no longer confined to a fixed viewpoint; eye level, focal length, viewing point and viewing angle can now be moved freely and changed with ease. Elaborate renderings achieve the quality of photorealistic simulations, and can represent any surface structure and any light source with all their shadows and reflections. In this way, digitalization has completely changed our habitual way of looking at things within only a few years. Hand-drawn perspectives have become perfect-looking simulations, and often also combinations of photomontages and simulations that no longer look "made", no longer seem like the result of an artistic effort, but intend to be as natural and convincing as photographs, from which, in well executed cases, they are retrospectively scarcely distinguishable. In the process photographs have lost much of their credibility.

Window in the Museum Serralves in
Oporto, Álvaro Siza, 1991–1999

Photograph, film, video

We are slowly becoming aware that we cannot just photograph reality with a camera, but that it can actually create reality. Neil French (after Vaske 2001, p. 112)

173

The tools introduced so far have been mainly tools for expressing inner ideas, but photography is seen almost exclusively as a tool of perception. Even though it is one of the most important means of communication today, and has also become a powerful tool for presenting design ideas because of the opportunities offered by digital image manipulation, designers give very little thought to photography's potential. It seems to work in a perfectly simple and obvious way, but in fact knowledge of the possibilities of this tool has been masked by everyday practice. The reasons for this lie in the history of its emergence and in our everyday reception of photographs, which despite the fact that we know better are intuitively seen as a convincing image of reality, completely faithful to the truth.

The photograph as a perspective view created by technical means goes back to the Camera Obscura, an aid used for drawing perspectives from nature. Everything that applied for the perspective as a design tool therefore also applies to the "automatically" created technical images. Photography was born partly out of a desire to avoid the need for laborious drawing work, the results of which were still often unsatisfactory. But "photorealistic" images had existed long before photography, even though the development of photography was welcomed as an epoch-making breakthrough in the 19th century. Meticulous water-colours by artists like Albrecht Dürer or brilliant still lifes by 16th and 17th century Dutch painters show that a perspective view, faithfully representing form, light and details, had been established since the Renaissance.

A version of the Camera Obscura reflecting the incident light on to a ground glass screen on the top of the box. International Museum of Photography, The George Eastman House, Rochester, New York

William Henry Fox Talbot: *Looking up to the Summit of Sharington's Tower at Lacock Abbey*, negative on paper, light-sensitive silver nitrate solution applied with a paintbrush, 10.5 x 11.7 cm, presumably summer 1835. International Museum of Photography, The George Eastman House, Rochester, New York (74:047:32)

FROM RECORD TO RE-PRESENTATION

If we regard perception as an essential, constantly recurring step in the "design cycle", it becomes clear that even a tool that merely records an image can be highly significant. For designers too, the descriptive-recording aspect is the most important function of photography, and still dominates its use today. As Rolf Sachsse shows in his wide-ranging study *Bild und Bau – Zur Nutzung technischer Medien beim Entwerfen von Architektur* (Image and Building – On the Use of Technical Media for Architectural Design, 1997), architects started using photography shortly after it was discovered, mainly to record existing buildings. They set up collections and archives whose stocks first complemented and then replaced 19th century pattern collections and drawing portfolios. Architectural photography was used for analysing form (and later colours as well), structure and typologies, for documenting historical and contemporary models and also for architects' own creative work. Because photographs can be reproduced as needed, they soon became a key means of communication, particularly so in advertising and propaganda to convincing effect.

Even if photographs are seen primarily as copies and records of something that already exists, the reduction from four to two dimensions opens up a large number of creative possibilities, which means that photographs

cannot necessarily be regarded as objective and neutral depictions. Every photograph is a work of art in its own right, and should be understood as distinct from the works it depicts. Like perspective, photography attracts its viewers' attention to the author's conscious or subconscious agenda. This manipulation of the view is the realisation of a subjective perspective perception. Thus for example viewing angles are selected that make a building look larger or more dynamic, or unusual lighting conditions that convey a particular atmosphere. Colour and light have a far greater physical presence in photographs than in reality.

Corner detail of a Baroque building in Oporto.

Perspective view and photomontage: proposal for an extension for the Palast der Republik in Berlin, aNC Arquitectos, Jorge Carvalho, 2005

The precision and richness of detail that photographs offer make it easy to forget how much they distort and highlight. Photography shares one problem with cartography: the problem of reproducing a spherical, in fact approximately hemispherical field of view on a flat surface. (Dechau 1995, pp. 19–33) Any zoom lens can demonstrate the resultant dilemma. It is possible to show either the angle of view (at about 28 mm focal length for a 35 mm camera) or the focal depth (at about 50 mm focal length) correctly for the view selected, but never both at the same time. And only those rectangles that are parallel to the plane of the image appear as rectangles, all the rest are distorted in perspective. Even if panoramic views and stereoscopic photography are used to compensate for these defects, the impression remains that fundamentally it is not possible to photograph architecture satisfactorily. The complexity of a complete spatial and temporal experience cannot be reduced to a two-dimensional image without losing something. Certainly photographs are better suited than most media to representing every aspect of the atmosphere and mood of rooms, but the continuity of time and space is reduced to a two-dimensional vignette whose boundaries will always be arbitrary.

On the other hand, it is precisely this arbitrary aspect that makes photography a possible design tool, not just for producing passive records, but active re-presentations. How can this tool be used in a prescriptive and creative way? Of course it does not have the same immediacy and directness as a sketch or a drawing. However, on a first, receptive level, a photograph (or a series of photographs) is itself a sketch, a sketch of a particular way of perceiving an object and its context, in other words, a design for an aesthetic way of looking. But a change of perspective is required if a photograph is to be used as a *prescriptive* tool. On a second level, the depiction of a way of perception becomes the projection of a model for a future design. Simply by re-presenting the depiction, by fitting it into a different context we already create a new reality.

Photographs can be modified and mounted into other shots or media. They can be used as a source for sketches or drawings, or the basis for drawing up a perspective. Likewise, perspectives that have been drawn or created digitally can be fitted into photographs. Photographs of models preserve delicate and unique objects that are difficult to transport, and can themselves be manipulated digitally in a variety of ways and then inserted back into shots of the surroundings. Mies van der Rohe's design presentations were characterized by a combination of constructed perspective drawings with photographs fitted into them.

SIMULATING IMAGES DIGITALLY

Creating and manipulating images digitally make it much easier to work like this. Digital photographs, in combination with digitally produced and mounted perspectives, are now among the most important design tools. Complex situations can be presented rapidly and convincingly with composed, digitalized photographs manipulated in image processing programs. Such presentations are so vivid that laymen can understand them as well. Images are stored digitally as a combination of mathematical parameters that are thus available in the form of individual data that can be changed individually.

"Digital technology relating to images could also be understood like this: we have penetrated into the nuclear physics of the image, as it were, and can now split and dissect every image right down to its atoms, and then reassemble the atoms, the pixels just as we wish." (Wim Wenders, after Maar 2004, p. 300)

Looking back at the time when architectural drawings were still done by hand shows how greatly the coloured, photo-realistic presentations that are customary today have changed the way we look at things. If we compare Frank Lloyd Wright's atmospheric perspectives or the enchanting sketches by an architect like Aldo Rossi with computer-generated renderings, it is clear that today's presentation scarcely give a sense of personal expression. They are intended to look objective and realistic, and not to be seen as subjective artistic ideas. These photo-realistic simulations of a future reality, usually prepared by neutral specialists, are not intended to be artistic drawings any longer. The best of them can scarcely be distinguished retrospectively from photographs of the real building. The atmosphere of a room, the impact made by a building, is no longer conveyed in the context of relatively abstract drawings with a personal style, but can be simulated with increasing precision. These techniques make it possible to make the complex interplay of many factors into a subject for discussion. Hence they are tending to make individual expression superfluous, and draw attention to concrete realization.

But most of all, digitalization has increasingly removed the boundaries between perspective, photography, film, television and video. These media, which used to be considered very different, if not antagonistic to each other, have fused into one as a result of technical qualities becoming equivalent and the possibilities of digital transmission. Film in particular was technically and financially far too demanding to be used as a design tool by architects. Now digitalized videos can be recorded, manipulated and duplicated at very little effort and cost, in comparison with film.

Even though we become aware of a building's essential architectural qualities only when we move around inside it, our ideas and thinking about architecture today are shaped by static images like the drawing, perspective, model and

above all photography. Even a hundred years after the invention of film and fifty years after the introduction of television our idea of the world and of architecture in particular is still dependent on it: stills cut out of the flow of events reify what is happening, "capture" it and reduce its complex sequences to a single perspective, a single image, condensed into an icon. Still images are there for us to perceive for as long and as often as we like, and of course this means that they are much easier to retain: *"Memory is a still"* says Susan Sontag. (after Maar 2004, p. 10)

Even today, architecture is still mediated above all via photographs in magazines, books or on slides. The spaces and sequences of movement that these generate are neglected, and so are the processes that an architectural object stimulates or prevents. Even Le Corbusier's promotion of the *promenade architecturale* was unable to change this. Rem Koolhaas describes his work as that of a filmmaker, thinking through his buildings as a sequence of scenes and cuts that he arranges along an elaborate path.

But even films about architecture often work with fixed cameras or even with filmed photographs, and manage without zooms, pans or tracking shots. Viewers are often quickly disoriented by tracking shots, as a camera has a much narrower field of view than the human eye. The sense of movement at the edge of the image is missing, and a feeling that one's body is moving and acoustic spatial perception are cut out as well. Pans with a wide-angle lens are also problematical for optical reasons. They stretch and distort the image of the architectural space so much that it no longer looks like a solid structure, but gives the impression that it is made up of some elastic material that can be stretched at will.

Now that recording video sequences is one of the standard functions on most digital cameras and many mobile phones, and professional video technology is available at

Sequence of movement when visiting the swimming pool on Leça de Palmeira beach, Álvaro Siza, 1959–1973

Dutch Embassy in Berlin, *promenade architecturale*.
OMA / Rem Koolhaas, 1999–2005

acceptable prices, a new design tool of the highest technical standard is present that unlike film can be used directly and personally. It is scarcely possible to anticipate the implications for design. It is possible to show movement through digital 3D models in video form, without undue effort or expense. Digitalization has made it considerably easier to produce, process and especially to simulate moving images, so it is now possible for the first time to shift ideas about architecture away from being static and towards movement and dynamics, processes of use, and spatial experience.

Calculation

The bird is an instrument that works according to a mathematical law.
Leonardo da Vinci (Codice Atlantico, 434 recto)

|8| There are two fundamentally different views of design. Architects and designers talk generally about "designing and presenting", and engineers about "designing and calculating". Formulae and algorithms, derived from mathematical, physical and economic theories, can be the basis for calculations that permit predictions about a design's future physical and economic performance. These formulae and algorithms and the statements derived from them count as verbal design tools, as we are dealing with texts (even though they are highly formalized) made up of logical combinations of verbal content. Designing architects tend to concentrate on visual design tools and are happy to neglect the fact that as a rule it is only statical and financial calculations that make it possible to realize a design, and that these can crucially influence the creative process leading to a building. Even Vitruvius criticized such behaviour, and demanded that architects should be

"more careful and thorough in reckoning and declaring their estimates, so that heads of households would proceed with their buildings within the budget they had prepared, or adding only a little more," and avoid "hope renounced and money squandered, financially and spiritually bankrupt." (Vitruvius X, Preface, 2)

Design as an activity always involves working things out and calculation to some extent. As a design tool, calculation provides access to a commercial and scientific view, a rational sphere. Engineers and scientists use calculations just as much as businessmen, who often have the last word when it comes to realizing a project. But even at the beginning of a piece of design work, for a competition, for example, calculating the building's functional programme has an important control function. It is not possible to arrive at proportions, figures like floor area, statical dimensions, building science, technical serv-

Calculating and drawing in the medieval stonemasons' guild

ices etc. without calculation. In the early stages of a design, it is relatively straightforward to estimate building costs in terms of area or building volume, but as a project develops, such matters become increasingly important. Most projects still fail because of problems here, ending with the terse argument: it doesn't add up.

Building costs do directly affect the volume and material quality of a project, but they influence its form only indirectly. Bernd and Hilla Becher's copious published documentations of industrial structures show how much scope is actually left for creative design, even if buildings are planned purely from an economic and functional point of view. (e.g. Becher 2003) The concept of economics itself, formed from the Greek word *oikos*, meaning house, relates to a central architectural theme. Even the radical approach developed by the architect Adolf Loos in the early 20th century was carried by economic arguments, as Fedor Roth was able to show in his book *Adolf Loos und die Idee des Ökonomischen* (Adolf Loos and the Idea of Economy, 1995).

Calculating building costs becomes a key factor in a design approach if the resources available are particularly tight, as is often the case for socially committed building projects. The concept of an *Architecture for the Poor* developed by the Egyptian architect Hassan Fathy (Fathy 1969) consists essentially of meticulous costings that make it possible to help village dwellers with very restricted resources to put a roof over their heads on an extremely tight budget.

The rule of economic dominance also extends to urban development paradigms. The crucial argument that enabled the Berlin architect Hardt-Waltherr

Reconstruction of the first Z1 computer built by Konrad Zuse in Berlin in 1938, input keyboard

Calculating mechanism

Memory unit

Hämer to persuade people to follow his sensitive urban renewal concept rather than the predominant seventies practice, vehemently promoted by both local authorities and the building industry at the time, of "area refurbishment" (i.e. demolishing, plot clearance and rebuilding), was based on model calculations showing that refurbishing late 19th century blocks could be just as cost-effective and economically viable – and much more socially sustainable. (Rosemann, in Hämer 2002, pp. 157–173)

CALCULATION IS INTERPRETATION

These examples show that working out building costs is anything but a mechanical activity. It requires intelligent interpretation of given facts, conceptual architectural thinking and a high degree of creativity if ambitious designs are to be realized. Few designers are aware how fundamentally the statical calculation approaches pioneered in the 18th and 19th century extended architecture's formal scope. As modern science developed, people started to research the properties of materials more precisely and to measure them systematically. From the mid 18th century, design and calculation methods emerged on the basis of these insights. Today's statics and strength theory developed from these methods to form the basis of modern engineering science, and have had an epoch-making impact on building design. (Straub 1949, p. 191 ff.) Similarly to the way in which the central competence of designers shifted from craft production to representing the design by means of drawing, perspective and models in the early Renaissance, in the 18th century scientific methods and insights came to form the basis of a new kind of design that was logically no longer practised by architects, but by the emerging profession of engineers, as it still is. Representing a building's statical behaviour with mathematical formulae and working out its form by calculation is fundamentally different from the architects' approach to design as a method, as the architect concentrates on functional and aesthetic premises. All modern building materials, such as cast iron, steel, glass, reinforced concrete, aluminium, plastics, paints and the way they are extracted, manufactured, processed and designed have been subject to optimization processes since these methods were developed, processes that in their turn make more and more new forms possible, and open up new technical and aesthetic scope. Today, building materials are just as much invented, designed or developed as the buildings themselves.

The results of calculations are often presented as exact figures and accepted in discussion as "hard facts". But as a rule they merely seem to be incontrovertible statements, and can certainly not be treated as absolutes, as they offer only limited certainty. Once designers have analysed such calculations in detail they often find plenty of reasons for questioning them. Here critical attention often has to be paid to the unspoken assumptions on which every calculation is based, precisely addressing those factors that cannot be expressed in figures and thus have not been accounted for in the calculations. These can include excessive safety factors for example, theories that apply only under certain conditions, and cost assumptions that are not based on current market conditions. Calculations, like most entirely rational ways of looking at things, can lead to one-dimensional thinking. This too taxes the designer's ability to keep an eye on things as a whole, and to weigh up ethical, aesthetic and general factors against technical, functional and particular interests.

Digitalization has made all calculations considerably easier through automation. We must not forget that the first computers were built by a civil engineer from Berlin, Konrad Zuse, who wanted to make hours and days of laborious calculation easier; at the time that still had to be done with paper and slide-rule. Since then, calculation possibilities have expanded exponentially. Calculations and the argu-

Pocket calculator.
Photograph: Stephanie Meyer, 2002

ments derived from them play an ever increasing role in discussions. Prestructured table calculations, some of which can be linked directly to digital design drawings, make it possible to sketch out calculations that are rapid but still have a high degree of precision. Simply changing one or two parameters can create new variants and calculate their consequences at the same time. Acoustics, energy consumption, the effect of daylight and artificial light, fire behaviour, visitor footfall and much else can be simulated in advance. And it is possible to demonstrate the sustainability of design decisions only through extensive calculations; here graphic simulations can help to visualise calculations more clearly.

But at the same time, such approaches make design less easy to grasp in full. The challenge lies in structuring – and using – tables, programs and simulations in such a way that it is possible to see how the results have been arrived at, as only then can their significance be correctly assessed.

Computer, program, simulation

Now that computers have become omnipresent a tool-ology seems more necessary than ever. Peter Jenny (1996, p. 229)

The imploring undertone alone in the statement that the computer is only a tool suggests that this is not the whole truth. Strictly speaking, this device is neither a tool nor a machine in the traditional sense, as it always needs peripheral devices to process material objects. Clearly the metaphor of the tool is stretched to its limits when considering computers. On closer examination, it appears very different when examined at various levels of abstraction. At the personal level it has become a fashion accessory, and at a global level it represents a medium that reduces any kind of data imaginable to a new and universal language.

"The computer" was originally a system made up of linked pieces of apparatus used for inputting, processing, saving and outputting electronic data. In the early days they were not called computers but calculating machines. The first freely programmable computer, the Z1, constructed by Konrad Zuse in 1938, was actually just a purely mechanical device driven by an electric motor. It presented and processed data using two metal strips about 2 cm wide crossing over each other. (Zuse 1970) A little later the terms computer system or electronic data processing system were used for devices made up of large numbers of sometimes room-filling components. Each individual component was an apparatus the details of whose way of working were opaque to the majority of its users, as were the structure and content of the programs controlling it.

Computers became objects recognizable in their entirety only in the very late 1970s, when the Personal Computer was introduced. The first was the Altair 8800 in 1975, the Apple II came on the market in 1977. The PC introduced by IBM on 12 August 1981 still had three components, the computer (with two built-in disk drives), the screen (which displayed figures and letters glowing in monochrome green) and the keyboard. Seeing the computer as a single object was then further reinforced by Notebooks, which combined computer, screen, data memory and keyboard together in one manageable object. Now, computers have been miniaturized to the point of

Reconstruction of the first Z1 computer built by
Konrad Zuse in Berlin in 1938, memory unit

Program reading unit

invisibility. They are found in this form in devices we no longer see as computers, like MP3 players, games consoles, navigation aids, digital cameras or mobile phones. Given the right programming and networks, these devices are all able to carry out a computer's essential functions. Mobile phones in particular are developing in this direction, with some manufacturers planning their models with connectability to larger keyboards and screens.

FROM CALCULATING MACHINE TO MASS MEDIUM

Seeing computers merely as tools because they are so useful and object-like would be to underestimate them completely. The computer pioneer Alan Turing formulated the idea in 1936 of a *"universal discrete machine that can perform the tasks of any other machines."* (after Davis 1958) Computers realize this idea as universal devices for processing electronic data. They do this on the basis of a code that is also universal, in which data are presented and processed according to any logical connection required. These connections form a system of mutually dependent mathematical languages in which all programs are written. Theoretically they are able to simulate all tools, machines, apparatuses, systems – and also all design tools – or to control them. Programming languages and operating systems translate each program into the appropriate machine language, which in its turn converts it

Designing Truth. As Hinrich Sachs's guest: Dr. Ansgar Philippsen, Structural biologist.
Stills from the film by Hinrich Sachs (2005)

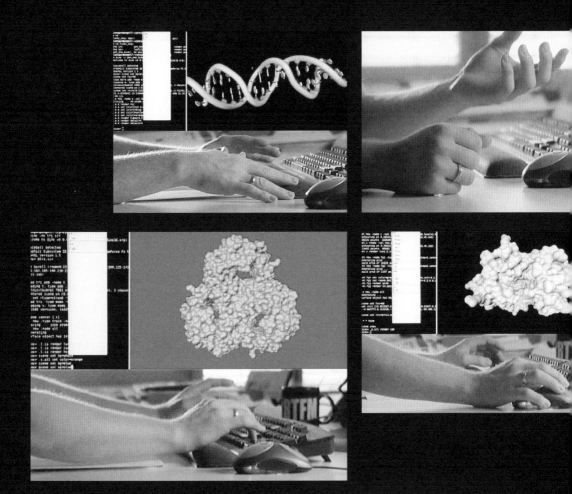

into binary code. This works on the basis of connecting the figures zero and one logically; they are represented by positive or negative electric charges, and as it were form the lowest common denominator, reducing language to a single symbol: on or off.

The universal nature of this mathematical language can be seen in the fact that all data, anything that can be described, defined and quantified, numbers, texts, drawings, images, music, films and so on can be translated into binary code. Here the data are transformed from analogue to digital, from the material, atomic plane to the immaterial electronic plane. Conversely, digital data can be turned back into analogue data by reversing the processes. Hence Friedrich Kittler appositely defines computers as *"general interfaces between systems of [mathematical] equations and sensory perception"*. (Kittler 2002, p. 319) What changes in this switch to the electronic plane? The basic change lies in the fact that the dimensions of the material plane no longer apply here. In this sense, it is possible to see the electronic plane, in which neither time nor space follow the same rules as on the atomic plane, as a fifth dimension that is largely detached from sensory perception. So the data and their processing have to be made accessible to perception via interfaces. But above all they can be manipulated in a quite different way that functions according to its own rules. They no longer offer any material resistance to the designer, but they do offer mathematical resistance: they are limited by the commands that can be used in any particular program, and the ways in which they can be connected, and they are subject to the limited capacities of the processors, memory and data transmission paths available in each case. The telegraph and the telephone, as electromechanical media, made it possible to overcome material, and thus also spatial borders by the late 19th century, and so did radio and television, the electronic media developed in the first half of the 20th century. But these early electronic mass media remained bound by the common time linking broadcaster and receiver, and they had to use analogue media like gramophone records, tape or film in order to convey the temporal dimension. Digitalization has meant that the dimensions of space and time can now be represented and transmitted, simulated and controlled at the same time.

For a long time the flaws in the first computer generations concealed the fact that the computer is not just a tool, but actually is a new medium, whose qualities and possibilities we are only just starting to explore. The first devices were still conceived purely as calculating machines that slowly developed into clumsy drawing machines and typewriters. It was not until the mass distribution of high-frequency processors in the 1990s that it became possible for the computer to establish itself as a mass medium.

What does it mean to treat the computer as a new medium? What content could be expressed in a new way with this aid? According to Marshall McLuhan, the "content" of a new medium is the previous medium:

"The content of writing is speech, just as the written word is the content of print, and print is the content of the telegraph." (McLuhan 1964, p. 8)

According to this, the "content" of the computer as a medium would be television, which reaches back to the media of film and radio in its turn. But this analysis does not quite work when applied to the computer. In fact the computer realizes for the first time an indissoluble combination of visual and verbal media: the networks of lines created by photographic exposure form the circuits on the silicon chips on the one hand and the program texts written in figures and letters on the other hand. This connection of visual and verbal elements is present in its most reduced form as screen and keyboard. But the computer is also the first medium that cannot only store and present data, but can process them automatically according to sequences that can be programmed at will. The actual new "content" of this medium is the data sets, equation systems and programs by means of which all other media, visual and three-dimensional as well as verbal, can be taken back to a universal system of languages and on this basis can be combined with each other, linked and controlled as wished.

DESIGNING DIGITALLY

How has the introduction of the computer affected design? Above all, the computer's introduction and general acceptance has meant the digitalization of all design tools. This has changed design fundamentally in recent years, even going so far as influencing the ways in which space and time are treated. Digitalization is a continuing process, driven by constantly rising computing capacity, connections that are constantly becoming faster and more comprehensive, and more and more programs, which are becoming increasingly sophisticated. This upheaval is comparable with the media changes at the beginning of the Renaissance. At that time, reduced-scale drawings and models, the use of central perspective and the rise of competitions and public criticism increased the dynamics of design to a hitherto unknown extent. Today it is new and constantly growing data processing possibilities that are opening up hitherto untrodden pathways for design and communication, and these are in their turn producing new forms of public life.

Now if we consider computers, or a super-medium based on computers, as a design tool, what we have is a meta-tool that combines all other design tools within itself, both verbal and visual-spatial. The ways in which this meta-tool works are naturally considerably more complicated than the individual design tools simulated by the various programs. Two different planes for looking at this should be distinguished: the plane of the individual design tools simulated by various specialized programs, and the media plane, on which it is possible to communicate data sets that are very much more complex, detailed and precise.

How does digitalization change design's traditional tools and cultural techniques? Digitalization enables computers to establish other ways of materializing inner ideas. Design ideas no longer assume material form only in analogue, atomic form, but as electrons, or as electronic charges. These can be manipulated following completely different rules – rules that designers can adapt to fit in with their ideas – from those to which atomic presentation forms are subject. The efficiency of the digital synthesis, made possible by today's high-frequency processors, whose pace *"far exceeds our perception time as much as the time that many thought processes need"*, (Kittler 2002, p. 319) leads to qualitative changes in the design process, whose boundaries are redefined and continually extended by digitalization.

At a time when all design tools are being reshaped digitally, it is therefore necessary to ask new questions about the nature of design. This question was not posed so acutely in the first phase of the transition to digital tools, as the program writers were mainly concerned with imitating analogue design tools as directly as possible. On this level, the computer was nothing more than a manageable typewriter, or a drawing tool that made laborious work easier.

The above-mentioned specific resistance that digitalized design tools offer to their users is not immediately apparent; it emerges only in the experience of using them. This resistance is fundamentally differently structured from that of analogue tools. There is no longer any resistance by the material, which in many respects represents a great liberation and speeds up the process. But this means that the sensual quality and directness of the material is lost as well – both factors that can be crucial in delicate design phases. In addition, every program implies a more or less concealed "ideology":

"They [the programs] contain latent styles and ideologies that powerfully condition every object constructed with them." (Eisenman 2003, p. 30)

Neither the authors nor the users of the programs may be aware of this latent ideology; it reveals itself only in systematic analysis.

The digitalization of all design tools means that all design content is translated into figures, algorithms and mathematical equations, in other words, into the computer's language. Only one parameter in these equations has to be changed to create what could well be a completely different result. Applying parameters to design processes makes it possible to change complex data structures without a great deal of effort – though only to the extent that the equations upon which they are based will allow. At this level, the programs are characterized by their ability to be expressed mathematically, by their regularity and repetition, and, in response to technical developments, by their increasing speed and complexity. The digital world's remorseless precision makes it possible to copy electronic data sets that are identical to the original. Data is much easier to manipulate, it can be copied, changed, moved around or deleted without trace; it is no longer "genuine", and no longer has the "aura" of an original. Photography had already questioned the concept of the original, and in the digital sphere it loses its meaning completely. This also changes our relationship to what we call "reality".

Computer programs are a special form of text that creates reality directly by "automatically" absorbing and processing data, and setting concrete processes in train. Digital networking brings design and production together directly if digital data is used to control production plants. Expert workers are no longer needed to read the plans and translate them for practical application, thus deploying their specialist knowledge and implicit skill. These working steps are omitted, so the appropriate knowledge and skill has to be transferred to programs and machines.

Handling complexity is getting easier. It is possible to program simple, readily intelligible, user-friendly interfaces that still contain great depths of information. It is becoming increasingly difficult to understand their structure because of increasing complexity, but it is also much easier to represent it, if desired. This facilitates handling complex design tools like the perspective view, the calculation or film and video, or makes it possible for the average user to gain access to such tools in the first place.

NETWORKING THE DESIGN TOOLS

Verbal design tools are now available, in the form of program texts that can describe complex sequences of events step by step, and capture highly detailed spaces point by point. Programs do not just make it possible to represent objects, but also to simulate events in time. Thus "meaning" in the sense of the future effect of design decisions can be represented, and so it can also be examined and monitored. It is only with these tools that it is possible to work on topics like sustainability. Simulating load-bearing patterns and response to fire, acoustics, aerodynamic flow, insulation and artificial lighting and the resultant energy balance, winter heat loss, use patterns and visitor footfall make it possible to optimize in cases where specialist experience and knowledge used to be required. Architects also classify digitalized, photorealistic perspective views as simulation; these can represent surface structures and light with all its mirror effects, reflections and degrees of diffusion much more realistically than a hand-drawn perspective view could achieve with the same amount of effort. So the appearance of a room or a building no longer has to be "represented", in fact programs are now conceivable that can simulate appearance according to objective standards. Simulations of this kind are tending to render the artistic, hand-made qualities of a sketch or a perspective drawing superfluous.

Can computers design? Computers have been stimulating designers' imagination ever since they were invented. Even the computer pioneer Konrad Zuse, who had originally been a civil engineer, believed that the calculating machines he had constructed would soon be able to draw up automatically complete working plans for a bridge, including all the detailed drawings, statical calculations and tendering documents. (Zuse 1970) The example of the computer in particular suggests the question of what designing is. Is the computer's processor the ideal tool for carrying out design *processes*? Is a computer designing when it executes a program that processes hundreds of parameters, combining and varying a certain number of modules for long enough until it arrives at an optimal solution? What is the difference between this and human design?

If we see design tools as representations of inner ideas that have moved ever closer to perfection in the course of technical development, then theoretically we could expect that these tools would become more and more like our brains as development progresses. But if we try to grasp the computer and its programs as an almost perfect copy of our thinking or even of the human mind, we realize that pretty much the opposite is the case. Even though we often use metaphors from the computer world when talking about our brain, the computer in fact provides a radical counter-image of the human brain: it can "calculate", i.e. carry out, store and reproduce logical operations with unimaginable speed and precision, but it is not capable of thinking, remembering or understanding, and thus also cannot develop consciousness. Discussions about artificial intelligence have sharpened our awareness of what actually sets human intelligence apart: "calculators" can beat a grand master at chess, but they couldn't understand a single sentence in a five-year-old's reading book.

But digitalization makes it possible to link all visual and verbal design tools together. The possibilities of rapid communication, of better and automated link-ups for individual tools and the automation of many processes make it possible to design on the basis of a database that is networked to a high degree of complexity. As ultimately all design tools share a common code, the boundaries between the tools blur, and become transparent. It is no longer possible to decide for certain whether a particular image presentation is based on a film or a video, a photograph or a perspective view, a drawing or a 3D model. And the boundaries between the professions and specialist disciplines are also becoming more transparent. The effects of this extend as far as the way we see the role of architects. The hierarchical idea of an orchestral conductor directing everyone involved in the project is increasingly obsolete. It is being transformed, writes Norman Foster, into the image of a 'jam session': spontaneous and flexible interaction between architects, specialist engineers, local authorities and building firms. (Jenkins 2000, p. 774)

Criticism

It is only by practicing constant comparison that we can achieve
a highly sophisticated ability to make distinctions. Jean-Christophe Ammann (1998, p. 21)

196   Clearly formulated criticism not infrequently offers a starting-point for a new
design approach, and criticism, whether in the form of self-criticism or criticism from others, has a fundamental part to play within the design process.
Leon Battista Alberti identifies "sound judgement and counsel" as the most
important prerequisite for an architect's work: *"The greatest glory in the art of*
building is to have a good sense of what is appropriate." (Alberti 1485, p. 518)
Criticism as the principal instrument for further progress (Popper) and
judgement as its basis are what help designers decide for or against a particular design idea.

Criticism can be described as "negative design". It works subtractively,
like a sculptor using his chisel to remove everything that does not belong to
his sculpture. Criticism is "no" as a necessary counter-pole to the countless
times we hear "yes" to our ideas: the ability to make distinctions, to weight,
balance, create connections, see the whole. An ability to make distinctions
and powers of judgement are skills that form the basis of any criticism.
When Immanuel Kant chose the title for his *Critique of Judgement* he is also
drawing attention to the fact that these two terms mean different things.
Criticism is first of all a verbal expression of a judgement, just as a sketch or
drawing expresses a design idea.

But the word criticism, derived from the Greek *kritike techne*, literally
translated as *"art of distinction, art of judgement"*, implies more than this first
meaning. Since Socrates it has been associated with the idea of enlightenment and science. Criticism means not just examining an achievement for its
significance and value, as Mies van der Rohe suggests, (Neumeyer 1986, p. 371)
but rather *"the enhancing, inspiring, upward-driving principle, the principle of*
insufficiency", says Thomas Mann (Reich-Ranicki 1994, p. 201) and thus the basis of
modern, competitive thinking (Popper).

If deployed cleverly and at the right moment, it becomes a Golden Axe,
in the words of the landscape architect Hermann Pückler-Muskau, tidying
up by imposing order on the undue proliferation of ideas. (Pückler-Muskau 1834,

p. 71) The problem with self-criticism, which is so central to design, is combining designer and critic in a single person without constantly getting in one's own way. The psychologist and thinking instructor Edward de Bono pointed out the danger of being blocked by criticism in the phase when ideas are being sought. He says that new ideas are present in our imagination for approximately ten minutes, and if they are not captured at this time they disappear again, rather like images in a dream. At the moment they come into being, ideas are as helpless as newborn babies. They cannot be criticized straight away, they have to be tended and nourished for a while, treated kindly and with understanding, before they are exposed to the cold wind of criticism. So a central rule of brainstorming is: no criticism! It will lead almost inevitably to creativity blocks if the designer's creative faculties and sense of self-worth are not sufficient to meet the criteria he has set. (De Bono 1970, p. 31 ff.) Switching criticism off, suspending it, is one way of getting round these blocks. The creative element of criticism can be found in

the fact that new design ideas are often first expressed in the form of criticism. As an example, let us take volume 1 of the leading German series in architectural theory, *Bauwelt-Fundamente*, entitled *Programme und Manifeste zur Architektur des 20. Jahrhunderts* (Programs and Manifestos on 20th-Century Architecture, 1970) edited by Ulrich Conrads. (Conrads 1964) Many of the essays published in this volume are hard, forthright criticism. Starting with Adolf Loos' *Ornament und Verbrechen* (Ornament and Crime) and moving on via Walter Gropius' tirade against *"these grey, hollow and insipid shams in which we live and work"* to Friedensreich Hundertwasser's *"rotting manifesto against rationalism in architecture"*, critiques and analyses are collected here that became the starting-point for developing new ideas.

Ben Shahn: Portrait of the physicist J. Robert Oppenheimer. Ink on paper, 1954

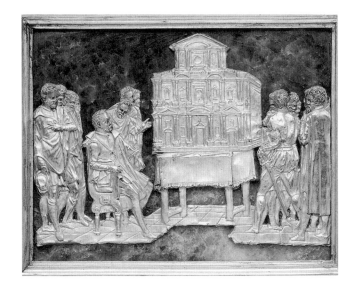

Giovanni da Bologna: Buontalenti presents the Grand Duke Francesco de Medici with a model for the façade of the Duomo in Florence.

If we see criticism as a design tool, we treat it differently, and perceive it differently. Like all verbal tools, it dissects the complex simultaneity of a design into a logical sequence of individual terms. It abstracts and reduces simultaneity in order to describe it with the aid of a linear series of terms on a time axis; it is therefore better suited to analysing and breaking down complexity than to creating it: *"If one says something, one is killing it at the same time"* declares the French designer Philippe Starck. (Vaske 2001, p. 253) Criticism is a linguistic tool, but language alone founders on design practice, which needs personal skill as well as theory. There is a *"sound barrier between theory and practice"* (Hinrich Sachs) which every designer can overcome only on his own and with his own practical abilities.

But criticism does not have to be conveyed in language. If a critic decides not to use language, choosing visual tools as a means of expressing himself instead, then all he can do is intervene in the creative process itself. By doing this he loses the distance that gives him the qualification for his position, but the creative element of criticism shifts into the foreground. Something that remains inaccessible to the publishing critic provides the teaching critic with an outstanding opportunity to overcome the distance to his students.

A TEACHING TOOL

Design is usually taught by setting tasks and then attempting to explain to students what they have done wrong and, far less frequently, what they have done right – a frustrating process for both sides. First-year students are often well aware of design problems, are able to identify them clearly as well, but do not yet have the creative resources needed to solve them. In a situation like this, severe criticism from outside is debilitating rather then motivating. Criticism is always a two-edged sword, and some blood is always left on the golden axe. It is both an instrument of might, and an instrument of promotion. But given the central importance of criticism as a design tool, it is impossible to do without it altogether. To quote the German classic author and critic Theodor Fontane:

"Bad is bad, and it has to be said. Others can come with explanations and mitigating factors afterwards." (Reich-Ranicki 1994, p. 124)

The dilemma is that criticism is necessary and frustrating at the same time. Hence one topic that appears constantly in architectural discussions is the absence, the lack of good criticism: genuine criticism is as rare as genuine art, says Mies van der Rohe. (after Niemeyer 1986, p. 371) The Brazilian architect Paulo Mendes da Rocha states:

"Genuine criticism of architecture is always lacking. [...] It gets lost in questions about context, about meaning, about questions that are very specific to architecture, and thus imposes a systematization that is fundamentally senseless. It fails to acknowledge that architecture is in fact a discourse that cannot be independent of human knowledge and conscience." (Spiro 2002, p. 250)

But what should criticism talk about? What are the essential criteria of architecture? Our first sense of criteria is that they are exclusive, negative, often nothing but a restrictive ban. This can sometimes develop into rules in the course of design work that can be formulated as positive instructions, and that leave much less open for further development. If such rules finally become common property, and thus banal, like the academic Beaux-Arts approach in the early 20th century, or the functionalism of the building industry in the 1960s and 1970s, they become merely restrictive and prevent any further development.

But paradoxically, very tightly formulated *contraintes*, self-imposed and rigid rules, can become inspiring triggers of creativity. The criteria formulated for film-making by Lars von Trier and Thomas Vinterberg that became familiar as *Dogme 95*, (Hallberg 2001) prescribe the use of hand-held cameras and filming in original locations, banning among other things the use of studio buildings and properties, alienation through time or geography, subsequently added sound, artificial lighting and optical tricks and filters. This questioned the essential mechanisms of current film production, especially its well-nigh boundless ability to manipulate, and the resultant low reality content of many films. At first it was still possible to dismiss the publication of the *Dogme 95* theses as an advertising gimmick by young Danish directors, but in 1998 the first film shot according to these criteria, *Festen (The Celebration)*, showed how thoroughly they had laid down the conditions for independent work. In an interview, Vinterberg said these criteria were like *"walls to play against,"* representing a sporting challenge and with a liberating effect, unlike others that are as constricting as *"a large, heavy duvet that you can't throw off"*. (Hallberg 2001, p. 104)

The ability to see the world as a whole and to relate the design to be evaluated to this whole—which, in itself, is never comprehensible in its entirety – is a requirement for critics even more than for designers. Making distinctions and passing judgements is closely linked to questions of perceptual ability, of awareness and of the horizon of experience on which a judgement is based. Anyone who takes criticism to heart would do well to consider the critics' viewpoint. Comparing several criticisms of the same design relativizes the various points of view and makes it clear how the individual authors are approaching things. It is only then that the educational function of criticism can develop fully.

Student at a design presentation

Criteria and value systems

What is good about good architecture? Hanno Rauterberg (2003)

The title of a famous drawing by Francisco de Goya is a play on words based on the ambiguity of *sueño*, which can mean both sleep and dream in Spanish: *El sueño de la razon produce monstruos.* In English the title is usually translated simply as "The sleep of reason produces monsters", without mentioning the second possible reading. Given the catastrophes – architectural, urban and others – of Modernism, shaped by cold rationality, the second possibility, calling it the *"dream of reason"*, which also produces monsters, can be equally significant. Most designers are convinced that the world would be a better place if it were run according to their ideas. They are surprised when their suggestions meet with resistance, and not infrequently provoke bitter disputes.

What are the essential criteria for "good" architecture? It is rare for the value systems underlying the work of architects or architecture critics to be stated explicitly. Journalistic criticism usually does not have the space to do so, and expert academic criticism, as practised for example in Edward Said's literature studies (Said 1983) or André Bazin's work on film (Bazin 1958) is scarcely to be found in architecture colleges and universities.

FIRMITAS, UTILITAS, VENUSTAS

The fundamental criteria in architecture are *"that it works, and that I like it"* – a throwaway line from a colleague. Mies van der Rohe identified two classes of criteria: he talked about *"good reasons"*, in which he included the technical aspects of building that are open to rational explanation, and *"real reasons"*, by which he meant the cultural and artistic aspects of architecture. Since Vitruvius, the three classical architectural criteria have been seen as *firmitas, utilitas, venustas* (lat. solidity, usefulness, grace). They are now as generally correct as they are useless when it comes to concrete questions. Both architects and critics like to cover up the impossibility of formulating binding criteria by uttering vehement postulates. None of the three terms can be clearly defined, and yet these criteria are not obsolete. It is much more valuable to shed light on the structure of the impossibility of defining them precisely. If we think about architecture on the basis of these three criteria, *firmitas*, *utilitas* and *venustas* become categories that each sum up a central architectural theme.

Firmitas, the "solidity" of a building is scarcely an architectural problem any longer today, but rather one for building science, left to engineering experts as a rule. Seen as a category, *firmitas* becomes a matter for construction work, a question of right and wrong. Authors like Theodor Fontane and Otl Aicher have spoken in favour of returning to the category of what is "correct" in case of doubt. (Reich-Ranicki 1994, p. 122) A construction holds together or it doesn't, it is watertight or it isn't. Questions of *firmitas*, because they can be considered objectively, seem to be the simplest to decide. But the scientific and technical insights on the basis of which they

Criteria for assessing architectural designs according to Jürgen Joedicke et al. The three vertical columns could also be headed *utilita*, *firmitas* and *venustas*, after Vitruvius.

	FUNCTIONAL CONCEPT	STRUCTURAL CONCEPT	CREATIVE CONCEPT
URBAN DEVELOP- MENT LEVEL	1. ACCESS (TRANSPORT) - ACCESSIBILITY BY PUB. TRANSPORT - DELIVERY ACCESS (LORRIES) - VEHICULAR ACCESS/PARKING - PEDESTRIAN ACCESS - TRAFFIC NOISE INSULATION - BUILDINGS AND OPEN SPACES - ARRANGEMENT (ORIENTATION, SHADE, OVERLOOKING	1. BASIC TECHNICAL CONCEPT FOR CONSTRUCTION AND SERVICES: SYSTEM, COLUMN SPACING, CEILING TYPES, HEATING VENTILATION 2. SUNSHADING 3. PLANNING VALUES	1. ACCESS ORIENTATION 2. OPEN SPACES - STRUCTURE AND EXPLOITATION - RELATIONSHIP TO PREV. DEVELOPMENT 3. SURROUNDINGS: - DESIGN COMPATIBILITY (MASS DISTRIBUTION, SCALE, SHAPE), SILHOUETTE, SIGHTLINES)
BUILDING LEVEL	1 INTERNAL TRANSPORT SYSTEM - FOR STAFF/VISITORS (ORIENTATION) - INTERNAL ORIENTATION (HORIZONTAL AND VERTICAL 2. FUNCTION STRUCTURE AND FUNCTION ALLOCATION 3. CONSIDERATION OF EXISTING TRAFFIC CONDITIONS	a) AREA RATIOS GROSS AREAS, CIRCULATION AREA/ USE AREA/FAÇADE AREA/USE AREA b) VARIABILITY - POSSIBILITY OF USE CHANGE WITH EXTRA BUILDING c) FLEXIBILITY - POSSIBILITY OF USE CHANGE WITHOUT EXTRA BUILDING	1. STRUCTURE, DISTRIBUTION AND HEIGHT FOR BUILDING MASSES 2. ARCHITECT. DESIGN AND CONSTRUCTION PRINCIPLE 3. IMAGE OF BUILDING (APPEARANCE AND EFFECT OF FORM) 4. INTELLIGIBILITY OF FUNCTION AREAS AND THEIR CONNECTIONS 5. CLARITY AND ARTICULATION OF INTERNAL ROUTING 6. ORIENTATION FOR VISITORS AND STAFF
TOPIC LEVEL	1. INTERNAL PATHWAYS (ALLOCATION AND ARRANGEMENT, DIMENSIONS) 2. FUNCTION AND ROOM ALLOCATION 3. ASSESSING USE POSSIBILITIES - TYPE AND SIZE OF USE AREAS - DIFFERENTIATION OF USE AREAS - ALLOCATION OF USE AREAS (COMBINATION AND EXTENSION POTENTIAL)	1. EXTENSION POTENTIAL (MICRO) 2. RELATIONSHIP BETWEEN PRIMARY/ SECONDARY CONSTRUCTION AND FINISHING ELEMENTS 3. FLEXIBILITY AND VARIABILITY FOR TECHNICAL AND SANITARY SERVICES	1. ELEMENTS CREATING SPACE: SHAPE, TYPE, NUMBER AND RELATIONSHIP WITH EACH OTHER 2. OVERALL SPATIAL EFFECT, INTERIOR, CHARACTERISTICS, FUNCTIONALITY 3. SPATIAL STRUCTURE - SPATIAL LINKS (HOR./VERT.) - LIGHTING, LIGHT MANAGEMENT 4. MATERIAL, COLOUR CHOICE
INNOVATION	E.G. TREND-SETTING INNOVATIONS, NEW CONCEPTUAL IMPULSES OR PLANNING IDEAS, SUGGESTIONS FOR FUTURE DEVELOPMENT		

are decided are in a constant state of flux. We only seem to be dealing with "hard facts" here, as they usually apply only under certain conditions.

Utilitas, seen as a category, addresses function and use, how the building relates to people; is the building good or bad? Good or bad for whom, or for what? A building impacts upon the interests of all parties involved in its manufacture and use: the client and his wife, the neighbours and their children, the architects, construction workers, experts at the planning permission authorities and at the bank, building caretaker, occupants, users and visitors, which occasionally also include firefighters, photographers and finally architecture critics. The question of usefulness is ultimately an ethical one, and its answers come from the sphere of politics. In concrete terms, it is all about the spatial organization of a building, the size and qualities of the rooms created, the way they relate to each other and to the outside world.

The concept of *"good architecture"* has a ring of political correctness to it, usually describing worthy, uncontroversial mainstream architecture. But *"the good cannot be defined"* (Aristotle, Nichomachean Ethics), and questions about the relationship between "utility value" and "artistic value" need constant readdressing. But in everyday life the use is often thrust one-dimensionally into the foreground, while the act of using is assessed only trivially. The business concept of return on investment is an attempt to express the usefulness of a building in figures. This is a calculation that is often based on factors that have little to do with the functional qualities of a building. The result of this calculation represents an abstraction that tells us little about the actual usefulness of a building – reducing it to an exclusively financial perspective.

Ultimately, insisting that a building has to fulfil certain functions is too trivial to be relevant as a criterion. The question is not "whether", but "how". How does the design strike a balance between the many different demands made on it? How, with what degree of wit, charm and elegance does it meet these, and what does it achieve over and above that?

Venustas finally, the category of beauty, of aesthetics, of subjective feelings includes the whole sphere of art. Erich Mendelsohn describes why it is impossible to define it conclusively as follows:

"Our aesthetic evaluation – evaluation in terms of beauty – is based only on requirements that appear to have become laws through traditional and categorical education. Because concepts of this kind are determined according to the state of human culture, to the particular moment in human cultural and historical development, and thus are variable, they cannot be set up as yardsticks of value." (Mendelsohn 1961, p. 22)

But to derive an appeal for a "taste dictator" from this would be to show a lack of political taste. Aesthetics often turns out to be social convention, a demarcation device, and an imposition of taboos on value judgements. Proclaiming that something is "beautiful" often means actually finding it merely "good" but not wanting to enter into any discussion about this evaluation. The question "Don't you think that's beautiful?" all too often implies that the person being asked does not have "good" taste if he says not, and consequently "doesn't fit in". The close connection between ethics and aesthetics, between politics and art, explains the great interest shown by political groups, which can be observed in all historical epochs, for manifesting their views aesthetically as well.

Vitrivius' criteria are therefore relevant, but not open to fulfilment in absolute terms. Ultimately it is not just about fulfilling them, but on a higher plane about the balance with which these requirements are registered, about the consistency of the decisions made on various planes. Alberti's key criterion of concinnitas, of the harmony of the parts with the whole (Grafton 2000, p. 28), is based on a definition of beauty as *"that reasoned harmony of all the parts within a body [...] so that nothing may be added, taken away, or altered, but for the worse".* (Alberti 1485, p. 156) This criterion is also to be found in Vitruvius, although stated considerably more moderately, who demands that *"should something need to be subtracted from or added to the proportional system, [...] it will seem to have been designed correctly with nothing wanting in its appearance."* (Vitruvius, VI 2,1) What Vitruvius and Alberti present here as an aesthetic criterion, which as such has long been contradicted by additive and

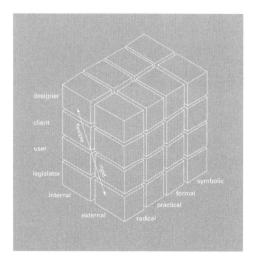

"The completed model of the design problems",
Brian Lawson, 1997

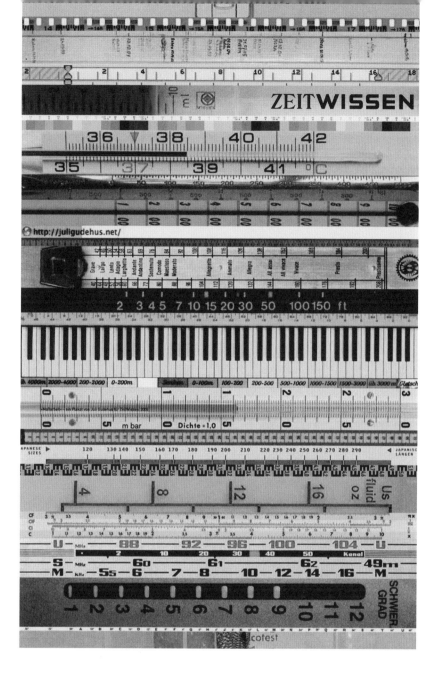

Juli Gudehus: *Precision work* (detail). Poster for the *ZEIT Wissen* scientific magazine, 2005.
Photographs: Annette Schuler

deconstructive formal languages, goes back to a general ethical maxim that had already been formulated by Aristotle:

"Thus a master of any art avoids excess and defect, but seeks the intermediate and chooses this – the intermediate not in the object but relatively to us. [...] so that we often say of good works of art that it is not possible either to take away or to add anything, implying that excess and defect destroy the goodness of works of art, while the mean preserves it." (Nichomachean Ethics, II, 5, 1106 b)

In a design, technical, ethical and aesthetic questions fuse into a unit that, if it is successful, belongs to the sphere of art and not to that of science. When science is good, it is "clear and distinct", but a good design is *"complex and contradictory"* (Venturi), eschewing both scientific clarity and the general validity claimed by scientific pronouncements.

The complex, contradictory, paradoxical demands made on a design can be listed, but they do not help very much when assessing it. They include far too many mutual dependencies, "if-then", "both-and" and "either-or" connections for the list of criteria to be formulated as a conclusive algorithm. Charles Eames produced the most convincing image of this set of problems with a diagram representing the superimposed forms, difficult to grasp, of design criteria. (Demetrios 2001, p. 177)

The overlap between three areas denoting design criteria identifies an area where the interests of client, office and society intersect. Charles Eames, 1969

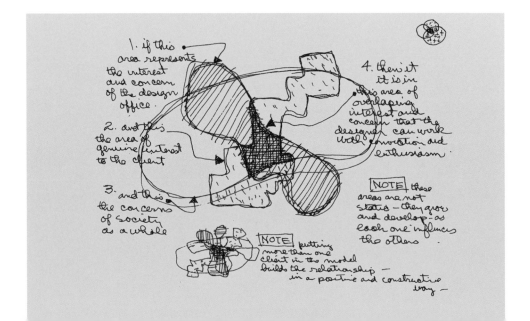

INNOVATION AND THE EMIGMATIC

Now there are two essential criteria for the value system within our culture that are not included in those postulated by Vitruvius and Alberti: the requirements that a work of art should be innovative and enigmatic. Rules can enshrine only the rationally accessible aspects of a design; only that can be enshrined about which we know enough to enshrine in rules. The new, the original, the innovative features of a design create their own rules. And it is precisely this that since the start of the modern age has been the essential criterion of a design: making *inventio* more important than *imitatio*, invention more important than imitation. (Groys 1992, p. 10) The criterion of the new also introduces the utopian element into a design. Designing something new means designing something that does not yet exist; at the time the design is made it is questionable whether this element can ever be realized at all. The frequently heard reproach that a design idea is "utopian" turns out to be a misunderstanding when seen against this background: designs are always utopian, and remain utopian until they are realized.

The criterion of the enigmatic includes the question of the meaning of a piece of work. This identifies a major part of the fascination a work of art exercises. Theodor Adorno (and also Vilém Flusser) talks about the *"enigmatic character"* of art: *"all works of art, and art as a whole, are enigmas"*, (Adorno 1970, p. 182) and he states categorically:

"But this characteristic of enigma can be identified as constitutive at the point where it is lacking: works of art that reveal themselves to contemplation and thought with nothing left, are not works of art." (Adorno 1970, p. 184)

At this point we come back, via Wittgenstein's definition of architecture as a gesture, (see p. 108) to Flusser's analysis of gestures–constituting the basis of designing – as enigmas. Deciphering them makes it possible *"to penetrate them ever more deeply, in order to be able to experience them ever more richly"*. (Flusser 1991, p. 90 f.)

Only simple regular things can be grasped rationally. The complex, multi-layered, holistic aspects of a design, which are ultimately the key to it, are accessible only to feeling, to instinct, to individual sensibility: *"love and hate cannot be calculated, and neither can functionality or aesthetic quality."* (Aicher 1991/1, p. 182) This is actually why criticism *"will not work with principles and a code of paragraphs*". (Theodor Fontane, after Reich-Ranicki 1994, p. 122). The role of criticism is to verbalize these aspects, to convey them, and thus make them accessible to rationality. Treating the criticism of buildings and designs as an art is certainly a provocation for all who believe (or pretend) to know what "good" architecture is. The relativity of all criteria and paradigms, the *anything goes* approach, forms a striking contrast with the uniformity and lack of ideas found in a large number of today's designs and buildings. Obviously it is precisely this freedom that frightens people, a fear that unfortunately means that today the principle of *imitatio* remains stronger than that of *inventio*.

The continuous analysis and discussion of criteria and values is more important in an open society than fixing them. The question of what factors are crucial for the tasks we face today has to be constantly asked and answered again. The key factor here is the individual's and indeed the whole of society's ability to learn. In design teaching, the students' ability to criticize should be trained, rather than simply subjecting them to criticism. Design becomes a process of arbitrating over conflicts of interests that are mediated by criticism. Enlightened design teaching does not restrict itself to postulating paradigms, but conveys the ability to reflect upon criteria and their significance. There are no rules or recipes for this. Every generation and every designer has to redefine what is good, true and beautiful.

"Knowledge, Information, Communication" theme park at the Expo Hannover 2000. Zentrum für Kunst und Medientechnologie Karlsruhe

Theory

Τηεορια *is not so much the single act of a moment, but an attitude, a state and a condition in which one keeps oneself.* Hans-Georg Gadamer (1983, p. 44)

209

A design theory emerges as a set of statements that attempt to explain how designs come into being, as systematically and with as few contradictions as possible. A distinction should be made between *general* and *special* design theories according to a theory's degree of abstraction and the area in which it claims to be valid. Special theories apply only to limited sets of designs, for example to designs by a particular individual, school or movement, or also to a particular design phase or a single design. The relevance of such theories – the central question for practicing designers – would be measured by the extent to which they can be applied and the quality and cultural importance of the designs that result from applying them. Their flaws show up in the contradictions that occur between design theory and practice, and also in the aspects of designing and designs produced that they cannot explain.

A satisfying design theory, or even just a pathway towards one, is not in sight at the time of writing for the architecture and other design fields. The

existing approaches contain flaws, gaps, logical contradictions and inconsistencies with practice. Given the complexity of the subject matter, this is entirely to be expected. But if progress is to be made towards a theory of design, then it is precisely the flaws in the existing theories that are of interest. Analysing them can provide indications as to how a theoretical approach can be improved and developed further.

All design activity is based on voluntary gestures. There are no causal explanations for these, as they are an *"expression of human freedom"* (Flusser). And yet there is a great deal to be known about design, there are

Otl Aicher in May 1990

more or less illuminating ways of talking about design. Among these, the approach taken by the German designer and theoretician Otl Aicher (1922–1991) stands out both because of the breadth of the themes considered and the radical nature of the position he adopts. His writings were hailed by architects and designers as an important contribution to design theory. (Kuhnert 1989, Foster 2002, De Bruyn 2003, Rathgeb 2006) But it is not easy to ascertain what this contribution constitutes and what makes it so significant. Aicher did not formulate his ideas as a systematic theory, but simply as collections of independent essays. Most of his texts were written in the 1980s; the first was published in 1978, and the most recent in 1991, the year of Aicher's death. They were brought together in two volumes in 1991, *analog und digital* (*analogous and digital*, 1991/1) and *die welt als entwurf* (*the world as design*, 1991/2), complemented by the volume *schreiben und widersprechen* (writing and contradicting) published posthumously by his wife Inge Aicher-Scholl in 1993. Aicher's texts are first and foremost statements by a designer, justifying his personal standpoint and relating it to his philosophical and political thinking. In the same period, Aicher published various other books containing further explorations of his design thinking, for example *gehen in der wüste* (walking in the desert) and *Die Küche zum Kochen*, with the ambitious subtitle *Das Ende einer Architekturdoktrin* (The Kitchen for Cooking. The End of an Architectural Doctrine, both 1982 – Aicher was not always able to insist on the lower case type he was so fond of), *kritik am auto* (criticising the car, 1984), *innenseiten des krieges* (inside the war, 1985), *Wilhelm von Ockham: Das Risiko modern zu denken* (William of Ockham: The Risk of Thinking Modern, with Gabriele Greindl and Willhelm Vossenkuhl, 1986) and the extensive basic work *typographie / typography (1988)*.

Otl Aicher grew up in a family of Catholic craftsmen in Ulm in Swabia, and spent most of his life in Ulm, Munich and the Allgäu. He was a young man in the National Socialist period, and a friend of Hans and Sophie Scholl, but without being involved in the White Rose campaigns. He served as a soldier from 1941–45, briefly studied sculpture in Munich after the war and then started work as a graphic designer. In 1952, he married Inge Scholl and the two of them founded the hochschule für gestaltung in Ulm, together with Max Bill. Aicher became one of the most important designers in postwar Germany with his corporate identity for Lufthansa and his designs for

the 1972 Munich Olympics. He set up his home and office in an old mill in the Allgäu, proclaiming the estate as the *"autonomous republic of rotis"*, after the Celtic place-name. Despite all his travels, his friendship with Norman Foster and also despite his philosophical thinking, Aicher ultimately remained rooted to his native soil and region and worked mainly in the German-speaking countries. His major writings have been translated into English, and a comprehensive monograph about his work was published in London recently. (Rathgeb 2006)

AICHER: THEORY FROM BELOW

Aicher developed his theories from opposition to great ideas, generally valid truths and abstract higher theories. However, he did not entirely avoid becoming involved in principles himself; Aicher asks for the world to be seen as a *"world from below"*: education from the point of view of children, the state from the point of view of its citizens, the economy from the point of view of workers and consumers. Aicher concludes from this that *"geist"* (spirit, mind) is *"geist from below, from making"*. (Aicher 1991/1, p. 147) From this perspective, making became the central theme for Aicher, as *"the world we live in is the world we have made"*. (Aicher 1991/2, p. 185) By making, he says, by the achievements of science and technology, industry and commerce, the world we live in is no longer nature embedded in the cosmos, but has become a design, a *"made model, one that even includes nature"*. (loc. cit., p. 188)

But Aicher feels that making is in danger itself. He senses that our civilization, above all its industrial economy, has a tendency to drive us out of all forms of work in favour of automated production. In this way we are losing not just a relationship with things, an understanding of cause and effect, of design and consequence, but also our own self-determination, which is reduced to making consumer decisions. As a result of this we are losing our trust in ourselves, our security in acting, making and saying, and becoming increasingly trusting of authority. Making, defined by Aicher as

"an action for which responsibility is taken by an individual, who participates in concept, design, execution and testing" and from which *"insights are gained for correcting concept and design,"* (loc. cit. p. 190 ff.)

is the prerequisite for freedom, which Aicher understands as a *"condition arising from making"*. (loc. cit., p. 154)

Aicher does not see design as creative work, as endowing prescribed ideas with material quality, but as developing them actively in a cycle of experiment, evaluation and modification, in a sequence of *"practical model experiments"*. This development process is not based on predetermined planning logic according to Aicher, but on working with models:

"model situations are designed, models are made, and the model shows whether the approach is correct, whether new questions arise, to be replied to by new models."
(Aicher 1991/1, p. 148)

Aicher is not describing an architectural model concept here, but a scientific one, which also, for example, includes sketches and drawings as *"graphic models"*. He defines models as *"structures made up of statements, concepts and conceptual operations"*. (Aicher 1991/2, p. 195)

Within the design process, Aicher allocates so much importance to comparing alternatives and evaluating them that he equates this with design: *"the designer's activity lies in creating order in a conflicting field of heterogeneous factors, evaluating them."* (loc. cit., p. 67) The difficulty with evaluation lies in the contradictory nature of criteria. The object to be designed should function technically, appeal formally, prove itself in use, be economical, and intelligible in its function, meaning and origin. These are qualities that are not prerequisites of each other, and are not causally interdependent; they are in a state of tension with each other, and create differences and conflicts that the designer has to resolve. In order for this to succeed, comprehensive working hypotheses and programmes have to be created, a whole philosophy has to be developed, according to Aicher, that makes it possible to make decisions not just as a question of taste, or drawing on a trend, for example, but to justify them with precisely derived arguments: *"the designer is the philosopher in the enterprise."* (loc. cit., p. 160 ff.) Aicher juxtaposes the *"reason of acting and making"* with *"logical deduction, with its claim to total truth"*. He makes a case for *"analogous thinking"*, which is visual and comparative, in contrast with *"digital thinking"*, which is verbal, strictly logical and based on precise numerical values. (Aicher 1991/2, p. 198 ff.) He illustrates the difference with a clock face, whose hands

Examples of analogue and digital time displays

make it possible to read the time clearly and directly, while the numerical readout on a digital clock has first to be read and then translated into a time.

This position is both philosophical and political: *"analogous thinking"* means not just preferring the concrete phenomenon for Aicher, the individual case, but also abandoning absolute systems for explaining the world. Rather than a general order determined by abstract logic, which always leads to subordination and domination, and whose culture is nothing more

Posters for events at the Volkshochschule Ulm, founded by Inge Scholl in 1946

than distraction by the good, the true and the beautiful, Aicher chooses the idea of a *"world as design"*. (loc. cit. p. 191)

The anarchic element that can be heard here condenses into a criticism of the state in Aicher's writing. He feels that anything defined by the abstract concepts of right and freedom can only be experienced as concrete right and concrete freedom. In most cases, he argues, the concrete is everyday and ordinary. Aicher sees the designer's most important task as being precisely here:

"what is hard work is the completely ordinary. and it is in the completely ordinary that life pays. culture develops in the ordinary. as form which one gives to one's life." (Aicher 1991/1, p. 171)

For Aicher, according the everyday such importance leads to the pre-eminence of the criteria of use, manufacture and functionality. Here he does not mean abstract ideals like Vitruvius firmitas or utilitas; using is also not to be seen in the technical sense as value-free, like the concept of function, but

Poster for the sport of wrestling, designed for the Munich Olympics in 1972

derives from concrete experience of dealing with a particular object or building personally. So Aicher's principle of functionality is not exclusive; on the
contrary, it leads to a decentralization of the claim to truth, as *"much is functional, and much is functional in a variety of ways"*. (Aicher 1991/2, p. 191) Rather
than the general category of truth, Aicher takes what is right as the truth
that is possible for mankind: *"it is concrete. it has circumstances, it is manageable, it is object-like, concrete, can be tested and discussed."* (Aicher 1985, p. 251) The
correct is distinct from the merely opportune if it meets a criterion *"outside
the case"*, (loc. cit., p. 252) for example when a technical solution also meets criteria that do not come from the technical sphere. But ultimately a substan-
tive system of requirements and consequences of the individual case has to
be built into its evaluation.

Aicher also subjects aesthetics to these criteria. He agrees that it is important to identify aesthetic concepts such as proportion, volume, progression,
penetration or contrasts and understand them experimentally, so that a
grammar, a syntax of designing can be derived from them and conceptual
control of aesthetic phenomena achieved. (Aicher 1991/2, p. 92) But he says that
in aesthetics there are no generally valid rules, each aesthetic proposition is
legitimate in its own right in the first place. As a consequence, freedom in
our society is often reduced to the aesthetic, which is then used as a pretext
for and obfuscation of real power. (loc. cit., p. 35, p. 88) His scepticism about the
instrumentalization of the aesthetic radicalizes Aicher to the extent of completely rejecting art. He says that art is unfit for functional design work. (loc.
cit. p. 23) It is also an escape, an obfuscation of the everyday, based on sepa-
ration into mind and matter. (loc. cit., p. 88) Aicher's rejection of art, however,
is based on a concept of art that is reduced to the *"aesthetic experiment"*, to the
"incomprehensible", (loc. cit. p. 31) that should *"remain outside work"*. (loc. cit., p. 24)
An attitude of this kind can be better understood if one considers that it
came into being in the years of crisis during and after the Second World
War. Aicher started to study sculpture at the Akademie der Bildenden
Künste in Munich in 1946, but gave it up in the following year. He had
come to think that any concern with art meant neglecting the ordinary. The
vehemence of his rejection gives a sense of the resistance he had to overcome in order to give up his original motivation. This was the situation that
led to his postulating a *"culture of the everyday"*, (Aicher 1991, p. 15 f.) which
became fundamental to his subsequent work:

"the real culture would be everyday culture and high culture merely one of its forms. thinking in this way would be a reversal of all values [...] artistic creativity would have to benefit everyday things, life as it is lived." (loc. cit., p. 17 f.)

Aicher reflects on the design methods of outstanding designers in the same way as he relates his theoretical thinking to philosophical positions. One of his early enthusiasms was for the architect Le Corbusier, whose work was banned by the National Socialists and seemed to Aicher at the time like a *"manifesto for the freedom of behaviour"*, with the free ground plan and the free façade as an *"inevitable expression of a liberated mode of living"*. (Aicher 1985, p. 206 f.) Here design's political dimension is clearly demonstrated.

Aicher's sport pictograms, designed for the Munich Olympics in 1972, were also used in Montreal in 1976. All the pictograms are based on the same grid. © 1976 by ERCO Leuchten GmbH

Grid serving as a basis for the sport pictograms

Aicher sees certain architecture practices as "cognition workshops" that draw their insights from making, from manufacturing and from comparing concepts, designs and models. (1991/1, p. 106 f.) Thus he describes the design methods in Norman Foster's practice (with whom he worked on several occasions, and who was a personal friend), whose special feature lies in working out alternative designs so thoroughly in terms of structure, organization and services that the results can be compared directly. The most labour-intensive part of a design process consists of

"reaching the distillate of the best possible solution in trials, experiments and studies, in numerous iterative cycles of investigation and evaluation using models and prototypes [...] with the help of one's own work and consultation with others".
(Aicher 1991/1, p. 101)

The designers whose work Aicher analyses also include the architect and designer Charles Eames, whom he calls the *"first modern non-ideological designer"*. He says that Eames develops his products thinking like a process engineer, without any stylistic guidelines, but with high aesthetic ambitions, from their function, from material and manufacturing methods, and from use. (loc. cit, pp. 54, 63 f., 92) He sees similar qualities in the designer Hans Gugelot, who saw style as the *"beginning of the corruption of design"*, (loc. cit. p. 71) and Johannes Potente, who designed door handles as an anonymous factory worker in the 1950s. (loc. cit., p. 130) Aicher also notes the aircraft engineer Paul McCready, who established several world records with aircraft driven by muscle power or by solar cells around 1980, and then devoted himself to questions of thought, culture and politics with the insights he had gained. (loc. cit., p. 79 ff.)

In philosophy, Aicher refers particularly to William of Ockham and Ludwig Wittgenstein, and also addresses the work of philosophers including Plato and Aristotle, Descartes, Kant, Buridan and Peirce. In the work of Wittgenstein, and particularly in his linguistic philosophy, Aicher finds a way of thinking that addresses the everyday and the ordinary, with use as the highest criterion. But this is not seen simply as a touchstone for distinguishing the true from the false, but as an activity for making what is right – as in a game, in which rules are established as a basis for developing a new reality. Aicher says that Wittgenstein sees language as action, as making that creates a life form. (loc. cit., p. 121)

OPEN QUESTIONS

So how can we answer the above question about Aicher's contribution to design theory? Unlike thinking as such, which would not be thinking if it did not move between contradictions, we expect a theory to provide the most systematic statements possible, free of contradictions and with a grip on realistic potential that can be tested. We can define Aicher's design theory as consisting of what can be derived from his texts as a conclusive set of statements. When summing up, it becomes clear that his theoretical approach definitely follows a logical structure: starting with the postulate that the world is to be considered as a *"world from below"*, Aicher's theory develops from the everyday, the concrete, from making that becomes design by becoming increasingly complex. Here again he sees the supreme criteria as use and functionality, and the aesthetic is also one of use, art being rejected as an obfuscation of the ordinary. Perception is based on an analogue approach, insight derives from making.

If like Aicher we opt for use and functionality as the supreme criteria, these must be distinguished from the one-dimensional criteria of sheer functionality. The argument of functionality was also used to justify the architectural deserts of a trivialized Modernism, and Aicher provides no appropriately differentiated definition of these terms. But in his own work,

Lettering for the Lufthansa corporate image

Logo for the ERCO corporate image

Lorry with the ERCO logo

Aicher was never in danger of going beyond the boundaries of the human. He was very well aware that every design, even the worst, would be "functional" for some of the people involved in realizing it. The question is much more whether the design is acceptable to all those affected by its implications. This also conveys Aicher's point that designers have to reconcile the differences and conflicts that a design brings with it. (Aicher 1991/2, p. 68 f.)

While Aicher's writings do certainly reveal his design theory to us, we can only form conclusions about his thinking as a whole by relating his many texts, design activities and his biography to each other critically. Seen from this distance, of course there are large numbers of contradictions, and he must have been strongly aware of this himself. They reflect the conflicts from which he developed his position. Thus the unresolved contradiction between Aicher's rejection of comprehensive theories and the theoretical content of his texts with their schoolmasterly didacticism, between his personal anarchy and the absolutist claims of a *"world as design"*, between use as the supreme criterion and an entirely engaging aesthetic, between his initial enthusiasm for and subsequent rejection of art, describes the field of tension in which Aicher operates. His theoretical utterances represent an attempt to articulate a radical position in this field, and to secure it by argument. Here Aicher is not ultimately concerned with creating a sophisticated theory, but with the clarity and sustainability of a position as a prerequisite for his ability to act as a creative designer. His texts are not to be read as incontrovertible dogma, which their tone definitely suggests, but as the voice of a designer assuring himself by argument. Here Aicher arrives at an attitude that is characterized by ideological abbreviations and simplifications, but one that emerges from thought and action that always perceives the corresponding counter-position as an option and includes it in the process of thought. The relationship between theory and practice remains ambivalent for him. In both his writings and his work Aicher makes clear that, as soon as there are more demanding problems to be solved, a theoretical horizon is required that very few designers are able to present explicitly, while at the same time design practice creates insight in a way that is often well ahead of any theory.

	Rotis Grotesk	Rotis Semigrotesk	Rotis Semiantiqua	Rotis Antiqua
45	R1 45 ran	R2 45 ran		
55	R1 55 ran	R2 55 ran	R3 55 ran	R4 55 ran
65	R1 65 ran	R2 65 ran	R3 65 ran	R4 65 ran
75	R1 75 ran	R2 75 ran		
46	R1 46 ran	R2 46 ran		
56	R1 56 ran	R2 56 ran		R4 56 ran

The Rotis typeface family consists of four fonts: a serif, a semi serif, a semi sans and a sans-serif, each available in four weights, from thin to bold, with the exception of the semi-serif, which is available in normal and bold only.

DESIGNING THEORY

Despite all the open questions, Aicher's thoughts on design theory imply new standards for what a design theory would have to achieve. Not so much in the position he takes up personally as in the breadth of his thinking, Aicher identifies a theory of design that redefines the range of questions to be answered. His texts show that a design theory cannot be reduced to problems of methodology or defining terms. Questions of perception, of creative and critical thinking, of production and evaluation, have to be placed in a logical context and should be related to practical questions as much as to political and philosophical positions. A theory of design would have to describe a meta-plane directed towards concrete action:

"design transcends theory and practice and opens up not just a new reality, but also new insights." (loc. cit., p. 196)

Starting with Aicher's statement that evaluation is a fundamental element of design, the question of what the essential elements of a design process are would have to be investigated, what they mean and how they relate to each other. The most important design tools would have to be identified, and it would be necessary to establish the sense in which they are to be perceived as design tools. To this end, the story of how they emerged would have to be told, the way they work analysed, and ultimately they would have to be discussed in relation to the questions Aicher raises about perception, thinking, production and evaluation. Then the problems of evaluating design would have to be set out, and the field of possible design criteria examined, with their common links, dependencies and hierarchies.

On one occasion, Aicher quotes these words by the philosopher Ludwig Wittgenstein: *"we are not permitted to set up any theory. all explanation must go, to be replaced only by description."* (Aicher 1991/1, p. 125) A *general theory* of design would have to describe the whole field of possibilities and conditions of design action, beyond ideology and dogma. But it would not be possible to reduce a theory of this kind, which would also have to contain a theory of thought and perception, to a catchy formula. Such a theory would be difficult to imagine as a more or less compact theory, but would have to consist of extensive, detailed descriptions. The task of a *special theory* would then be to define and justify certain positions in this field by selecting appropriate elements from a general theory and relating them to each other logically. In this way it would ultimately create the prerequisites for a designer's ability to act.

Aicher's "autonomous republic of rotis" in the Allgäu consists of an old mill and modern studio buildings designed by Aicher. Photograph: Otl Aicher

Trying to address the whole

A study of design and its tools would not be of interest if it did not come up with any new insights and methods, indications of how to improve practice and theory, or any suggestions for further research. I hope that the first part of this book has shown that design procedures have to be considered from a wide variety of viewpoints if they are to be grasped in their full complexity. It became clear in this context that design tools occupy a key position in all design processes, in individual acts of design as well as in long-term processes involving large numbers of people. Part two investigated the most important of these tools in greater detail. These analyses have followed the author's personal interests in that they have turned out to be more detailed and systematic for some tools than for others, and some have been dealt with only cursorily, or as yet not at all. Further studies of the individual tools could be related to certain epochs, individual designers, schools or projects. Questions concerning the digitalization of individual design tools are of great interest for the future development of design. The second part of this book has also shown how digitalization has fundamentally transformed the way of working with these tools.

This book contains approaches to a design theory that makes certain assumptions based on the method of critical rationalism put forward by Karl Popper, (Popper 1974, p. 164) deducing a series of objective statements from it. These have been thought through to the extent that it is possible to name practical examples that support these statements, or conversely make it possible to question them empirically. Even though the subject of design and its tools embraces a very large and diffuse field, in which it is impossible to avoid subjective experiences and individual, arbitrary decisions, I think it is possible to arrive at objective statements that can be examined critically in this way. Of course, like all theories in research they always remain open to doubt and, in order to push forward research in the field, they should be doubted and examined, and then rejected or confirmed and improved.

It would certainly also be rewarding to apply the approach developed here to related questions. Thus for example it would be possible to examine how a particular person handles design tools in professional practice, and to derive ideas on how to optimize their use from an analysis of that practice.

It would also be revealing to observe in the long term how a particular team uses the individual tools in the course of a certain project, what mutual influences there are within that use and what influence this has in its turn on the development of the design. New design strategies could be developed from a careful combination of selected tools, and then tried out experimentally in design seminars, for example.

In current design teaching, models, methods, constructive rules and technical regulations are very well presented in general. But there is often a lack of discussion about the possibilities and conditions of design activities. This is also because apart from the "classics", most of whom are out of date, there is scarcely any contemporary research on this subject. Hence a purely practice-oriented form of design teaching has become widespread, confining itself to formulating problems and criticizing students' attempts to solve them. One consequence of this is that students favour feasability without fundamentally tackling the actual complexities of design. The very approach taken by this introduction questions such current practices in both design and design teaching. It does this on the one hand by confronting the habitual use of individual tools, which is often subject to very little reflection, with a systematic analysis of those tools, and by indicating a wide range of tools and possible ways of acting. It divides the tools into two groups, corresponding to two contrasting but complementary ways of thinking: verbal and visual-spatial thinking. Both kinds of tool are used in design: the visual tools to show what cannot be described (the beautiful), and the verbal tools to describe the invisible (the backgrounds and contexts). Analysis has shown that certain tools, like the sketch, for example, the simple verbal tools as well as criticism acquire key functions in design that suggest they should be reassessed in both design practice and theory.

But it has also become clear that the computer has now become more than just another more convenient tool for designers. In fact it is a new medium that digitalizes all the traditional design tools and unites them within it, completely changing them in the process. These changes are not a unique transformation, but a continuous process in parallel with technical developments, constantly redefining design conditions at certain time intervals, and demanding continuous assessment.

The approach used here could lead to a next working step developing study programmes as an introduction to architectural design, ensuring that trainee designers on the shorter BA courses become familiarized with all the major design tools, undergoing training that will qualify them for professional practice. Architecture students should develop the competence to work in a whole series of different media, and also an awareness of the possibilities and problems presented by digital design. A curriculum of this kind would stimulate innovative intellectual approaches by moving step by step from simple to more complex tools, and by systematically switching between customary and unusual design tools, and working with visual and verbal tools in combination. In this way the basic course would be more unambiguously directed at the design perspective, and at the same time open up a considerably broader range of possible activities for designers. At a time that is crying out for new, additional qualifications, professional specialization and broader fields of activity, it is very important to convey creative ideas for design thinking and action. Without the ability to design, the enormous technical and cultural developments of the 19th and 20th centuries could never have been achieved. However impressive this progress may be, its impact on the environment, natural resources and society is equally alarming. Without the ability of thinking the – never completely comprehensible – whole by design, and of questioning and pushing forward the currently established rules by design, we would remain locked into the status quo.

Appendix

BIBLIOGRAPHY

The bibliography contains the original editions or editions in the original language. The date in brackets indicates the year of the first edition. In some instances, English or German translations have been included as well. Unless otherwise mentioned, English translations of the quotations are by the translator of this book.

Abbreviations:

DiskAB 4 (1984): *Diskussionen zur archäologischen Bauforschung 4: Bauplanung und Bautheorie der Antike.* (Symposium publication) Berlin: German Archaeological Institute, 1984

IstMitt 30 (1980): *Istanbuler Mitteilungen, vol. 30, 1980.* German Archaeological Institute, Istanbul Department. Tübingen: Wasmuth, 1980

LasCasas (1997): *Las Casas del Alma. Maquetas arquitectónicas de la Antigüedad (5500 a.C./ 300 d.C.)* (Exhibition catalogue), Barcelona: Centre de Cultura Contemporània, 1997

Part A: Design (pp. 9–79)

ABEL, GÜNTER (Ed.) (2005): *Kreativität. XX. Deutscher Kongress für Philosophie.* Berlin: Universitätsverlag der TU Berlin, 2005

ACKERMANN, KURT, et al. (1985): *Industriebau.* Stuttgart: DVA, 1985, 4th ed. 1994

ACKERMANN, KURT, et al. (1988): *Tragwerke in der konstruktiven Architektur.* Stuttgart: DVA, 1988

ACKERMANN, KURT, et al. (1993): *Geschossbauten für Gewerbe und Industrie.* Stuttgart: DVA, 1993

ADAMCZYK, GRAZYNA (Ed.) (1998): *Rezeptfreies Entwerfen. Auf der Suche nach persönlichen Gesichtspunkten im Entwurfsprozess.* Edited by the Institute of Urban Design at the University of Stuttgart. Stuttgart, 1998

ADLER, DAVID A. (1986, 1999): *Metric Handbook Planning and Design Data.* Architectural Press, 1986, 1999

ADORNO, THEODOR W. (1970): *Ästhetische Theorie.* Edited by Gretel Adorno and Rolf Tiedemann. Frankfurt am Main: Suhrkamp, 1970, 9th ed. 1989

ADORNO, THEODOR W. (1971): *Erziehung zur Mündigkeit. Vorträge und Gespräche mit Helmut Becker 1959-69.* Edited by Gerd Kadelbach. Frankfurt am Main: Suhrkamp, 1971, 16th ed. 1999

AICHER, OTL (1989): *"Entwurf der Moderne"*, in: Arch+ 98, Aachen: Arch+, 1989

AICHER, OTL (1991/1): *analog und digital.* Berlin: Ernst & Sohn, 1991. English edition: *analogous and digital,* translated by Michael Robinson. Berlin: Ernst & Sohn, 1994

AICHER, OTL (1991/2): *die welt als entwurf.* Berlin: Ernst & Sohn, 1991. English edition: *the world as design,* translated by Michael Robinson. Berlin: Ernst & Sohn, 1994

AICHER, OTL (1993): *schreiben und widersprechen.* Berlin: Janus, 1993

AICHER, OTL; GREINDL, GABRIELE; VOSSENKUHL, WILHELM (1986): *Wilhelm von Ockham: Das Risiko modern zu denken.* Munich: Callwey, 1986

ALBERTI, LEON BATTISTA (manuscript ca. 1443-1452) (1485): *De re aedificatoria libri decem.* Florenz: Alamanus, 1485. Quoted from the English edition: *On the Art of Building in Ten Books,* translated by Joseph Rykwert, Neil Leach, Robert Taverner. Cambridge, Mass. and London: MIT Press, 1988

ALEXANDER, CHRISTOPHER; ISHIKAWA, SARA; SIVERSTEIN, MURRAY (1977): *A Pattern Language.
Towns, Buildings, Construction.* New York: Oxford University Press, 1977

ALTSCHULLER, GENRICH SAULOWITSCH (1979): *Tvorcestvo kak tocna ja nauka.* Moskau, 1979.
Corresponding English publication: Altshuller, Genrich: *Creativity as an Exact
Science.* New York: Gordon & Breach, 1984

AMMANN, JEAN-CHRISTOPHE (1998): *Das Glück zu sehen. Kunst beginnt dort, wo der
Geschmack aufhört.* Statement series S 26. Regensburg: Lindinger & Schmid, 1998

ANDREAS VESALIUS (1543): *De Humani Corporis Fabrica.* Basel, 1543

ARASSE, DANIEL (1997): *Leonardo da Vinci. Le rythme du monde.* Paris, 1997

ARISTOTLE (2001): *Problems,* translated by W.S. Hett and H. Rackham. Cambridge,
Mass. and London: Harvard University Press, 1970, 2001

ARISTOTLE (1908): *Nicomachean Ethics,* translated by W. D. Ross, Oxford:
Clarendon Press, 1908

ARNHEIM, RUDOLF (1974): *Art and Visual Perception. A Psychology of the Creative Eye,*
Berkeley: University of California Press, 1974

ARNHEIM, RUDOLF (1969): *Visual thinking.* About the Unity of Image and Concept,
Berkeley: University of California Press, 1969

ARNHEIM, RUDOLF (1986): *New Essays on the Psychology of Art.* Berkeley: University of
California Press, 1986

ARNHEIM, RUDOLF (1996): Preface to the new German edition: *Anschauliches Denken.
Zur Einheit von Bild und Begriff.* Cologne: DuMont Schauberg, 1996

BACHMANN, WOLFGANG (2006): "Der Kampf der Baukulturen", in: Baumeister, no. 5/2006, p. 1

BALMOND, CECIL; SMITH, JANNUZZI (2002): *informal.* Munich: Prestel, 2002

BATESON, GREGORY (1972): *Steps to an Ecology of Mind. Collected Essays.* San Francisco:
Chandler, New York: Ballantine, 1972. Quoted from the edition Fragmore: Paladin
1973

BATESON, GREGORY (1979): *Mind and Nature. A Necessary Unity.* New York: Dutton, 1979

BECHER, BERND & HILLA (2003): *Typologien industrieller Bauten.* München:
Schirmer/Mosel, 2003

BEHNISCH & PARTNER, Architekten (1987): *Designs 1952–1987.* (Exhibition catalogue)
Stuttgart: Cantz, 1987

BEHNISCH & PARTNER, Architekten (1996): *Bauten und Projekte 1987–1997.* Ostfildern-Ruit:
Hatje, 1996

BEHNISCH, GÜNTER; DURTH, WERNER (2005): *Berlin – Pariser Platz. Neubau der Akademie der
Künste.* Berlin: Jovis, 2005

BENSE, MAX (1998): *Ausgewählte Schriften in vier Bänden,* vol. 3: *Ästhetik und Texttheorie.*
Weimar: Metzler, 1998

BINDING, GÜNTHER (1993): *Baubetrieb im Mittelalter.* Darmstadt: Wiss. Buchges., 1993

BLASER, WERNER (1977): *Mies van der Rohe. Principles and School.* Basel,
Stuttgart: Birkh user, 1977

BONO, EDWARD DE (1970): *Lateral Thinking. A Textbook of Creativity.* London, 1970,
quoted from the edition London: Penguin, 1990

BOURDIEU, PIERRE (1984): *Homo academicus.* Paris, 1984

BOURDIEU, PIERRE (1992): *Les règles de l'art. Genèse et structure du champ littéraire.*
Paris: Éditions du Seuil, 1992

BROADBENT, GEOFFREY (1973): *Design in Architecture. Architecture and the Human Sciences.*
London, New York: John Wiley, 1973, reprint 1975, 1981, 1988

232

Bruyn, Gerd de; Trüby, Stephan (Ed.) (2003): *architektur-theorie.doc – texte seit 1960*.
In cooperation with Henrik Mauler, Ulrich Pantle. Basel, Boston,
Berlin: Birkhäuser, 2003

Burckhardt, Lucius (2004): *Wer plant die Planung? Architektur, Politik und Mensch*.
Edited by Jesko Fezer and Martin Schmitz. Kassel: Schmitz, 2004

Cafee, Richard (1977): „*The Teaching of Architecture at the Ecole des Beaux-Arts*",
in: Drexler 1977, p. 61–109

Calvino, Italo (1988): *Lezioni americane. Sei proposte per il prossimo millenio*.
Milano: Garzanti, 1988.

Chastel, André (Ed.) (1987, 1990): *Leonardo da Vinci (1651): Trattato della pittura*.
(Manuscripts until 1519) Edited by Francesco Melzi. Paris: Fresne, 1651, German
edition: Nuremberg, 1724. Quoted from the German edition: *Sämtliche Gemälde und
die Schriften zur Malerei, kommentiert und eingeleitet von André Chastel*.
München: Schirmer/Mosel, 1990

Ching, Francis D.K. (1979): *Architecture. Form Space & Order*. New York, 1979

Ching, Francis D.K. (1989): *Drawing. A Creative Process*. New York, 1989

Ching, Francis D.K. (1998): *Design Drawing. A comprehensive introduction to drawing and more*.
New York, 1998

Ching, Francis D.K. (2002): *Architectural Graphics*. 4th ed., New York, 2002

Clair, Jean (Ed.) (2005): *Melancholie. Genie und Wahnsinn in der Kunst*. (Exhibition
catalogue) Ostfildern-Ruit: Hatje Cantz, 2005

Conrads, Ulrich (Ed.) (1964): *Programme und Manifeste zur Architektur des 20. Jahrhunderts*.
Collected and commented by Ulrich Conrads. Bauwelt-Fundamente, vol. 1,
Frankfurt am Main/Berlin: Ullstein, 1964. Quoted from the unaltered reprint of the
2nd ed. 1981. Basel, Boston, Berlin: Birkhäuser, 2001

Croset, Pierre-Alain (1987): "*Occi che vedono*", in: Casabella no. 531–532, Milano 1987,
p. 4–8 (Le Corbusier, Carnet T 70, no. 1038, 18.8.63)

Damasio, Antonio R. (1994): *Descartes' Error. Emotion, Reason and the Human Brain*.
New York: Putnam, 1994

Damasio, Antonio R. (1999): *The Feeling of What Happens. Body and Emotion in the Making of
Consciousness*. New York: Harcourt Brace, 1999

Demetrios, Eames (2001): *An Eames Primer*. London: Thames & Hudson, 2001

Dominick, Peter G.; Demel, John T., et al. (2000): *Tools and Tactics of Design*.
London: Wiley, 2000

Dörner, Dietrich (1989): *Die Logik des Misslingens. Strategisches Denken in komplexen
Situationen*. Reinbek bei Hamburg: Rowohlt, 1989, 13th ed. 2000

Dorst, Kees (2003): *Understanding Design. 150 Reflections on Being a Designer*.
Amsterdam: BIS, 2003

Drexler, Arthur (Ed.) (1977): *The Architecture of the École des Beaux-Arts*.
London: Secker & Warburg, 1977

Durand, Jean-Nicolas-Louis (1802): *Précis des Leáons d'Architecture données à l'École
Polytechnique*. Paris, 1802

Ebert, Theodor (1995): "*Phronêsis. Anmerkungen zu einem Begriff der Aristotelischen
Ethik (VI 5, 8–13)*", in: Höffe 1995

Eccles, John C. (1973): *The Understanding of the Brain*. New York, 1973

Eccles, John C. (ed.) (1966): *Brain and Conscious Experience*. New York: Springer, 1966

EDWARDS, BETTY (1979): *Drawing on the Right Side of the Brain. A Course in Enhancing
Creativity and Artistic Confidence.* Los Angeles, 1979

EIERMANN, EGON (1994): *Briefe des Architekten, 1946–1970.* Edited by the Institute of
Building History of Karlsruhe University. Stuttgart: DVA, 1994

EISENMAN, PETER (1992): *Interview with Frédéric Levrat,* in: L'Architecture d'aujourd'hui,
no. 279, Feb. 1992, p. 100–108

EISENMAN, PETER (2005): *Ins Leere geschrieben. Schriften & Interviews 2.* Vienna: Passagen, 2005

ENGEL, HEINO (2003): *Methodik der Architektur-Planung.* Berlin: Bauwerk, 2003

ERMEL, HORST; BECK, CHRISTIAN, et al. (2004): *Grundlagen des Entwerfens.* Vol. 1:
Gestaltungsmethodik. Department of Architecture, Environmental Planning and
Building Engineering at the University of Kaiserslautern. Darmstadt: Das Beispiel, 2004

ERMEL, HORST; BRAUNECK, PER, et al. (2004): *Grundlagen des Entwerfens.* Vol 2: *Funktion.*
Department of Architecture, Environmental Planning and Building Engineering at the
Universtiy of Kaiserslautern. Darmstadt: Das Beispiel, 2004

EVERS, BERND; THOENES, CHRISTOF (Eds.) (2003): *Architectural Theory from the Renaissance to the
Present.* Cologne: Taschen, 2003

FERGUSON, EUGENE S. (1992): *Engineering and the Mind's Eye.* Cambridge,
Mass.: MIT Press, 1992

FIEDERLING, OTTO (1975): *Theorie des Entwerfens.* Hannover, 1975

FISCHER, VOLKER; HAMILTON, ANNE (Hg.) (1999): *Theorien der Gestaltung. Grundlagentexte
zum Design,* vol. 1. Frankfurt am Main: Form, 1999

FLUSSER, VILÉM (1989): *"Vom Unterworfenen zum Entwerfer von Gewohntem",* in: Intelligent
Building. Symposium at the Faculty of Architecture at the University of Karlsruhe,
Institute of Building Design, Prof. Fritz Haller, Karlsruhe 1989, chapter 11, p. 1–9

FLUSSER, VILÉM (1991): *Gesten. Versuch einer Phänomenologie.* Bensheim and Düsseldorf:
Bollmann, 1991, 2nd ed. 1993

FLUSSER, VILÉM (1992/2): *"Virtuelle Räume – Simultane Welten",* in: Arch+ 111,
Aachen: Arch+, 1992, p. 17–81

FLUSSER, VILÉM (1994): *Schriften,* edited by Stefan Bollmann and Edith Flusser, vol. 3:
Vom Subjekt zum Projekt. Menschwerdung. Bensheim and Düsseldorf: Bollmann, 1994

FLUSSER, VILÉM (1999): *The shape of things.* English translation. London: Reaktion, 1999.

FLUSSER, VILÉM (2001): *From Subject to Project: Becoming Human.* English translation.
London: Free Association Books, 2001

FLUSSER, VILÉM (2002): *Writings,* edited by Andreas Strähl, translated by Erik Eisel.
Minneapolis: University of Minnesota Press, 2002

FONATTI, FRANCO (1982): *Elementare Gestaltungsprinzipien in der Architektur.*
Vienna: Tusch, 1982

FOSTER, NORMAN (2000): *Rebuilding the Reichstag,* edited by David Jenkins, Weidenfeld &
Nicolson 2000

FRÉART, ROLAND (1650): *Parallèle de l'architecture antique avec la moderne.* Paris, 1650,
quoted from: Laugier 1753, p. 83

FUHRMANN, PETER (1998): *Bauplanung und Bauentwurf. Grundlagen und Methoden der
Gebäudelehre.* Stuttgart: Kohlhammer, 1998

GADAMER, HANS-GEORG (1983): *Lob der Theorie. Reden und Aufsätze.* Frankfurt am Main:
Suhrkamp, 1983, 3rd ed. 1991

GADAMER, HANS-GEORG (Ed.) (1998): *Aristoteles' Nikomachische Ethik IV.*
Frankfurt am Main: Klostermann, 1998

GÄNSHIRT, CHRISTIAN (2000): *„Entwerfen und Forschen. Architektur und die Idee der Universität"*, in: Cloud-Cuckoo-Land. International Journal of Architectural Theory, no. 2/2000

GARDNER, HOWARD (1993): *Creating Minds. An anatomy of creativity seen through the lives of Freud, Einstein, Picasso, Stravinsky, Eliot, Graham and Gandhi.* New York: Basic Books, 1993

GAST, KLAUS-PETER (1998): *Louis I. Kahn, Die Ordnung der Ideen.* Basel, Boston, Berlin: Birkhäuser, 1998. English edition: Louis I. Kahn, The Idea of Order. Basel, Boston, Berlin: Birkhäuser, 1998

GAST, KLAUS-PETER (2000): *Le Corbusier: Paris-Chandigarh.* Basel, Boston, Berlin: Birkhäuser, 2000

GERKAN, MEINHARD VON (1995): *Architektur im Dialog. Texte zur Architekturpraxis.* With contributions by Werner Strodthoff, Klaus-Dieter Weifl, Jan Esche and Bernd Pastuschka. Berlin: Ernst & Sohn, 1995

GROAT, LINDA; WANG, DAVID (2002): *Architectural Research Methods.* New York: Wiley, 2002

HÖFER, CANDIDA (2003): *A monograph.* With a text by Michael Krüger. London: Thames & Hudson, 2003

HÖFFE, OTFRIED (Ed.) (1995): *Aristoteles. Die Nikomachische Ethik.* Berlin: Akademie, 1995

HOFMANN, WERNER (2003): *Goya. Vom Himmel durch die Welt zur Hölle.* Munich: Beck, 2003

JANSEN, JÖRG, et al. (1989): *Architektur lehren. Bernhard Hoesli an der Architekturabteilung der ETH Zürich.* Zurich: gta, 1989

JASPERS, KARL (1946): *Die Idee der Universität,* Berlin, 1923, new edition Berlin/Heidelberg, 1946, reprint: Heidelberg/Berlin/New York: Springer, 1980

JENCKS, CHARLES, KROPF, KARL (Eds.) (1997): *Theories and Manifestoes of Contemporary Architecture.* Chichester: Academy, 1997, 5th ed. 2003

JENKINS, DAVID (Hg.) (2000): *On Foster … Foster on.* Introduction by Deyan Sudjic. Munich, London, New York: Prestel, 2000

JENNY, PETER (1996): *Das Wort, das Spiel, das Bild: Unterrichtsmethoden für die Gestaltung von Wahrnehmungsprozessen.* Zurich: vdf, 1996

JOAS, HANS (1996): *Die Kreativität des Handelns.* Frankfurt am Main: Suhrkamp, 1996

JOEDICKE, JÜRGEN (1976): *Angewandte Entwurfsmethodik für Architekten.* Stuttgart: Krämer, 1976

JOEDICKE, JÜRGEN (Ed.) (1970): *Entwurfsmethoden in der Bauplanung. Arbeitsberichte zur Planungsmethodik, vol. 4.* Stuttgart/Bern: Krämer, 1970

KALAY, YEHUDA E. (2004): *Architectures' New Media. Principles, Theories, and Methods of Computer-Aided Design.* Cambridge, Mass.: MIT Press, 2004

KEMP, WOLFGANG (1974): *Disegno. Beiträge zur Geschichte des Begriffs zwischen 1547 und 1607,* in: Marburger Jahrbuch für Kunstwissenschaft, vol. 19, Marburg, 1974, p. 219–240

KLEINE, HOLGER; PASSE, ULRIKE (Ed.) (1997): *Nach dem Bauhaus – 13 Positionen zur Entwurfsgrundlehre.* Foreword: Matthias Sauerbruch. Berlin: Technische Universität, 1997

KNAUER, ROLAND (1991, 2002): *Entwerfen und Darstellen. Die Zeichnung als Mittel des architektonischen Entwurfs.* Berlin: Ernst & Sohn, 1991, 2002

KOELBL, HERLINDE (1998): *Im Schreiben zu Haus. Wie Schriftsteller zu Werke gehen. Fotografien und Gespräche.* Munich: Knesebeck, 1998

KRÄMER, SYBILLE; BREDEKAMP, HORST (Ed.) (2003): *Bild – Schrift – Zahl.* (Kulturtechnik series) Munich: Wilhelm Fink, 2003

KRAUSSE, JOACHIM; LICHTENSTEIN, CLAUDE (Eds.) (2001): *Your Private Sky: R. Buckminster Fuller. Discourse.* Baden: Lars Müller, 2001

KRUFT, HANNO-WALTER (1986): *Geschichte der Architekturtheorie. Von der Antike bis zur Gegenwart.* Munich: Beck, 1985, 4th ed. 1995. English edition: *A History of Architectural Theory. From Vitruvius to the Present.* Philip Wilson, 1994

KÜCKER, WILHELM (1989): *Die verlorene Unschuld der Architektur. Aufsätze und Reden 1980 bis 1987.* Bauwelt-Fundamente, vol. 84. Braunschweig: Vieweg, 1989

LAMPUGNANI, V. MAGNAGO; HANISCH, RUTH; SCHUMANN, U. MAXIMILIAN; SONNE, WOLFGANG (Ed.) (2004): *Architekturtheorie 20. Jahrhundert – Positionen, Programme, Manifeste.* Ostfildern-Ruit: Hatje Cantz, 2004

LAPUERTA, JOSE MARIA DE (1997): *El Croquis – Projecto y Arquitectura (Scintilla Divinitatis).* Madrid: Celeste, 1997

LAUREL, BRENDA (Ed.) (2003): *Design Research: Methods and Perspectives.* Cambridge, Mass.: MIT Press, 2003

LAWSON, BRYAN (1980, 1990, 1997, 2006): *How Designers Think. The Design Process Demystified.* Oxford: Architectural Press, 1980, 1990, 3rd ed. 1997, 4th ed. 2006

LAWSON, BRYAN (1994): *Design in Mind.* Oxford: Butterworth-Heinemann, 1994

LAWSON, BRYAN (2004): *What Designers Know.* Oxford: Architectural Press, 2004

LENK, HANS (2000): *Kreative Aufstiege. Zur Philosophie und Psychologie der Kreativität.* Frankfurt am Main: Suhrkamp, 2000

LEONARDO DA VINCI (2005): *Treatise on Painting,* translated by John Francis Rigaud, Dover, New York, 2005

LEPIK, ANDREAS (1995): *"Das Architekturmodell der frühen Renaissance. Die Erfindung eines Mediums",* in: Evers 1995, p. 10–20

LINDINGER, HERBERT (Ed.) (1987): *Hochschule für Gestaltung Ulm – Die Moral der Gegenstände.* Berlin: Ernst & Sohn, 1987

LINKE, DETLEF (1999): *Das Gehirn.* Munich: Beck, 1999

LISSITZKY-KÜPPERS, SOPHIE (1967): *El Lissitzky. Maler, Architekt, Typograf, Fotograf.* Dresden: Verlag der Kunst, 1967, quoted from the English edition: *El Lissitzky,* translated by Helene Aldwinckle, London: Thames & Hudson, 1968

LOIDL, HANS; BERNARD, STEFAN (2003): *Freiräume(n). Entwerfen als Landschaftsarchitektur.* Basel, Boston, Berlin: Birkhäuser, 2003. English edition: *Open(ing) spaces. Design as Landscape Architecture.* Basel, Boston, Berlin: Birkhäuser, 2003

LORENZ, PETER (2004): *Entwerfen. 25 Architekten, 25 Standpunkte.* Munich: DVA, 2004

MATTENKLOTT, GUNDEL; WELTZIEN, FRIEDRICH (Eds.) (2003): *Entwerfen und Entwurf. Praxis und Theorie des künstlerischen Schaffensprozesses.* Berlin: Dietrich Reimer, 2003

McLUHAN, MARSHALL (1964): *Understanding Media.* Toronto, 1964

MEISS, PIERRE VON (1984): *De la Forme au Lieu. Une introduction á l'étude de l'architure.* Lausanne: 1984, 1993

MICHELS, KAREN (1989): *Der Sinn der Unordnung. Arbeitsformen im Atelier Le Corbusiers.* Braunschweig/Wiesbaden: Vieweg, 1989

MITTELSTRASS, JÜRGEN (1994): *Die unzeitgemäße Universität.* Frankfurt am Main: Suhrkamp, 1994

MOON, KAREN (2005): *Modeling Messages. The Architect and the Model.* New York: Monacelli, 2005

MORAVANSKY, ÀKOS; GYÖNGY KATALION M. (Eds.) (2003): *Architekturtheorie im 20. Jahrhundert. Eine kritische Anthologie.* Vienna, New York: Springer, 2003

MUSSO, ARNE; LAFRENZ, CHRISTIAN; WILKER, WOLFGANG (1981): *Zur Anwendung von Bewertungssystemen im Bauwesen.* Berlin, 1981

NÄGELI, WALTER; VALLEBUONA, RENZO (1993): *A Factory in Melsungen.*
Berlin: Wasmuth, 1993

NESBITT, KATE (Ed.) (1996): *Theorizing a New Agenda for Architecture. An Anthology of Architectural Theory 1965–1995.* New York: Princeton Architectural Press, 1996

NEUFERT, ERNST (1936) (1979) (1992) (2005): *Bauentwurfslehre. Grundlagen, Normen, Vorschriften.* Berlin: Bauwelt-Verlag, 1936, continued by Peter Neufert, 33rd ed. Braunschweig, Wiesbaden: Vieweg, 1992. English edition: *Architects' data.* London: Lockwood, 1970, 2nd international English edition London: Granada, 1980, Collins 1985.

NEUMEYER, FRITZ; CEPL, JASPAR (Eds.) (2002): *Quellentexte zur Architekturtheorie.* Munich: Prestel, 2002

ONIONS, C.T. (1996): *Oxford Dictionary of Etymology,* edited by C.T. Onions, 1996

OSTENDORF, FRIEDRICH (1913): *Sechs Bücher vom Bauen. Enthaltend eine Theorie des Architektonischen Entwerfens.* Vol 1: *Einführung.* Berlin: Ernst & Sohn, 1913, 2nd ed. 1914

PACIOLI, FRA LUCA (1509): *De Divina Proportione.* Florenz: Paganius, 1509

PANOFSKY, ERWIN (1924): *Idea. Ein Beitrag zur Begriffsgeschichte der älteren Kunsttheorie.* Hamburg, 1924. Quoted from the English edition: *Idea. A concept in Art Theory,* translated by Joseph J.S. Peake. New York, San Francisco and London: Harper & Rowe, 1968

PESSOA, FERNANDO (manuscript until 1933) (1990–91): *Livro do desassosego. Vol. 1 + 2. Por Vicente Guedes, Bernardo Soares. Leitura, fixação de inéditos, organização e notas Teresa Sobral Cunha, Lisboa: PreceÁa, 1990–91.* Quoted from the English edition: *Book of Disquiet,* composed by Bernardo Soares, translated by Alfred MacAdam. Cambridge, Mass.: Exact Change, 1998

PFAMMATTER, ULRICH (1997): *Die Erfindung des modernen Architekten. Ursprung und Entwicklung seiner wissenschaftlich-industriellen Ausbildung.* Basel, Boston, Berlin: Birkhäuser, 1997

PIANO, RENZO (2001): *La responsabilit dell'architetto. Conversatione con Renzo Cassigoli.* Firenze-Antella: Passigli, 2001

POPPER, KARL R. (1974): *Unended Quest. An Intellectual Autobiography.* London, Glasgow: Fontana, Collins, 1974

PORTER, TOM; GREENSTREET, BOB; GOODMAN, SUE (1980): *Manual of graphic techniques for architects, graphic designers and artists.* No place, 1980

PRECHTL, PETER (1999): *"Ideenlehre",* in: Prechtl, Burkard 1999, pp. 248–250

PRECHTL, PETER AND BURKARD, FRANZ-PETER (Eds.) (1999): *Metzler Philosophie Lexikon,* Stuttgart, Weimar: Metzler, 2nd ed. 1999

PROMINSKI, MARTIN (2003): *Komplexes Landschaftsentwerfen.* (Diss.) Berlin: Technische Universität, 2003

PROUVÉ, JEAN (2001): *Jean Prouvé par lui-míme. Propos recueillis par Armelle Lavalou.* Paris: Linteau, 2001

RAMBOW, RIKLEF (2000): *Experten-Laien-Kommunikation in der Architektur.* Münster, New York, Munich, Berlin: Waxmann, 2000

RICE, PETER (1994): *An Engineer Imagines.* London: Artemis, 1994

RITTEL, HORST W. (1992): *Planen, Entwerfen, Design. Ausgewählte Schriften zu Theorie und Methodik.* Edited by Wolf D. Reuter. Stuttgart, Berlin, Cologne: Kohlhammer, 1992

ROBBINS, EDWARD (1994): *Why Architects Draw. Interwiews with Edward Cullivan, Spencer de Grey, Jorge Silvetti, Renzo Piano, Álvaro Siza et al.* Cambridge, Mass.: MIT Press, 1994, pb 1997

RODRIGUES, ANA LEONOR M. MADEIRA (2000): *O Desenho. Ordem do Pensamento Arquitectónico.* (Diss.) Lisboa: Estampa, 2000

RODRIGUES, JACINTO (1992): *Álvaro Siza, obra e méthodo*. Porto: Civilização, 1992

RYFF (OR RIVIUS), WALTHER HERMANN (1547): *Der furnembsten/notwendigsten der gantzen Architectur angehörigen Mathematischen vnd Mechanischen kuenst/eygentlicher Bericht* […] *Durch Gualtherum H. Riuium Medi. & Math.*, Nuremberg: Johan Petreius, 1547, reprint: Hildesheim and New York: Olms, 1981

RYFF (OR RIVIUS), WALTHER HERMANN (1548): *Vitruvius Teutsch, erstmals verteutscht und in Truck verordnet durch D. Gualtherum H. Rivium Medi. & Math.*, Nuremberg 1548, reprint with an introduction by Erik Forssman: Hildesheim and New York: Olms, 1973

SANER, HANS (1970): *Karl Jaspers*. Reinbek bei Hamburg: Rowohlt, 1970, 10th ed. 1996

SANOFF, HENRY (1970): *Techniques of Evaluation for Designers*. Raleigh, 1970

SATTLER, BARBARA JOHANNA (1998): *Der umgeschulte Linkshänder oder Der Knoten im Gehirn*. Donauwörth: Auer, 1998, 5th ed. 1999

SCHILDT, GÖRAN (Ed.) (1998): *Alvar Aalto in his own words*. New York: Rizzoli, 1998

SCHNEIDER, BEAT (2005): *Design – Eine Einführung. Entwurf im sozialen, kulturellen und wirtschaftlichen Kontext*. Basel, Boston, Berlin: Birkhäuser, 2005

SCHNEIDER, FRIEDERIKE (1994, 2004): *Floor Plan Manual Housing*. Basel, Boston, Berlin: Birkhäuser, 1994, 3rd ed. 2004

SCHÖN, DONALD A. (1983): *The Reflective Practitioner. How Professionals Think in Action*. New York: Basic Books, 1983, 1991, reprint: Adlershot: Ashgate, 1995, 1996, 2003

SCHÖN, DONALD A. (1987): *Educating the Reflective Practitioner*. San Francisco: Jossey-Bass, 1987

SCHÖNWANDT, WALTER (1986): *Denkfallen beim Planen*. Bauwelt-Fundamente, vol. 74. Braunschweig: Vieweg, 1986

SCHRICKER, RUDOLF (1986): *Darstellungsmethoden*. Stuttgart: DVA, 1986

SCHRICKER, RUDOLF (1999): *Raumzauber. Entwerfen oder "…wie die Dinge entstehen". Gestalten von Räumen und Produkten*. Stuttgart: DVA, 1999

SCHUMACHER, JOACHIM (1974): *Leonardo da Vinci. Maler und Forscher in anarchischer Gesellschaft*. No place, 1974, revised edition, Berlin: Wagenbach 1981

SCHUSTER, KLAUS-PETER (1991): *Melencholia 1 – Dürers Denkbild*. 2 vols. (Diss.) Berlin: Mann, 1991

SCHUSTER, KLAUS-PETER (2005): *"Melencholia 1 – Dürer und seine Nachfolger"*, in: Clair 2005, p. 90–103

SEYLER, AXEL (2003): *Wahrnehmen und Falschnehmen. Praxis der Gestaltpsychologie. Formkriterien für Architekten, Designer und Kunstpädagogen. Hilfen für den Umgang mit Kunst.* Frankfurt am Main: Anabas, 2003

SILVER, NATHAN (1994): *The Making of Beaubourg. A Building Biography of the Centre Pompidou, Paris*. Cambridge, Mass.: MIT Press, 1994

SIMONS, KATRIN (1993): *El Lissitzky Proun 23 N oder Der Umstieg von der Malerei zur Gestaltung*. Frankfurt am Main and Leipzig: Insel, 1993

SIZA, ÁLVARO (1990): *"Freibad in Leça de Palmeira"*, in: Bauwelt no. 29/30, Berlin: 1990

SIZA, ÁLVARO (1997): *Writings on Architecture*. Edited by Antonio Angelillo. Milano: Skira, 1997

SMITH, ALBERT (2004): *Architectural Model as Machine: A new view of models from antiquity to the present day*. Architectural Press, 2004

SPENGEMANN, KARL-LUDWIG (1993): *Architektur wahrnehmen. Experimente und Untersuchungen*. Bielefeld: Kerber, 1993

SPERRY, ROGER W. (1968): *"Hemisphere Disconnection and Unitiy in Concious Awareness"*, in: American Psychologist 23, 1968, pp. 723–733

SPERRY, ROGER W. (1973): *"Lateral Specialisation of Cerebral Function in the Surgically Separted Hemispheres"*, in: *The Psychophysiology of Thinking*. Edited by F.J. McGuigan and R.A. Schoonover. New York: Academic Press, 1973, pp. 209–229

SPITZ, RENE (2002): *hfg ulm, der Blick hinter den Vordergrund. Die Politische Geschichte der Hochschule für Gestaltung 1953–1968*. Stuttgart: Menges, 2002. English edition: *hfg ulm: The View Behind the Foreground. The Political History of the Ulm School of Design. 1953–1968*. Stuttgart: Menges, 2002

TAUT, BRUNO (1936, 1977): *Kenchiku Geijutsu-Ron*. Tokyo: Iwanami Shoten, 1936. Quoted from the German edition: *Architekturlehre. Grundlagen, Theorie und Kritik aus der Sicht eines sozialistischen Architekten*. Edited by Tilman Heinisch and Goerd Peschken. Hamburg, Westberlin: VSA, 1977

THACKARA, JOHN (2005): *In the Bubble. Designing in a complex world*. Cambridge, Mass.: MIT Press, 2005

TRAUFETTER, GERALD (2006): *"Stimme aus dem Nichts. Hirnforscher entdecken die Macht der Intuition"*, in: Der Spiegel, no. 15/2006, Hamburg: Spiegel, 2006, pp. 158–171

UHL, OTTOKAR (2003): *Gegen-Sätze. Architektur als Dialog. Ausgewählte Texte aus vier Jahrzehnten*. Foreword: Kathinka Schreiber. Edited by Elke Krasny and Claudia Mazanek. Vienna: Picus, 2003

VASKE, HERMANN (2001): *Standing on the Shoulders of Giants. Gespräche mit den Besten der Werbung*. Berlin, 2001

VESTER, FREDERIC (1999): *Die Kunst vernetzt zu denken – Ideen und Werkzeuge für einen neuen Umgang mit Komplexität*. Stuttgart: DVA, 1999, 4th ed. 2000

VITRUVIUS [VITRUVIUS POLLIO, MARCUS] (manuscript c. 33–22 BC) (1487): *De architectura libri decem*. No place: Veroli, 1487. Quoted from the English edition: *Ten books on architecture*, edited by I.D. Rowland and T. Noble Howe, Cambridge: Cambridge University Press, 1999

WACHSMANN, KONRAD (1959): *Wendepunkt im Bauen*. Wiesbaden: Krausskopf, 1959; 2nd ed. Stuttgart: DVA, 1989. English edition: *The Turning Point of Building*. New York: Reinhold, 1961

WATSON, DONALD; MICHAEL J. CROSBIE; CALLENDER, JOHN HANCOCK ET AL. (Eds.) (1997): *Time Saver Standards for Architectural Design. Technical Data for Professional Practice*. McGraw-Hill, 7th ed. 1997, 8th ed. 2004

WEISS, L. (1975): *Bewertung im Bauwesen*. Zurich, ETH: Institute of Building Research HBF, 1975

WELSCH, WOLFGANG (Ed.) (1988): *Wege aus der Moderne. Schlüsseltexte der Postmoderne-Diskussion*. Weinheim, 1988, 2nd ed. Berlin, 1994

WICK, RAINER K. (1982): *Bauhaus-Pädagogik*. Cologne: Dumont, 1982, 4th ed. 1994

WIESING, LAMBERT (Hg.) (2002): *Philosophie der Wahrnehmung. Modelle und Reflexionen*. Frankfurt am Main: Suhrkamp, 2002

WILSON, EDWARD O. (1998): *Consilience. The Unity of Knowledge*. New York: Knopf, 1998

Part B: Design tools (pp. 81-224, arranged according to chapters)
Publications mentioned in several chapters have been included in the previous general part of the bibliography.

ARNHEIM, RUDOLF (1979): *"The Tools of Art – Old and New"*, in: Technikum. University of Michigan, 1979, quoted from Arnheim 1986, pp. 166 ff.

BREDEKAMP, HORST (2003): *"Kulturtechniken zwischen Mutter und Stiefmutter Natur."* in: Krämer, Bredekamp (2003), pp. 117–142

DIDEROT, DENIS; D'ALEMBERT, JEAN-BAPTISTE LE ROND (Eds.) (1751–72): *Encyclopédie, ou dictionnaire raisonné des sciences, des arts et des métiers.* Paris, 1751–72

FEHRENBACH, FRANK (Ed.) (2002): *Leonardo da Vinci. Natur im Übergang. Beiträge zu Wissenschaft, Kunst und Technik.* Munich: Fink, 2002

FULLER, R. BUCKMINSTER (1969): *Operating Manual for Spaceship Earth.* Simon & Schuster/Southern Illinois University, 1969

GÄNSHIRT, CHRISTIAN (1999): *"Sechs Werkzeuge des Entwerfens"*, in: Cloud-Cuckoo-Land. International Journal of Architectural Theory, no. 1/1999

GROTE, ANDREAS (1966): *der vollkommen Architektus. Baumeister und Baubetrieb bis zum Anfang der Neuzeit.* 2nd ed. Munich: Prestel, 1966

HAMBLY, MAYA (1988): *Drawing Instruments 1580–1980.* London: Sotheby's, 1988

HANSMANN, WILFRIED (1999): *Balthasar Neumann.* With photographs by Florian Monheim. Cologne: DuMont, 1999

HERMANN-FIORE, KRISTINA (2002): *"Leonardos Gewitterlandschaft und Dürers Nemesis. Zur kosmischen Vision der Landschaft um 1500"*, in: Fehrenbach 2002

MAU, BRUCE (2000): *Life Style.* Edited by Kyo Maclear with Bart Testa. London: Phaidon, 2000

MÜLLER, KARL (1905): *Kunststeinbau. Stummer Lehrmeister für die gesamte Kunststeinbranche.* Gommern, 1905, 2nd reprinted ed. Holzminden: Hennig, no date

RÖTTINGER, HEINRICH (1914): *Die Holzschnitte zur Architektur und zum Vitruvius Teutsch des Walther Rivius.* Studien zur deutschen Kunstgeschichte 167, Straßburg, 1914

ZIMMER, GERHARD (1984): *"Maßstäbe römischer Architekten"*, in: DiskAB 4, 1984, pp. 265–276

Gesture

FLUSSER, VILÉM (1991): *Gesten. Versuch einer Phänomenologie.* Bensheim und Düsseldorf: Bollmann, 1991, 2. Aufl. 1993 (for publications in English see Bibliography Part A)

GÄNSHIRT, CHRISTIAN (2003): *"Geste und Sprache als grundlegende Entwurfswerkzeuge"*, in: *Architekturjahrbuch des Instituts für Entwerfen*, BTU Cottbus, 2003, pp. 34–39

STURM, HERMANN (Ed.) (1998): *Geste & Gewissen im Design.* Cologne: DuMont, 1998

VERSCHAFFEL, BART (2001): *Architektur als Geste.* With a foreword by Ákos Moravánsky. Luzern: Quart, 2001

WITTGENSTEIN, LUDWIG (manuscripts 1914–1951)(1977): *Vermischte Bemerkungen.* Werkausgabe Band 8, Frankfurt am Main: Suhrkamp, 1984, 6th ed. 1994. Quoted from the English edition: *Culture and Value*, translated by Peter Winch. Chicago: The University of Chicago Press, 1980.

Sketch

BERGEIJK, HERMAN VAN; HAUPTMANN, DEBORAH (1998): *Notations of Herman Hertzberger.* Rotterdam: NAI Publishers, 1998

EDWARDS, BETTY (1999): *The New Drawing on the Right Side of the Brain. A Course in Enhancing Creativity and Artistic Confidence.* New York: Tarcher/Putnam 1999

FOSTER, NORMAN (1993): *Sketch Book*. Edited by Werner Blaser. Basel, Boston,
Berlin: Birkhäuser, 1993

HAHNLOSER, HANS ROBERT (1935): *Villard de Honnecourt*. Critical complete edition of the
Portfolio ms.fr 19093 of the Bibliothèque Nationale, Paris. Vienna: Schroll, 1935, 2nd
revised ed. Graz, 1972

HOLLANDA, FRANCESCO DE (c. 1550): *Dialogos em Roma*. German edition: *Vier Gespräche über
die Malerei zu Rom 1538. Originaltext mit Übersetzung, Einleitung, Beilagen und Erläuterungen
von Joaquim de Vasconcellos*, Vienna 1899

KOSCHATZKY, WALTER (1977): *Die Kunst der Zeichnung. Technik, Geschichte, Meisterwerke*.
Salzburg: Residenz, 1977, Munich: DTV, 1981, 7th ed. 1991

MENDELSOHN, ERICH (1930): *Das Gesamtschaffen des Architekten. Skizzen, Entwürfe, Bauten*.
Berlin: Mosse, 1930

POSENER, JULIUS (Engl. manuskript 1957) (2004): *Heimliche Erinnerungen. In Deutschland
1904 bis 1933*. Translated into German by Ruth Keen. Edited by Alan Posener.
Munich: Siedler, 2004

SIZA, ÁLVARO (1994): *City Sketches / Desenhos urbanos*. Edited by Brigitte Fleck, foreword:
Norman Foster, texts by Brigitte Fleck, Álvaro Siza and Wilfried Wang. Basel, Boston,
Berlin: Birkhäuser, 1994

WISNIEWSKI, EDGAR (1993) *Die Berliner Philharmonie und ihr Kammerkonzertsaal.
Der Konzertsaal als Zentralraum*. Berlin: Mann, 1993

Language

BIRNBACHER, DIETER; KROHN, DIETER (Eds.) (2002): *Das sokratische Gespräch*.
Stuttgart: Reclam jun., 2002

FULLER, R. BUCKMINSTER (1944): *"Dymaxion Comprehensive System. Introducing
Energetic Geometry"*, unpublished manuscript 1944, p. 1–15, in: Krausse 2001,
pp. 169–181

GUDEHUS, JULI (1992): *Genesis*. Baden: Lars Müller, 1992

KRAUSSE, JOACHIM; LICHTENSTEIN, CLAUDE (Hg.) (1999): *Your Private Sky: R. Buckminster
Fuller. The Art of Design Science*. Baden: Lars Müller, 1999

LOOS, ADOLF (1924): *"Von der Sparsamkeit"*, in: Wohnungskultur (journal) no. 2/3, Vienna,
1924. Quoted from Loos 1983

LOOS, ADOLF (1983): *Die Potemkinsche Stadt. Verschollene Schriften 1897–1933*,
edited by Adolf Opel. Vienna: Prachner, 1983

MACCORMAC, EARL (1985): *A Cognitive Theory of Metaphor*. Cambridge, Mass., 1985

NIEMEYER, OSCAR (1993): *Conversa de arquiteto*. Rio de Janeiro: Revan, 1993.
Porto: Campo das Letras, 1997, 1999

STEINGRUBER, JOHANN DAVID (1773): *Architectonisches Alphabet*, Schwabach, 1773

VALÉRY, PAUL (1921): *"Eupalinos ou l'Architecte – Dialogue des Morts"*, in: in: La Nouvelle
Revue Française 90, Paris 1921, pp. 237–285. Quoted from the English edition:
Selected Writings of Paul Valéry, New York: New Directions, 1950

WITTGENSTEIN, LUDWIG (1921): *"Tractatus logico-philosophicus. Logisch-philosophische Abhandlung"*,
in: Annalen der Naturphilosophie. No place: Ostwald, 1921, Frankfurt am Main:
Suhrkamp, 1963, 22nd ed. 1989

Design drawing

HESBERG, HENNER VON (1984): *"Römische Grundrisspläne auf Marmor"*, in: IstMitt 30, 1980, pp. 120–136

LE CORBUSIER (1923): *Vers une Architecture*. Paris, 1923, quoted from the edition Librairie Arthaud, Paris, 1984, and from the English edition: *Towards a New Architecture*, translated by Frederick Etchells, London and New York: Architectural Press, 1927, 1963

NERDINGER, WINFRID (Ed.)(2005): *Frei Otto – Das Gesamtwerk. Leicht bauen, natürlich gestalten.* Edited by Winfrid Nerdinger, Irene Meissner, Eberhard Müller und Mirjana Grdanjski. (Exhibition catalogue) Basel, Boston, Berlin: Birkhäuser, 2005

PEVSNER, NIKOLAUS; HONOUR, HUGH; FLEMING, JOHN (1966): *Penguin Dictionary of Architecture.* Harmondsworth: Penguin, 1966

RAUTERBERG, HANNO (2005): *"Barock aus dem Rechner"*, in: Die Zeit no. 45/2005, 3.11.2005, p. 54

VIEIRA, JOAQUIM (1995): *O Desenho e o Projecto São o Mesmo? Outros Textos de Desenho.* Porto: FAUP, 1995

Model

EVERS, BERND (Ed.) (1995): *Architekturmodelle der Renaissance. Die Harmonie des Bauens von Alberti bis Michelangelo.* (Exhibition catalogue) Munich, New York: Prestel, 1995

GRAEFE, RAINER (Ed.) (1989): *Zur Geschichte des Konstruierens.* Stuttgart: DVA, 1989

LEPIK, ANDREAS (1995): *"Das Architekturmodell der frühen Renaissance. Die Erfindung eines Mediums"*, in: Evers 1995, pp S. 10–20

OECHSLIN, WERNER (1995): *"Das Architekturmodell zwischen Theorie und Praxis"*, in: Evers 1995, pp. 40–49

OTTO, FREI (1989): *„Was könnten die alten Steinbaumeister gewusst haben, um entwerfen und bauen zu können?"*, in: Graefe 1989, pp. 196–210

SCHAERF, ERAN (2002): *Blue Key. Journal for Demographic Design.* (Exhibition catalogue) Cologne: Walther König, 2002

STACHOWIAK, HERBERT (1973): *Allgemeine Modelltheorie.* Vienna, New York: Springer, 1973

Perspective view

ALBERTI, LEON BATTISTA (manuscript 1435) (1540): *De Pictura.* Basel: Bartholomaeus Westheimer, 1540. Quoted from the English edition: *On painting*, translated by Cecil Grayson, with an introduction and notes by Martin Kemp. London: Penguin, 1991

EDGERTON, SAMUEL Y. (1975): *The Renaissance Rediscovery of Linear Perspective.* New York, San Francisco and London: Icon, 1926, 1975

FOURNIER, DANIEL (1761): *A Treatise on the Theory of Perspektive*, 1761

GOSZTONYI, ALEXANDER (1976): *Der Raum. Geschichte seiner Probleme in Philosophie und Wissenschaften.* 2 vols., Freiburg, Munich: Alber, 1976

KLOTZ, HEINRICH (1997): *Der Stil des Neuen. Die europäische Renaissance.* Stuttgart: Klett-Cotta, 1997, 2nd ed.

LINDBERG, DAVID C. (1976): *Theories of Vision from Alkindi to Kepler*, Chicago and London: The University of Chicago Press, 1976

PANOFSKY, ERWIN (1927): *"Die Perspektive als symbolische Form"*, in: Vorträge der Bibliothek Warburg 1924–25, Leipzig: 1927, pp. 258–330

RICHARDSON, JOHN (1996): *A Life of Picasso.* New York: Random, 1996, Quoted from the German edition: *Picasso. Leben und Werk, vol. 2, 1907-1917.* Munich: Kindler, 1997

Photograph, film, video

DECHAU, WILFRIED (1995): *Architektur abbilden.* Stuttgart: DVA, 1995

FLUSSER, VILÉM (1983): *Für eine Philosophie der Fotografie.* Göttingen: European Photography, 1983, 8th revised ed. 1997. English edition: Flusser, Vilém (2000): *Towards a Philosophy of Photography.* London: Reaktion, 2000

MAAR, CHRISTA; BURDA, HUBERT (2004): *Iconic Turn. Die neue Macht der Bilder.* Cologne: DuMont, 2004, 3rd ed. 2005

SACHSSE, ROLF (1997): *Bild und Bau. Zur Nutzung technischer Medien beim Entwerfen von Architektur.* Bauwelt-Fundamente, vol. 114. Braunschweig, Wiesbaden: Vieweg, 1997

SCHAAF, LARRY J. (2000): *The Photographic Art of William Henry Fox Talbot.* Princeton: Princeton University Press, 2000

Calculation

FATHY, HASSAN (1969): *Gourna: A Tale of Two Villages.* Cairo: Ministry of Culture, 1969, Quoted from the edition: *Architecture of the Poor.* Cairo: The American University in Cairo Press, 1989, 3rd printing 2000

HÄMER, HARDT-WALTHERR (2002): *Stadt im Kopf.* Edited by Manfred Sack. Berlin: Jovis, 2002

ROTH, FEDOR (1995): *Adolf Loos und die Idee des Ökonomischen.* Vienna: Deuticke, 1995

STRAUB, HANS (1949): *Geschichte der Bauingenieurkunst. Ein Überblick von der Antike bis in die Neuzeit.* No place, 1949, 4th enlarged ed., edited by Peter Zimmermann, Nikolaus Schnitter and Hans Straub Jr., Basel, Boston, Berlin: Birkhäuser, 1992, 1996

Computer, program, simulation

BARZON, FURIO (2003): *La carta di Zurigo.* Turino: Testo & Immagine, 2003, English edition: *The Charter of Zurich.* Basel, Boston, Berlin: Birkhäuser, 2003

DAVIS, MARTIN (1958): *Computability and Unsolvability,* New York: McGraw-Hill, 1958

EISENMAN, PETER (2003): "A Matrix in the Jungle", in: Barzon 2003, pp. 28–37

FOSTER, NORMAN (2000): "Design in a Digital Age", in: Jenkins 2000, pp. 773–785

KITTLER, FRIEDRICH (2002): *Short Cuts.* Vol. 6 of the Short Cuts series, edited by Peter Gente and Martin Weinmann, Frankfurt am Main: Zweitausendeins, 2002

ZUSE, KONRAD (1975): *Der Computer, mein Lebenswerk.* Munich, 1970

Criticism, criteria and value systems

BAZIN, ANDRÉ (1958–1962): *Qu'est-ce que le cinéma?* Vol. I–IV, Paris: Éditions du Cerf, 1958–1962

CONRADS, ULRICH; FÜHR, EDUARD; GÄNSHIRT, CHRISTIAN (Ed.) (2003): *Zur Sprache bringen. Kritik der Architekturkritik.* Münster, New York: Waxmann, 2003

GÄNSHIRT, CHRISTIAN (2003): "Goldene Axt und intelligentes Gefühl. Kritik als Werkzeug des Entwerfens", in: Cloud-Cuckoo-Land. International Journal of Architectural Theory, no. 2/2002

GRAFTON, ANTHONY (2006): *Leon Battista Alberti. Master Builder of the Italian Renaissance.* New York: Hill and Wang, 2000

GROYS, BORIS (1992): *Über das Neue. Versuch einer Kulturökonomie.* Munich, Vienna: Hanser, 1992, Frankfurt am Main: Fischer, 1999, 3rd ed. 2003

HALLBERG, JANA; WEWERKA, ALEXANDER (Ed.)(2001): *Dogma 95. Zwischen Kontrolle und Chaos.* Berlin: Alexander, 2001

KANT, IMMANUEL (1790): *Kritik der Urteilskraft*. Berlin, Libau: Lagarde und Friedrich, 1790, Frankfurt am Main: Suhrkamp, 1974

MENDELSOHN, ERICH (1961): *Briefe eines Architekten*. München: Prestel, 1961, quoted from the edition Basel, Boston, Berlin: Birkhäuser, 1991

NEUMEYER, FRITZ (1986): *Mies van der Rohe: Das kunstlose Wort*. Berlin: Siedler 1986 English edition: *The Artless Word. Mies Van Der Rohe on the Building Art*. Cambridge, Mass.: MIT Press, 1991

PÜCKLER-MUSKAU, HERMANN FÜRST VON (1834): *Andeutungen über Landschaftsgärtnerei, verbunden mit der Beschreibung ihrer praktischen Anwendung in Muskau*. Stuttgart: Hallberger'sche, 1834, zitiert nach: Stuttgart, DVA, 1977

RAUTERBERG, HANNO (2003): *"Raus aus den alten Rastern! Zeitgenössisch bauen, was heißt das?"*, in: Die Zeit no. 26/2003, 21.6.2003

REICH-RANICKI, MARCEL (1994): *Die Anwälte der Literatur*. Stuttgart: DVA, 1994, Munich: DTV, 1996, 2nd ed. 1999

SAID, EDWARD W. (1983): *The World, the Text and the Critic*. Cambridge, Mass.: Harvard, 1983

SPIRO, ANNETTE (2002): *Paulo Mendes da Rocha. Buildings and Projects*. Sulgen: Niggli, 2002

Theory

ADLER, KATHARINA; AICHER, OTL (1981): *das Allgäu (bei Isny)*. Isny: o.V., 1981

AICHER, OTL (1980): *zeichensysteme*. München: Koch, 1980

AICHER, OTL (1982): *Die Küche zum Kochen – Das Ende einer Architekturdoktrin*. Munich: Callwey, 1982

AICHER, OTL (1982): *gehen in der wüste*. Frankfurt am Main: Fischer, 1982

AICHER, OTL (1984): *kritik am auto*. München: Callwey, 1984

AICHER, OTL (1985): *innenseiten des krieges*. Frankfurt am Main: Fischer, 1985

AICHER, OTL (1988): *typografie*. With a contribution by Josef Rommen. Berlin: Ernst & Sohn / Maak, 1988, 3rd revised ed. 1992

FOSTER, NORMAN (2000): *"Otl Aicher, 1991"*, in: Jenkins 2000, pp. 592–595

GÄNSHIRT, CHRISTIAN (2005): *"A Theory of design? On the Writings of Otl Aicher"*, in: GAM Graz Architecture Magazine no. 02, Vienna, New York: Springer, 2005, pp. 174–191

KUHNERT, NIKOLAUS: *„Otl Aicher / Entwurf der Moderne"*, in: Arch+ 98, Aachen: Arch+, 1989, pp. 20 f.

RATHGEB, MARKUS (2006): *Otl Aicher*. London: Phaidon, 2006

ILLUSTRATION CREDITS

Entries with year and date refer to sources mentioned in the bibliography. Every effort has been made to trace the copyright holders of images. In the case of unintentional omissions we would ask the copyright holders to contact the publisher or the author. The author holds the rights of all illustrations not mentioned below.

Aicher, Florian 213, 214, 215, 219, 220, 222, 224
Arch+ no. 137, 1997, p. 23 161 (below)
Arch+ no. 137, 1997, p. 27 161 (above), 163
Arch+ no. 137, 1997, p. 36 164
Arch+ no. 98, 1990, p. 25 209
Audi AG 158 (above)
Behnisch, Günter 144, 156
Buether, Axel 111
Carvalho, Jorge 176
Chevallier, Pascal, WIB Paris 131
Clair 2005, p. 136 74
Clair 2005, p. 190 76
Demetrios, Eames 206
Diderot 1751, Pl. XI. 87
Eccles 1973, p. 264 62
Eisenman, Peter 146
Engel 2003, p. 52 69
ERCO Leuchten GmbH, © 1976 217
Evers 1995, p. 265 155
Evers 1995, p. 285 198
Evers 1995, p. 312 116
Fuhrmann 1998, p. 67 202
Grote 1966, p. 5 84
Grote 1966, p. 6 40
Grote 1966, p. 74 181
Gudehus, Juli 71, 132, 205
Hahnloser 1972, appendix, fol. 29 115
Hambly 1988, p. 20 81
Hammel, Tobias 113, 136
Hansmann 1999, p. 11 98

International Museum of Photography, The George Eastman House, Rochester, New York 173, 174
Jenny, Peter 96
Jörns, Michael 105
Kemp 1974, p. 223 86
Kristen, Marianne 20, 135
LasCasas 1997, p. 208 157
LasCasas 1997, p. 74 82
LasCasas 1997, p. 75 82
Laugier 1753, p. 83 44
Lawson, Brian 204
Lequeu, 1782 100
Lindinger 1987, p. 146 219
Meyer, Stephanie 54, 127, 158 (below), 184
Müller 1905, p. 35 93
Ostendorf 1913, pp. 134, 137 137
Otto 1989, p. 209 152
Pieper, Christian, www.jp3.de 92, 108, 125
Piranesi 1761, Pl. XIII 166
Reti 1987, p. 71 41
Rittel 1992, p. 75 ff. 66
Sachs, Hinrich, © VG Bild-Kunst 106, 189
Santos, José Paulo dos 141
Scheidegger, Ernst, © Neue Züricher Zeitung, 2007 149
Siza, Álvaro 47, 72, 119, 120, 138, 169
Stachowiak 1973, p. 131, 160 150
Steingruber 1773 129
The Royal Collection, © 2006, Her Majesty Queen Elizabeth II 13, 83
VG Bild-Kunst, © 2007 cover, 61, 197
Wachsmann 1959, p. 204 68

INDEX OF NAMES

Aalto, Alvar 32, 72, 121ff.
Abel, Günter 37
Adamczyk, Grazyna 36
Adler, David A. 30
Adorno, Theodor 12ff., 53, 207
Aicher, Otl 20f., 32, 36, 38, 48, 50-55,
    61ff., 70, 88, 97, 101, 122, 130, 133, 151,
    155, 171, 202, 207, 209-224
Aicher-Scholl, Inge 210, 214
Alberti, Leon Battista 44f., 128, 150f, 153,
    158, 162f., 165, 196, 204, 207
Alembert, Jean Baptiste le Rond d' 87
Alexander, Christopher 31
Altschuller, Genrich Saulowitsch 29
Ammanati, Bartolomeo 86
Ammann, Jean-Christophe 78, 196
aNC Arquitectos 176
André-Salvini, Beatrice 82
Aquinas, Saint Thomas 42
Archimedes 76
Aristotle 22f., 41, 73, 203, 206, 218
Arnheim, Rudolf 20, 36, 57, 61, 97, 160
Augustine, Saint 41

Bachmann, Wolfgang 11
Balmond, Cecil 32
Bateson, Gregory 12, 16, 63
Bazin, André 201
Becher, Bernd and Hilla 26, 182
Behnisch and Partners 144, 156
Behnisch, Günter 26, 50, 70, 73, 117, 144,
    154ff.
Bense, Max 38
Blaser, Werner 33
Blow, Isabella 131
Bologna, Giovanni da 198
Bono, Edward de 35, 61, 101, 121f., 197
Bourdieu, Pierre 10, 37
Braque, George 170
Bredekamp, Horst 36, 87, 97
Broadbent, Geoffrey 34
Broca, Paul 63

Bronzino, Agnolo 86
Brunelleschi, Filippo 142, 153, 155, 161f.
Bruyn, Günter de 38, 210
Buether, Axel 110
Burckhardt, Lucius 95
Buridan, Johannes 218

Cafee, Richard 33
Calatrava, Santiago 32
Callender, John Hancock 31
Callimachus 43f.
Carvalho, Jorge 176
Cellini, Benvenuto 45f., 85f.
Cepl, Jaspar 37
Cézanne, Paul 170
Ching, Francis D. K. 31f.
Columbus, Christopher 161
Conrads, Ulrich 38, 197
Crescas, Chasdai 160
Crosbie, Michael J. 31

Daguerre, Louis Jacques Mandé 165
Damasio, Antonio R. 35, 63, 77, 122
Demetrios, Eames 32, 206
Descartes, René 218
Dewey, John 37
Diderot, Denis 57, 87
Doerner, Dietrich 35
Dominick, Peter G. 33
Doni, Anton Frencesco 46
Dorst, Kees 30
Durand, Jean-Nicolas-Louis 15, 28
Dürer, Albrecht 73, 75, 83, 85f., 162, 164,
    173
Durth, Werner 26

Eames, Charles 32, 206, 218
Eccles, John C. 35, 60f., 101, 122
Edgerton, Samuel Y. 160, 162, 165, 171
Edwards, Betty 101, 122f.
Eiermann, Egon 10
Eisenman, Peter 32, 37, 145f., 154, 193
Engel, Heino 29, 68
Ermel, Horst 31

Evers, Bernd 37
Eyck, Jan van 161
Fathy, Hassan 182f.
Ferguson, Eugene S. 37
Fiederling, Otto 25
Fischer, Volker 38
Flusser, Vilém 18, 20, 36, 40, 52-55, 57,
    88-93, 96, 99, 105-108, 130, 139, 149,
    155, 207, 209
Fonatti, Franco 31
Fontane, Theodor 199, 202, 208
Foster, Norman 26, 32, 65, 114, 195, 210,
    212, 218
French, Neil 173
Fuhrmann, Peter 32
Fuller, R. Buckminster 32, 98, 128, 137

Gadamer, Hans-Georg 9, 22f., 209
Gardner, Howard 73
Gast, Klaus-Peter 32
Gehry, Frank 147
Gerkan, Meinhard von 29
Ghiberti, Lorenzo 155, 161
Goodman, Sue 31
Goya, Francisco de 27, 201
Greindl, Gabriele 210
Groat, Linda 24
Gropius, Walter 197
Gudehus, Juli 71, 133, 205
Gyöngy, Katalion M. 38

Hämer, Hardt-Waltherr 182f.
Hamilton, Anne 38
Hammel, Tobias 113, 136
Hanisch, Ruth 38
Hasselbach, Julia von 108
Hertzberger, Herman 32
Herzog & de Meuron 29
Hoesli, Bernhard 33
Höfer, Candida 26
Hollanda, Francesco de 115
Honnecourt, Villard de 114f.
Horkheimer, Max 53

Jansen, Jürg 33

Jaspers, Karl 13, 15, 17
Jenny, Peter 61, 96, 110, 186
Joas, Hans 37
Joedicke, Jürgen 29, 48, 202

Kafka, Franz 53
Kahn, Louis I. 32
Kalay, Yehuda E. 34
Kant, Immanuel 196, 218
Kemp, Wolfgang 45f., 48
Kittler, Friedrich 99, 190, 192
Kleine, Holger 33
Knauer, Roland 31
Koelbl, Herlinde 33
Koolhaas, Rem 37, 42, 170, 179, 180
Krämer, Sybille 36, 97
Kristen, Marianne 20, 135
Kruft, Hanno-Walter 37f.
Kubrick, Stanley 98f.
Kücker, Wilhelm 29
Kuhnert, Nikolaus 210

Lampugnani, Vittorio Magnago 38
Lapuerta, Jose Maria de 31
Laurel, Brenda 18, 24
Lawson, Bryan 32, 35, 204
Le Corbusier 15, 32, 37, 59, 110, 129, 143,
    179, 217
Lenk, Hans 37, 129f.
Leonardo [da Vinci] 13f., 41, 59f., 81, 83,
    114, 134, 164, 181
Lepik, Andreas 142, 153
Lequeu, Jean-Jacques 100
Lindberg, David C. 171
Lissitzky, El [Lasar Markowitsch Lissizki]
    60f.
Loidl, Hans 33
Loos, Adolf 37, 125, 182, 197
Lorenz, Peter 33

MacCormac, Earl 129f.
Mann, Thomas 196
Mattenklott, Gundel 36
Mau, Bruce 97
McCready, Paul 218

McLuhan, Marshall 67, 99f., 103, 191
Meiss, Pierre von 31
Mendelsohn, Erich 115, 117, 122, 203f.
Meyer, Stephanie 54, 184
Michelangelo [Buonarroti] 114, 117, 142,
    156
Michels, Karen 32
Mies van der Rohe, Ludwig 33, 64, 176,
    196, 199, 201
Moholy-Nagy, Lázló 14
Moon, Karen 31
Moravansky, Ákos 38
Musso, Arne 70

Nägeli, Walter 26
Nesbitt, Kate 37
Neufert, Ernst 28, 30
Neumann, Balthasar 97f.
Neumeyer, Fritz 37
Neweczeral, Alfred 96
Niemeyer, Oskar 130f.
Nouvel, Jean 60

Ockham, William of 210, 218
Oechslin, Werner 151, 154
Ostendorf, Friedrich 49f., 137, 144
Otto, Frei 152f.

Panofsky, Erwin 41, 43, 167
Passe, Ulrike 33
Peirce, Charles Sanders 218
Pelletier, Louise 97
Pérez-Gómez, Alberto 98
Pessoa, Fernando 16
Pfammatter, Ulrich 33
Philippsen, Ansgar 189
Piano, Renzo 26, 32
Picasso, Pablo 170
Pieper, Christian 92, 108, 125
Piranesi, Giovanni Battista 167
Plato 41-43, 133, 218
Plotin 41
Poelzig, Hans 14
Popper, Karl R. 196, 225
Porter, Tom 31

Prominski, Martin 28
Prouvé, Jean 32, 143f.
Ptolemaeus, Claudius 160
Pückler-Muskau, Hermann von 196

Rambow, Riklef 36
Rathgeb, Markus 210
Rauterberg, Hanno 147, 201
Reich-Ranicki, Marcel 196, 199
Rice, Peter 32
Rittel, Horst W. 18, 34, 38, 40, 51f., 65f.,
    70
Robbins, Edward 32
Rocha, Paulo Mendes da 199
Rodrigues, Ana Leonor 31, 144
Rodrigues, Jacinto 32
Rogers, Richard 26, 32
Rossi, Aldo 37, 178
Ryff [Rivius], Walther Hermann 40, 75, 83,
    85

Sachs, Hinrich 106, 189, 198
Sachsse, Rolf 175
Said, Edward 201
Sanoff, Henry 70
Santos, José Paulo dos 141
Sattler, Barbara Johanna 62, 101
Scamozzi, Vincenzo 153
Scharoun, Hans 122
Schneider, Beat 26, 38
Scholl, Sophie and Hans 210
Scholl, Inge 210, 214
Schön, Donald A. 29f.
Schricker, Rudolf 31, 33
Schumann, U. Maximilian 38
Seyler, Axel 36
Shahn, Ben 197
Silver, Nathan 26
Siza, Álvaro 13f., 21f., 28f., 32, 46, 72, 114,
    119, 121, 138, 155f., 169, 172, 179
Smith, Albert 31
Socrates 41, 133, 196
Solà-Morales, Manuel de 139
Solis, Virgil 75, 83, 85f.
Sonne, Wolfgang 38

Sontag, Susan 179
Spengemann, Karl-Ludwig 36
Sperry, Roger W. 35, 61f, 122
Stachowiak, Herbert 150f.
Starck, Philippe 198
Stein, Gertrude 113
Steingruber, Johann David 129

Talbot, William Henry Fox 165, 174
Taut, Bruno 76, 129
Thackara, John 38
Thoenes, John 37
Toscanelli, Paolo dal Pozzo 161
Trier, Lars von 200
Trüby, Stephan 38
Tucholsky, Kurt 53
Turing, Alan 187

Uhl, Ottokar 48ff.
Ungers, Oswald Mathias 37

Valéry, Paul 125
Vallebuona, Renzo 26
Vasari, Giorgio 45f., 86
Venturi, Robert 37, 206
Verberne, Paul 158
Vesalius, Andreas 75f.
Vester, Frederic 35
Vinterberg, Thomas 200
Vitruvius 40, 43-45, 76, 83, 85, 125, 135, 140, 150f., 181, 201f., 204, 207, 215

Wachsmann, Konrad 67f.
Wang, David 24
Warren, Waldo 128
Watson, Donald 31
Weiss, L. 70
Weltzien, Friedrich 36
Wenders, Wim 176
Wernicke, Carl 62
Wick, Rainer K. 33
Wilson, Edward O. 16
Wittgenstein, Ludwig 108, 125f., 218, 223
Wright, Frank Lloyd 178

Yeang, Ken 32

Zuccari, Frederico 45, 48
Zuse, Konrad 183ff., 194

INDEX OF SUBJECTS

Abstraction 67, 88, 95, 109, 119, 125, 128,
    134, 137, 139, 142, 151–153, 169, 203
Académie Royale d'Architecture (Paris) 14
Accademia del Disegno (Florence) 45, 86
Act
    of designing 72–78, 225
    artistic 29
Action 11f., 17f., 77
    theory 37
Aesthetics 126, 177, 184, 203f., 216, 221
Akademie der Bildenden Künste (Munich)
    216
Algorithm 29, 101, 147, 181, 193, 206
Apparatus 53, 55f., 92f., 96, 101, 186
Architects' and engineers' fees regulations
    (Germany) 68
Architectural Association (London) 15
Architectural theory 23, 37f., 43, 83, 126
Architecture critic 203
Architecture teaching 14, 33, 156
Art 14f., 17f., 24f., 27, 35f., 40f., 87, 99,
    110, 115, 122, 126, 160f., 164, 196, 199,
    203f., 206ff., 216, 221
    works of 46, 106, 125, 207
    rejection of 53, 216
Art academy 9
Art college 9, 15
Arts and Crafts movement 14
Awareness 195, 200, 227
Axonometry 118, 170

Bachelor's course 9, 227
Balance 204
Baroque 87, 97, 168, 175
Basic architectural course 227
Bauhaus 14, 33, 170
Brain 35, 61f, 101, 122, 195
Brainstorming 197
Brief 67, 127f.
Building costs 181ff.

Calculation 101, 125f., 147, 181–185, 203
Camera 171

Camera Obscura 173
Celebration, The (Festen) 200
Central perspective 162–164, 192
Chaos theory 34
Clarity (see also: Vividness) 49, 55, 138,
    185
Code, binary 190
cogitatione (lat.) 43
Commerce 212
Communication 36, 95, 99, 167, 175, 192,
    195, 208
    visual 161, 171f.
Competition 40, 54, 142, 181, 192
Complexity 18, 30, 35f., 50, 56, 65, 73, 76,
    95, 100f., 103f., 110, 118, 168, 176, 193,
    195, 198, 209, 219
Computer 34, 64, 93, 102, 113, 126, 145,
    147, 186–195
    as medium 191, 226
    Z1 183, 186, 187
Computer-Aided Design 34
Concept 131, 147, 151, 183
concinnitas (lat.) 204
Consideration, levels of 51, 59
Constraint 66, 157, 200
Contradiction 18, 67, 73, 85, 94, 206, 209f.,
    213, 219, 221
Conversation 127
    Socratian 133
Cost analysis 146
Creataphor 37, 130
Creative process 34, 58, 198
Creativity 37, 73, 75, 79, 118, 130, 157, 183,
    200
Creativity block 197
Criteria 34, 38, 49f., 106, 200-207, 213, 216
Criticism 34, 79, 101f., 125, 133, 141ff.,
    192, 196–200, 214
    ability 208
Cultural techniques 23, 27, 36, 81, 94, 99,
    103f., 108, 117, 192
Culture theory 36
Cybernetics 34

Data sets 192f.
Data structure 146
Database 195
Decision theory 49
Decision-making 29, 48f., 65, 70
Description 125ff., 223
Design 38
   (definition) 40, 43, 45f., 48f., 52, 57
   negative 196
Design cycle 78ff., 98f., 110, 175
Design decision 71, 154, 185, 194
Design drawing, see: Drawing
Design History Society 39
Design idea 22, 49, 78, 95, 99, 101, 110,
   114, 130, 146, 150, 173, 196, 207
Design method 20, 33ff., 48, 66ff., 217f.
Design methodology 28f.
Design Methods Movement 28
Design practice 198
   academic 143
Design principles, formal 31
Design process, see: Process of designing
Design task 127
Design team 67
Design teaching 12–16, 18, 20, 23f., 28–33,
   39, 209, 223
Design tools 81–104, 223, 225
   (definition) 94, 97, 101
   of the Renaissance 141
   (table) 102
   verbal / visual 100–104, 125, 133
designatio (lat.) 126
Development 65, 213
Diagram 146, 150, 206
Digital 53, 96, 122f., 145, 148, 159, 171,
   178, 180, 186–195, 225
Dimensioning 152
Discussion 101, 127, 131, 141
disegno (it.) 86, 126, 134f.
   (definition) 45f.
Dogma 95 200
Drawing 31ff., 45, 68, 81, 97, 99, 101, 113,
   126, 134–148, 178
   (definition) 113

Drawing program 123, 147
Dymaxion 128

École des Beaux-Arts (Paris) 14f., 33, 136,
   143
École Polytechnique (Paris) 15f., 28, 33
Economics 182
Emotion 35f., 43, 59, 73–78, 168
Encyclopédie 87
Engineering school 9
Enigmatic, the 207
Enlightenment 14, 28, 83, 87, 196
Ethics 22, 126, 184, 203f., 206
European Association for Architectural
   Education 39
Evaluation 26, 29f., 70f., 213, 223
Everyday culture 217
Everyday, the 109, 215f., 219
Experiment 213, 216, 226
Expression 60, 78f., 95, 107ff.

Feeling (see also: Emotion) 122
   of happiness 43
Film 101, 154, 170ff., 190, 200
firmitas (lat.) 201f., 215
Floor plan, see: Plan
Focal length 167, 171, 176
Form 54f., 57, 101, 104, 109
Formal language 28, 154f., 157
Formula 101
Function 213, 216
Functionality 53, 108, 207, 216, 219

Geometry 75, 83, 97, 100f., 135, 137f., 142,
   147f.
   Euclidian 137f.
Gestalt psychology 36
Gesture 40, 55, 73, 78, 81, 100, 105–111,
   113, 154, 209
   architecture as 108f., 207
   communicative 105
   as enigma 207
   of making 20, 54, 88–90
   of melancholy 73ff
   theatrical 109

Grid 163, 165, 169
Ground plan, see: Plan

Hemisphere 62, 122
hochschule für gestaltung (Ulm) 33f., 38, 210
Idea 46, 49f., 76, 81, 89f., 113, 121, 141f., 197, 213
  (definition) 41f.
  finding of 197
  theory of (Plato) 41
  of university 10
Ideology 54, 104, 193, 223
Image manipulation, digital 173
Images, banning of 128
imitatio (lat.) 207f.
Imitation 31, 43, 207
Imprecision 22, 40, 52, 117f., 150
Inner ideas 59f., 101, 105, 110, 192, 195
Innovation 207
Inspiration 78, 85, 143
Institute of Design (Chicago) 67
instrumentum architecturae (lat.) 97
Interviews 32
Intuition 78
Invention 29, 43, 59, 87, 207
inventione (lat.) 43, 45, 207f.
Isometry 119, 170

Judgement (see also: Decision) 99, 196

Language 100, 125–133, 198
Linear perspective 98, 160–172
Loading experiments 153
Logic 95

Machine 91f., 98, 186, 193
  universal 187
Mainframe computer 145
Making 86, 94, 155, 212ff., 219
  (definition) 88, 130, 212
Manifesto 197, 217
Master-pupil relationship 14, 28
Master's course 9

Material 31, 54, 88f., 114, 143, 151–159, 179, 183f., 218
Materialisation, Material form 97, 99, 117, 125, 159, 192, 213
Meaning 55, 91, 95, 97, 101, 105ff., 125, 135, 194, 196, 213
  change of 150, 152
  level of 18, 77f., 103, 105, 107, 109, 117
Media theory 36
Medium 31, 67, 81, 99-104, 114, 130, 135ff., 142, 147, 153, 167f., 175ff., 186, 191f., 227
Melancholy 73–75, 85
Mental strategies 35
Metaphor 30, 37, 78, 88, 94, 95, 129–133, 195
  theory of 130
  of the tool 186
Method 27, 32, 34, 99, 133, 225f.
Methodology 17, 29, 223
mimesis (lat.) 41
Model 31, 44ff., 66ff., 88, 100f., 126, 128, 141, 146, 149–159, 192, 212f., 218
  (definition) 150, 213
  and original, representation of 150
  digital 3D 146f., 171, 180, 195
  material used for 154ff.
  photographs of 177
  sketch 123
  theory 34, 151
Modernism 16, 20, 52f., 170, 201, 219

Negation 52f., 55
Networking 194f.
Neurology 35, 77
Norms 108

oikos (gr.) 182
Olympics (Munich) 145, 155, 212, 215, 217

Paradox 18, 206
  of constraints 200
  of meaning 56

of rationality 51
of the sketch 117
Parameter 147f., 177, 185, 193ff.
Perception 36, 41, 59–64, 78f., 98, 103,
    110, 118-123, 136, 163-175, 179, 200, 219
    (definition) 36
Perceptual apparatus 163, 168
Periodicals 38f.
Perspective view 31, 101, 118, 119, 141,
    154, 160–172, 177f.
Perspective, three-dimensional illusion of
    163f.
Phenomenology 105
Philosophy 15, 36f., 41, 55, 73, 213, 218
    linguistic 218
Photogram 59
Photography 26, 33, 97, 100f., 115, 123,
    128, 148, 164 f., 167 f., 171–180, 193
    digital 177
Photomontage 123, 170f., 176
Pictorial / picture space 160, 162, 165
Pitch (stairs) 28
Plan 30, 43, 82, 103, 114, 118, 129,
    134–147, 165, 167, 217
Planning 29, 34, 50ff., 213
    (definition) 50f.
poiesis (gr.) 22 f., 41
Portfolio of drawings 114
Postmodernism 171
Practice 31, 36, 88f., 143, 209, 221, 225 f.
    reflective 30f., 107
praxis (gr.) 22f.
Prescriptive 95, 118, 177f.
Principles 27f., 30–33, 207
Problem 127
    wicked and tame 18, 34, 51, 71
Process 225, 227
    of designing 28f., 36f., 48f., 54, 65-71,
    78f., 99, 109, 117, 192
    of designing, simultaneous 67
    determined, strongly / weakly;
    undetermined 71
    iterative 65
    as in court of law 65

linear sequence 65f
Processor 102, 195
Programmes 40, 101, 123, 133, 185–195,
    197, 213
    to program 147, 194
promenade architecturale (fr.) 110, 179
Prototype 64, 142, 149, 151, 153
Psychology 35–37, 121, 197
Pyramid, visual 162f.

Rapid Prototyping 159
Rationalism 197
    critical 225
Rationality 15, 61, 125, 137, 143, 165, 201,
    208
Realization 15, 18, 57, 70, 143, 178, 181,
    183, 221
Reduction 60, 118, 137, 138, 175
Renaissance 87, 114, 153, 168, 173, 183,
    192
Rendering 178
Representation 97, 103, 142, 146, 151
    by parameters 147
Research (see also: Science) 10, 12 f., 15,
    17, 26, 34, 38f., 91, 225f.
    methods for 24
Resistance 89, 144, 155, 157, 171, 193f.,
    201, 216
    of digital tools 192
    of material 157, 190, 193
    mathematical 190
Revolution
    French 14
    Industrial 88, 91
rotis
    autonomous republic 212, 224
    typeface 222
Rules 27f., 30f., 33, 37, 68, 81, 108, 163f.,
    192, 199, 207f., 216, 218, 226f.

Sample 149ff.
Schematic outline 81, 99
Science (see also: Research) 10, 13, 15–19,
    23, 30, 34, 38, 40, 51, 87, 115, 134, 164,
    196, 206, 212
    of design / design science 18, 38

Sensibility 59, 207
Shape, giving shape 154
  (definition) 56
Simulation 102, 146, 171, 178, 180, 185 f.,
  194
Sketch 30f., 49, 98f., 100, 113-124, 141
  (definition) 113
  first 123
Sociology 37
Space Odyssey, A: 2001 97f.
Space 31, 98, 110, 118, 130, 136, 145,
  158f., 160–168, 176, 179, 188, 190f., 194
Specialist college 9
Stairs 28
Standards 25, 30f.
Stereotopic photography 176
Stonemasons 126, 142
Strategy 78f, 99, 129f.
Study programme 226
Sustainability 185, 194
Synthèse des Arts 15

Table calculation 185
Teaching 9–15, 18, 29f., 34, 199, 208, 226f.
techne (gr.) 22f.
Technical college 9
Tectonics 19
tekton (gr.) 18, 130
Tendering 146, 194
Tensegrity 128
theoria (gr.) 209
Theory 9, 15 f., 23, 30, 32, 36ff., 67, 88f.,
  101f., 108, 125, 183, 198, 209–224
  from below 212
  creation of 221
  of design 20, 24f., 34, 52, 54, 79, 91,
  108, 209–225
  as instrument of power 53, 212
Thinking 88, 91
  analogous / digital 63, 101, 214
  intuitive 59
  lateral/vertical 35, 61f, 121
  linear 62
  with the scalpel 157

verbal 63, 101, 122, 130, 226
visual 36, 63
visual-spatial 63, 101, 121–123, 226
Thought 58–63, 122
  mode of 121f.
  rational 35, 77
  traps 35
Tools (see also: Design tools) 90f.
  ambivalence of 90–93
  of building 82
  of drawing 99
  making of 89, 97
  of shoemaker 94
Trade journals 38f.
Transcendence 53, 57
Typology 26, 175

University 9–15
  original idea of 10
Use 52, 94–99, 104, 118, 140 f., 175f., 203,
  213, 215–221, 226
utilitas (lat.) 201ff., 215
Utopia 207

Value system 79, 201, 207
Vanishing point (Scaenografia) 140, 162
velum (lat.) 128, 164f.
venustas (lat.) 201ff.
Video 101, 146, 170ff.
Vividness (see also: Clarity) 134, 149, 151,
  168, 177

White Rose 210
Whole, the 15, 19, 20f., 77, 160, 184, 196,
  200, 204, 225-227
Working drawing 140,142
Working model 151, 155